THE ROAD TO SOMEWHERE

Related titles from Palgrave Macmillan

Julia Casterton, *Creative Writing: A Practical Guide*, 3rd edition
John Singleton and Mary Luckhurst (eds), *The Creative Writing Handbook*, 2nd edition
John Singleton, *The Creative Writing Workbook*

The Road To Somewhere

A Creative Writing Companion

Edited by

ROBERT GRAHAM, HEATHER LEACH
Manchester Metropolitan University, Cheshire

HELEN NEWALL
Edge Hill College of Higher Education

and

JOHN SINGLETON

Conceived by

Julie Armstrong
Robert Graham
Heather Leach
Helen Newall
John Singleton

First published 2005 by
PALGRAVE MACMILLAN
Houndmills, Basingstoke, Hampshire RG21 6XS and
175 Fifth Avenue, New York, N.Y. 10010
Companies and representatives throughout the world

PALGRAVE MACMILLAN is the global academic imprint of the Palgrave Macmillan division of St. Martin's Press, LLC and of Palgrave Macmillan Ltd. Macmillan® is a registered trademark in the United States, United Kingdom and other countries. Palgrave is a registered trademark in the European Union and other countries.

ISBN 1–4039–1639–X hardback
ISBN 1–4039–1640–3 paperback

This book is printed on paper suitable for recycling and made from fully managed and sustained forest sources.

A catalogue record for this book is available from the British Library.

A catalog record for this book is available from the Library of Congress.

10   9   8   7   6   5   4   3   2   1
14   13   12   11   10   09   08   07   06   05

Printed in China

Contents

Editors' Acknowledgements

Robert Graham: Rachel, Poppy and Noah for TLC; John Singleton for offering the break in showbiz; Edge Hill's Research Development Fund for the award during 2002 and 2003; Alistair McCulloch, John Simons, Gill Davies, Andy Butler and Creative Writing students at Edge Hill, 1996–2004, especially the kind few who gave permission for quotations from their reflective work; Jenny Newman and Roger Webster at Liverpool John Moores University.

Helen Newall: Brian, Laurie and Alastair; Tony Lindsay for help with the Scriptwriting chapter; Russ Tunney at the Nuffield Theatre, Southampton; Jenny Newman and Jim Friel at Liverpool John Moores University.

Heather Leach: Grateful thanks to all those students who let me practise on them, to my colleagues at MMU Cheshire who helped me find time to write, and to my dear husband, Roger, for his love and support.

Helen Newall wrote the *Agony Aunt* sections.
Robert Graham wrote the *Basics* and *Style* sections.

Notes on Contributors

Robert Graham is Subject Leader for Creative Writing at MMU Cheshire. His short stories have appeared in a variety of magazines, including *Metropolitan*, *Tandem*, and *She*, and in anthologies such as *Northern Stories Vol. 5* and *Pool*. He has also had work broadcast on Radio 4's afternoon short story slot. He is the co-author, with Keith Baty of the spoof biography, *Elvis – The Novel* (The Do-Not Press, 1997). Over a dozen of Robert's plays for youth theatres have been staged, including *If You Have Five Seconds To Spare* (about fans of The Smiths) which Contact Theatre, Manchester, produced in a critically acclaimed run. The finest publishers in the land are currently turning down his first novel, *Holy Joe*. Nevertheless, he is at work on *It's A Family Show!* his second novel.

Helen Newall teaches Drama and Scriptwriting at Edge Hill College of Higher Education. Her short stories have appeared in *Pool*, *Pretext* and *Mslexia*. She spent two years teaching in Botswana. Her work has been performed in venues as various as Chester Cathedral, The Bridgewater Hall, Manchester, and the Millennium Dome. She has worked for Performance Theatre Company, London; The Byre Theatre, St Andrews; Cheshire County Youth Theatre; HTV Television Workshop, Bristol; Action Transport Theatre Company, Cheshire; Carl Davis and the Liverpool Philharmonic Orchestra; The Chester Gateway Theatre (where she was Writer in Residence for two years); The Little Strumpets Theatre Company, Lancaster; and, most recently, The Nuffield Theatre, Southampton.

Heather Leach teaches Creative Writing at MMU Cheshire. Her short stories have appeared in a variety of publications including *The Big Issue*, *Metropolitan*, *The City Life Book of Manchester Stories* and others. She also writes articles and scholarly papers on a variety of themes, and is particularly interested in writing that crosses disciplinary and formal boundaries. Before teaching she was a youth and community development worker for many years in Manchester. She is currently planning to write a radio play, about Hulme, with Helen Newall.

John Singleton was formerly Subject Leader of Creative Writing at MMU Cheshire and has taught in schools and universities both in the UK and America. He has written extensively on the subject of creative writing and his books include: *The Creative Writing Handbook* with Mary Luckhurst and *The Creative Writing Workbook*, both published by Palgrave. His young-children's fiction has been published by Andersen Press and his latest teenage novels – *Star* (2003) and *Skinny B, Skaz and Me* (2005) are published by Puffin Books.

Julie Armstrong teaches creative writing at MMU Cheshire and has taught in schools, FE colleges and Universities. She taught EFL in Amsterdam and Brussels. Her poetry and short stories have appeared in a variety of magazines and anthologies including *No Earthly Reason*, Crocus Books, Forward Press, *Poetry Now*. Yorkshire TV commissioned her and her partner to write three interactive TV drama scripts. She is currently working on a novel.

Robert Sheppard is Creative Writing Co-ordinator, and the course tutor of the MA in Writing Studies, at Edge Hill College of Higher Education. His recent poetry books include *Tin Pan Arcadia* (Salt) and *The Lores* (Stride). He has a forthcoming volume on contemporary poetry, *The Poetry of Saying* (Liverpool University Press).

Scott Thurston began writing in the literary scene situated around Gilbert Adair's 'Subvoicive Poetry' reading series and Bob Cobbing's 'New River Project' workshops in London in the late 1980s. His books include: *Turns* (with Robert Sheppard) (Ship of Fools/ Radiator: Liverpool, 2003), *Two Sequences* (RWC: Sutton, 1998), *State(s)walk(s)* (Writers Forum: London, 1994) and *Poems Nov 89–Jun 91* (Writers Forum: London, 1991). He teaches English and Creative Writing at The University of Salford and runs the little magazine *The Radiator*.

Introduction: Imaginary Roads

Heather Leach

The idea of life as a story and of the story as journey seems to be hard-wired into our consciousness and culture, which is why this book is called *The Road to Somewhere*. Remember Red Riding Hood going deep into the dangerous forest; Dick Whittington on the path to London; Frodo the Hobbit and his Lord of The Rings quest; the Starship Enterprise, boldly going? Thousands of years ago, most human beings gave up the nomadic hunter-gatherer life and settled into villages but perhaps old memories of walking from place to place, of owning nowhere yet belonging everywhere, are still locked into the synapses of our brains. Like dogs, whose legs twitch as they run in dreams, so we still wander the world, the imaginary Universe, in our stories of journeys.

How This Book Can Be Used

Each of us must find our own way to the art of writing: to the voice that is ours alone. But writing is a practical craft as well as an art, and like all crafts, it can be learned, given time, effort and motivation. This book is organised like one of those old stories with a beginning, middle and end. *Getting Going* is about starting out on the writer's path. *Journey Essentials* and *Keeping Going* offer ideas and practical help on developing the skills and endurance needed for the long haul. *Going Where?* is about destinations – a signpost pointing in a number of directions.

The book is intended to be useful to student writers and their teachers in creative writing courses in universities, colleges, schools, and writers' groups, as well as to individuals looking for practical guidance. Hopefully some parts are so inspirational you'll immediately throw the book down and rush off to write. Other sections are meant to stimulate reflection and discussion. Each chapter has exercises and examples to help get you started; and there are resources for further reading and research.

Circular Routes

This book is not a route-map, a writing-by-numbers A–Z plan. Writing, like all creative human activities, cannot be fixed or determined in advance, and linear metaphors of journeys are not always appropriate for the contemporary world. Think instead of the cities where most of us live, of the webs and labyrinths of the Internet: who can tell where they begin and end? Creative writing is not only a road to somewhere, it is also that somewhere itself; an activity worth doing whatever the outcome or destination; a journey to be taken for the sake of the journey.

I
Getting Going

1 Becoming a Writer
Heather Leach

One Writer's Beginning

I used to work in an office. I used to sit at a desk next to a window, which looked out into an odd half-secret space, an inner enclosure. Around the walls were other windows, usually blinded. I was often bored, sifting my way through reports and policies, writing my own in the same rational calm language that slowly gets things done or undone. There was a door at the bottom of the courtyard which I supposed was used by maintenance and repair people but I never saw them and so as far as my office day was concerned this strange interior space was inhabited only by birds: pigeons; starlings; sparrows; occasionally a pair of magpies (one for sorrow, two for joy). Throughout a whole year I watched them come flying down out of the trapezoid sky, their anxious fluttering and flapping amplified by the walls as they hustled for space on ledges and buttresses. In the rain and cold they rested there in rows, patient, silent, looking back at me, their thick white droppings staining the already soot-stained stone.

I began to hate my job. Not the point of it, the meaning, which was worthy and honest, but the practice, the necessary but relentless daily discipline, the painstakingly detailed attention that was needed to carry it out. I hated as well the kind of person that this work was slowly turning me into. And the place, the room: that too. It was square with all the usual office accoutrements: desk, telephone, coat-stand, strong overhead lighting, cream cleanable walls. There were no computers then, no fax machines, but you get the picture. Oh yes, and there was also a picture on the wall in front of me, one picture per office each labelled *our wonderful rural heritage*: foot and mouth-less fields; unmechanised farms, rainless summers.

The more I hated the job and the room, the more I watched the birds. They inhabited their strange interior space with ingenuity, one or two even managing to make a scruffy nest in a corner, although I never saw any fledglings. As the year went by it became a kind of fetish to look out, to say hello to the birds before I did anything else. I found that, with effort, I could climb onto a chair and force the stiff window handle downwards and so lift the latch. The window hinge itself was rigid with years of disuse but I managed a few inches, enough to get my head through, enough to get a breath of acrid feathery air. In winter, when I looked down, there was often a body lying below me on the concrete ground, a small dark shadow, its frozen wings folded. By the next day these corpses had always gone.

In telling this story of the birds, I am trying to put together an account of the year that I started to be a proper writer. But as this is a book about the forms and processes of writing itself, I have to confess that I'm making it up as I go along. What's emerging, I see, is a fairly familiar story: the one about the sad would-be writer/artist/singer/actor who sits day after day trapped at a tedious desk, dreaming of creativity/fame/riches. The birds, of course, represent – but it should be quite obvious now what they represent – all the slightly embarrassing but pleasantly satisfying clichés that we already know: our wonderful literary heritage; lightness, freedom, flight; somewhere over the rainbow; all that stuff.

This is the way stories go, I find. You begin at the top of the page with a few words, not always quite sure where you're going, but if you persist, if you battle your way through the uncertainty, letting words come by themselves, sooner or later a narrative picks you up, huge rivers of language and form carrying you with them down to a sea of stories. So far: so good. Let's go with the flow, man. Except that each writer needs to find their own direction, to know when to go with the current and when to resist it, not to float or to drift but to swim, sometimes even upstream.

In my office story what should come next is a moment of revelation, clear insight, a bird-inspired epiphany. In fact, as I remember, there was no sudden sense of understanding that year, no dramatic change. I simply began to sit down at a table at home and instead of thinking about how I'd like to be a writer, I actually began to put words onto paper and to keep on doing it. If you want to write there's no escape from the desk. Nothing transformed me overnight, and nothing will transform you except *the act itself: writing*. Two things make you into a writer: writing regularly; and reading as much as you can so that you will learn to be aware of the currents of language and culture; aware enough to be able to distinguish between drifting and swimming. There's a lot more to it of course, but that's where we all begin: at the page, the screen. Curious, thrilled, afraid. The words appear one after another. You cross them out, erase them, write more, and gradually something begins to form itself, a knot of thought, an image: the way birds patiently stand side by side, for example, thinking of nothing, their claw feet blanket-stitching a ledge.

This room where I am now is small, square, plain. There's no coat-stand but there is a computer, plus desk, telephone and chair. Sometimes I hate having to sit here day after day; sometimes I hate the relentless discipline, the painstaking hours. I left that other office ten years ago and I'm usually sceptical of magical stories but I have to tell you that the birds came with me. They've appeared in a number of stories that I've written, bit parts only, but significant, often shifting the eye of the main character away from the action on the ground, out of the frame, into the sky. Here too, in this writing, they appear again, witnesses, protagonists. I look down at my hands, fingers tapping out this exact word, this particular full stop. To the left is a window and every so often I glance up from the screen, resting my eyes, pausing for thought: just a suburban garden, conifers, bushes, a child's boat-shaped sandpit. But then I look across and see you, reader, looking back at me. Between us is the place where the birds are, a place of beaks and claws. Of wings.

Getting Started

There are many ways of becoming a writer. Some people begin as children, keeping a diary or writing poems that explore feeling and thought. Others get hooked on reading, drawn into fictional worlds that, unlike the mundane and confusing *real* world, offer clear beginnings and definite endings. You might already have a great plot idea, a detailed plan that is working itself out in your head. Or maybe you have a cause, a strong viewpoint that you want to get over to others, a message to change the world. Some people dream of riches and fame: perhaps you can write a killer script that film studios will fight over, or become the next

J.K.Rowling and make millions by writing children's books. Maybe you simply want to write down your life, to pass on everything you know, all the things that have happened to you, your own take on the world, your particular voice. Writers come in all shapes, colours, ages and sizes. There is no right way or wrong way to be a writer.

If you're reading this book, then you've almost certainly put pen to paper, fingers to keyboard and made some kind of a start at writing. Before you go much further let me tell you something really worth knowing: all you need to do to become a writer is to get the words down: your own words on paper or screen: your own voice. That's all it takes. When you're writing, in the act of writing itself, you're a fully paid up and welcome new member of a club without any rules and without any rulers. You're the equal of all other writers, dead and alive, from Tolstoy to Tolkein. Let me say it again. It's as simple as this: *writers write*. Full stop.

So why write a book about it? Why join a writers' group or pay hard-earned money for a writing course? Good questions. I think the answer is that most of us want to do more than just write. We want to be able to produce something that other people might want to read, that they might even be willing to pay for: a fantastic, unputdownable story; a magical, terrible poem; a best-selling script; writing that's up there with the best; dramatic, emotional, brilliant, funny. This is harder, but a great many of the skills and abilities can be learned if you are willing to put in time and commitment. Below is a list of the absolutely essential activities that you need to develop and practise the actions and attitudes that need to become part of your life.

Try This: Begin With A Word

Take any printed page and, with eyes closed, let your finger pick out a word at random
   or
   Ask the person next to you to give you a word.
   The next step is to follow the word and see where it takes you. Don't think too hard or try to write cleverly or beautifully. Spend five minutes on your word. Write for the whole time, then stop.

Write Regularly

Think of writing as a muscle. It needs to get lean and fit. Writing leads to more writing: as you write, new ideas will spring up, words will lead to other words, stories will start, voices will speak. Don't wait for inspiration. Like Father Christmas, inspiration knows where you live and if you begin it will eventually find you all by itself. *Regularly* means different things to different people – every day is good but may not be possible. Don't beat yourself up if you can't manage that, but once a week is probably a minimum. Try writing at different times and in different places and find out which works best for you. Write about anything and everything. Don't think about whether the outcome is good or bad: this is practice not performance. Work that muscle. Hard.

Read

If I had a nickel for every person who told me he/she wanted to become a writer but 'didn't have time to read,' I could buy myself a pretty good steak dinner. Can I be blunt on this subject? If you don't have time to read, you don't have the time (or the tools) to write. Simple as that. Reading is the creative centre of the writer's life. (Stephen King: *On Writing*) [1]

This is the second commandment: *writers need to read*. Full stop squared. But *what* should you read? First: read for pleasure. Forget all those rules about 'serious' literature, the classics, et cetera, and simply read what you like. If, at present, you only like one particular form or genre – fantasy, romance, history, sci-fi, celebrity biography, for instance – then read that form with enjoyment, regardless of what anyone else thinks or says. Try not to get stuck, however, in a reading groove; keep pushing back the boundaries of what you enjoy. If you try something new and don't like it, fine, but make sure you give it a chance. Be aware that difficulty or confusion may be yours not the writer's, and that greater attention and persistence on your part may light up parts of yourself you didn't know existed. Make a particular point of reading the forms you are trying to write: if it's poems, read poetry; if it's fiction, read short stories and novels. As you read, not only will you be enjoying the story, poem, whatever it is, you'll also be absorbing the way language works, all the things it can do. Read on the bus; in bed; on the loo; read anywhere and everywhere. Writers need your cash. Libraries are free. Use them or lose them.

Know Your Stuff

The stuff I'm talking about here is language: words, sentences, paragraphs, story, dialogue, image: all that stuff. This is your material. I was tempted to write *raw* material, but, of course, by the time we get our hands on it, it isn't at all raw, having been already well cooked in history and culture. We are born into a world where words shape much of the way we think, feel and understand: a great ocean of words, constantly moving, constantly changing. There's far too much language for any one person to grasp it all and most of us will need a lifetime to grasp a small part, but this doesn't matter. What does matter is to develop a pleasure in language for its own sake, an energetic curiosity about its current and tides, its layers and depths. Reading will certainly help and the good news is that you have already gained many of the language skills that you need.

The not-so-good news is that to become a writer, particularly a good writer, you need to develop and extend these skills well beyond the average. I say *not-so-good*, because, for many of us, the phrase *language skills* has the stink of grammar about it: all those dry, complicated rules, structures and formalities that make the heart sink. There's no way round the fact that writers need a *working* knowledge of many of these forms and structures; you need to be able to use language skilfully, which means you should be able to understand the way it works, to know when something isn't quite right and to have ideas about how you could make it better. Just as the car mechanic needs to know that the name of that thing which mixes air and petrol is the carburettor, so the writer needs, for example, to know that words that describe nouns are usually called adjectives. The mechanic doesn't necessarily need to have the exact chemical formula for combustion at her oily fingertips, but she has to be able to distinguish, and therefore to name, the parts of the car. The writer needs to develop a working vocabulary, a way of knowing and naming the parts of language.

Try This: Put Words Together

Make a list of words that you like or which are at the forefront of your mind. Use words that refer to things or people, rather than ideas or emotions. Sometimes the simplest words are the most productive. For example my list at this moment could be:

Shed
Coffee
Tesco's
Birds
Rain

Write for five minutes including as many of the words as you can. Try not to think too hard. Just visualise what the words represent and write about them. You can use my list if you're stuck.

Learn

One last thing: in some ways this should come first, even before writing and reading because if you are able to learn for yourself then all the other essentials will fall into place. It is probably true that no one can *teach* you to become a writer, although they can give you a very good leg-up: a course or group can provide motivation and space as well as a responsive audience: a good teacher can help you with a range of useful skills. But what you also need to develop for yourself is an experimental and actively involved attitude going out from you into the world. Watch what people do and find out what motivates them. Ask questions and listen to the answers. Think a lot. Read with your mind and heart fully in gear. Look closely at things. Be curious. *Learn.*

Try This: The Three-Word Trick

Take three words from any source and write a paragraph or two, which includes all three words. The more unconnected these words are to each other, the better. If you're in a group you can have a great time seeing who can make up the weirdest three-word list. Examples:

reindeer; bin-bag; Eurotrash.
cheese; Superman; nits.

---

brother; rats; room.
valentine; telescope; referee.
Write for ten minutes making sure you use all three words.

A variation on the above is to add an emotion to the list:
reindeer; bin-bag; Eurotrash; + *boredom*.
cheese; Superman; nits; + *hopeless desire*.
brother; rats; room; + *terror*.
valentine; telescope; referee; + *obsession*.
Now write two pages weaving all four elements together. Try not to actually *use* the emotional word – *show* the emotion through action and implication. You can use the same words, lists and emotions to write in a variety of forms: prose, dialogue, poetry.

But What's the Point?

Many writers have used variations on these methods with surprising and productive results. When the short-story writer, Kathleen Mansfield, was at a loss for an idea, she used to call downstairs to her husband, John Middleton Murry. He'd shout back a word: *table; party*: and this would be enough to get her writing again. The random approach takes away your responsibility to think of something 'significant' or 'important,' helping you to relax, to allow the associative – partly unconscious – qualities of mind to get to work.

Some people love this kind of exercise and some hate it. A word of warning to the first group: Einstein said that he made some of his greatest discoveries simply by staring out of windows, but even so, he still had to do the sums, work out the theories and he already knew the language of physics inside out. James Joyce, one of the pioneers of the stream of consciousness technique, did not *write Ulysses* randomly: he attempted to write it so that it *appeared to be* the random thoughts of his characters. Which is hard. We need playfulness but it isn't *all* we need. Sorry to be a spoilsport.

Perhaps you're one of the second kind of people – you may already know what you want to write about – you've got a definite story to tell – maybe you've got a project planned and you'd really rather get on with that. I'd like to persuade you to at least give the playful method a try. Try it out on a piece of writing that's stuck. Pick a list of words at random and try to integrate them into the next chapter, scene, verse. It could give you a surprising kick-start.

There's a traditional Eastern phrase: *Don't Push the River*, meaning that some things have to be left to happen by themselves. The ability to play, to swim in the river of language, may not be all we need but it's a good place to start.

Further Reading

Natalie Goldberg (1986) *Writing Down the Bones* (Boston: Shambala).
   Lots of ideas to get you started – inspirational.
Stephen King (2000) *On Writing*. New English Library (London: Hodder and Stoughton).
   An autobiography of writing: helpful but uncompromising advice for beginner writers.

2 A Writer's Territory
Julie Armstrong

What Is a Suitable Place for a Writer to Work?

There are no right or wrong answers: the most suitable place to write is the one that best suits you. However, it is important that the place you choose is the one in which you can immerse yourself in the act of writing most deeply. Some writers prefer bustle, others tranquillity: somewhere they can *dream* uninterrupted.

Lesley Glaister says she likes to write in bed, Wendy Perriam too. It appears that there is something about the womb-like space of a bed that inspires creativity. Maybe because bed is a place where we can withdraw from the rest of the world and enter the fantasy space of our heads. It's a place for dreaming, and dreaming is linked to writing.

Caryl Phillips prefers to write in hotels where he can be anonymous. Nobody knows where he is and nobody can get hold of him. This illustrates the need some writers have for privacy, as well as space and solitude. While retreating from the world in order to write is important for some, there are always exceptions: Natalie Goldberg, for example, loves to write in cafés and restaurants; she finds the activity around her increases her concentration. However, even in a public space, writing can be a way of creating private space. We can watch the world going on around us and disappear into ourselves.

As a novice writer you might still be looking for that special place to write, a place in which you can reach your true potential as a writer. How can you discover the right environment for you?

Experimentation is the key. What suits one writer does not necessarily suit another, and preferences may change with the weather and time of day. Learn to be flexible. Write in different places and circumstances. Working in lots of different places lends itself to changing moods and experiences; it will increase sensory stimulation and enrich your writing, enabling you to step outside yourself and see things afresh. Keep an open mind: experimentation is useful for those who think they've already found the perfect space: perhaps there's another one out there with an even better atmosphere!

Try This: Exploring Territory

Arrange to meet yourself in different places: take your journal with you. Try a café or a pub, a park; some writers find bus or train journeys conducive to writing. Visit a cemetery, zoo, gallery, funfair, museum. Notice what's going on around you. Record what you think, see, hear and feel. Develop an eye for detail. Be observant.

Try working on something you've already started at home: perhaps the change of working environment will give you a new perspective on the work in progress. Now try writing in different rooms in your home. Which environment suited you best and why?

A Room with a View

Virginia Woolf wrote of having *A Room of One's Own*. To have such a space, shut away from the world, would be ideal for most writers, but this may not be feasible for everyone. It is possible, however, to create a writing territory for yourself. It can be as simple as a desk in a corner; a garden shed; a shared room the use of which you negotiate with a partner or friend. Wherever it is, it's the space offering the best internal view: where the dreams and ideas flow unhindered.

Having experimented with different places, try settling with one of them for a while. Whether you have chosen to write in a crowded pub or in an isolated room, you should be able to connect with the place and more importantly, with yourself. Then you will be able to engage fully with the act of writing. And if and when that place starts to feel stale, move on, or move the furniture.

Try This: A Temporary Territory

Some writers are like bower birds, and their desk space is cluttered with objects pertinent to the work in hand. If you have no room of your own, you might have space for a notice-board. Collect postcards, snippets of cloth, stamps, clippings from magazines – whatever floats your boat – and pin it all to the board. And if there's no room for a notice-board, then a shoebox of treasures will do: lay them out around you, to make a temporary writing environment, and then put them back in the box when you've finished.

Travelling Writers

Write anywhere and everywhere. Make time to devote to your writing practice. Don't be too rigid. Sometimes the place in which you are working will be suitable for short bursts of writing, at other times, for more sustained pieces. What is important is knowing what kind of writing you'd like to do, and knowing therefore where to go to best suit that activity. However, you'll only discover these writing places through trial and error.

Once you've found a writing space, limber up to work with a few writing exercises and then write! If you are constantly distracted, then the place isn't working for you. Get your mind used to the idea that this is a working space.

Experimenting with different territories is a way of rejuvenating yourself and your work, a way of experiencing the writing moment and making it full of vitality. The place you ultimately enjoy writing in most will be an environment where you feel comfortable, safe and inspired.

Further Reading

Virginia Woolf (2000) *A Room of One's Own* (London: Penguin Classics). What Woolf has to say about women writers needing a space is true for all writers, and it's a very good read if only to think about Shakespeare's sister.

The Origin of Ideas

Dear Auntie, Where do ideas come from?

Ideas are a tricky little kettle of fish. Some writers like to lay traps for them and surprise them at dawn. Others go hunting at night with sharpened pencils and alcohol. But ideas are not always on the run: sometimes, they chase you, and they can ambush you at surprising moments: they hide in atmospheric pieces of music, in beautiful pictures, and childhood memories. They can be particularly troublesome at night when they have been known to disturb the sleep of unwary writers. To protect yourself from such nocturnal encounters always keep a pen and notebook by your bed: this almost certainly guarantees that no ideas will ever come to you at night.

3 Creativity
Heather Leach

What Exactly Is This Thing Called Creativity and Have I Got It?

Have you noticed that there's something a bit odd about wanting to become a writer? Not the ambition but the language we use to express the ambition. It's the word writer itself that is oddly ambiguous. Think about it. You almost certainly have substantial experience as a writer of notes, lists, plans, postcards, letters – maybe even essays, reports, projects, and so on. You're already a writer. Of course. What we're talking about here is not that kind of writing – the ordinary everyday stuff that most people do – but the kind of writing that has the word creative in front of it: stories; novels; poetry; scripts. That word creative can have the strangest effects: some would rather go apple-ducking in a tub full of spiders than be labelled creative; while others (dream-struck and wild-eyed) are only too eager to set off on the path to Creativity World. If you ask any group of people (even would-be writers), whether they'd describe themselves as creative, the majority will regretfully say something like: 'no, not really, maybe sometimes, not very... No, I don't think I am'. There'll be one or two brave souls who go against the grain, owning up to a special kind of mind, personality or experience that they label as creative. Yet ask the same people to define what they mean by the word and there'll be a wide range of divergent responses, many tentative and vague, many others dependent on outdated stereotypes and clichés. In this section I want to explore some ideas about creativity and to suggest ways of developing your own creative abilities.

Right from the start, let's kill off the idea that creative people possess talents and character traits that the rest of us don't have. Not true. Just as plants grow, so people invent, imagine, create: it's what human beings do. While one person was daubing mud on cave walls, someone else was busy working out a new and quicker method for scraping the hairy bits off meat. Repeat after me: I am creative; he is creative; she is creative; we are all creative. We can't help it, it's in the blood and we've got the genes to prove it.

Creativity Wars

There are many definitions of creativity. It's one of those words, like love or community, that can mean all things to all people, and is often an ideological battleground. It can be easy to get the impression that ideas don't matter much, especially conflicting ideas. But ideas are strong: they persist, passed down through the cultural generations: teachers, books, mass media all act as carriers; ideas infect us like viruses, we inherit them like genes.

One of the most persistent, sometimes pernicious, ideas is that you can only be truly creative if you are in touch with a more mysterious world than that of everyday reality. This idea of the creative artist as semi-mystical, linked to nature, fairy, dream, and so forth, gained its greatest power during the eighteenth and nineteenth centuries, partly as a resistance to what was seen as the overwhelmingly mechanistic power of state and industry. Here is the origin of all those jokes about starving in garrets and waiting for the muse to turn up. Writers, particularly poets, became caricatured in the public mind as idiosyncratic creatures, sometimes thrillingly strange, at other times nerdishly weird.

This theory almost seamlessly transformed itself in the twentieth century (and is still going strong in the twenty-first), into the idea of creativity as linked to a deep inner self, a self that lies, oil-rich but dangerous, beneath the surface of consciousness. Freud's theory of the unconscious attempted to bring the scientific method to bear on human motivation and behaviour, to make a map of the mind, but he was well aware that he was not the first, 'Everywhere I go,' he said, 'a poet has been before me.'

As a theory, Freudianism isn't particularly fashionable at the moment and has always been disputed, but its influence is still pervasive: *Unlock the Secrets of Your Creative Mind*, shout a hundred self-help books, *Discover your Hidden Artistic Talents*, yell a thousand more. Many writers, most notably the Surrealists, have tried to draw on this unconscious power, using exercises such as automatic writing and associative wordplay. The idea that the creative process isn't fully conscious is both useful and nerve-racking. I'll come to the useful part bit, but just spend a moment or two thinking about the nerve-racking bit. If something is not in your control, how do you develop or improve it? If writing is something that the deep inner self has to do down there in the seething dark, then what has it got to do with you, the conscious sensible person reading this? How does the unconscious learn and develop? What does it eat and how should we feed it?

As a counter to this, others have argued for a more rational understanding of the creative process. The novelist Jane Rogers argues that writers are not arty but crafty: down to earth materialists. 'Self-expression may be a beautiful thing,' she says with a barely concealed sneer, 'and it can certainly have therapeutic value, but perhaps it should be confined to private diaries.' Rogers thinks that writers need to focus primarily on learning the practical tools of their trade: '...plot and characterisation...narrative structure; poetic form...' and so on.[1] George Orwell, in his brilliant article, 'Politics and the English Language', argues that the more unconscious we are, the more likely we are to produce sloppy, clichéd writing:

> Written English is full of bad habits which spread by imitation and which can be avoided if one is willing to take the necessary trouble. If one gets rid of these habits one can think more clearly...the worst thing you can do with words is to surrender to them. (George Orwell)[2]

The strongest lesson I think we might take from these debates is that creativity is made up of a range of skills, qualities and practices. It is no longer useful to define creativity in a language that has lost its power and our thinking will be more meaningful and interesting, in my view, if we use a contemporary language: the language of mind, culture, learning and consciousness rather than that of muse, magic and spirit.

Consciousness Studies

In recent years, scientists have begun investigating consciousness itself and some argue that creativity is an essential element of the mind/brain complex: that without the ability to make imaginative leaps, human beings would never have become human. At some point or other in the far distant past, one of our ancestors looked at an object, a feather say, and thought it might look stylish in his hair. This is the crucial metaphorical association: feather becomes ornament; one thing is imagined symbolically, in terms of another. This ability to associate leads to the ultimate symbolic system: language. Susan Greenfield in her book, *Brain Story*, suggests that the creative use of language is essential to any understanding of human evolution:

> Language has made us what we are. It freed us from stereotyped gestures and allowed us to use symbols to think metaphorically – to see one thing in terms of something else and to use, not just words but art to represent complex relationships, which in turn, have inspired innovative ideas.[3]

Greenfield, along with many other scientists studying the brain, believes that we are a long way from discovering the roots of consciousness, but that we are uncovering a whole range of insights which can help us understand the way our creative minds work. She points out that many people now consider Freud and his theories of the unconscious to be 'unscientific' but that there is much evidence for subconscious processes. She uses the example of a top tennis player who,

> has a serve of up to 120mph (193 kph) – once the ball has left the racket, his or her opponent has under 400 milliseconds to work out where the ball is going to land. The decision about how to return the shot has to be made subconsciously. Amazingly, when a player returns the ball they are not even consciously aware that the serve has started...None of the expert players I interviewed claimed to make a conscious decision about how to return a fast serve. Yet such a response is far more than just a reflex – it involves thinking strategically about exactly where to place the shot. Returning a tennis ball is a complex process – all done entirely subconsciously.[4]

There clearly are strong creative drives and energies available to all of us: powerful skills and talents that go beyond the more limited everyday abilities. Think about a skill you already have that uses this mix of the conscious and unconscious: driving for example; riding a bike; playing a musical instrument. It isn't possible to practise at a competent level while thinking in a mechanistic way about every move. You need to learn the skill and (this is the hard bit) you need to *allow* yourself just to do it: to drive; balance; play: to stop pushing the river.

Left Brain/Right Brain?

One popular theory of creative consciousness is that the brain is divided into two hemispheres controlling distinct aspects of human behaviour. The left brain is said to be more verbal and analytical, while the right brain is more emotional, visual and musical. Betty Edwards, author of the best-selling book, *Drawing on the Right Side of the Brain*, uses these ideas to set out a programme, which can enable beginners to become skilled at drawing. In the first edition of the book, she argues that:

> One of the key discoveries of the research revealed the dual nature of human thinking – verbal, analytic thinking mainly located in the left hemisphere, and visual, perceptual thinking mainly located in the right hemisphere.[5]

In later editions, she acknowledges that more recent research appears to show that the two aspects of mind cannot be precisely located in the left or right side, but that this dual nature is a useful way of understanding the way our minds work.

Dorothea Brande also posits the theory that our mind is split in two: one side, the unconscious mind, is the home of all creativity, while the other, the conscious mind, is where our critical senses reside.[6] She emphasises the importance of using the unconscious to write and the conscious to redraft. Very briefly, the unconscious mind is best tapped when we are closest to being unconscious: the early moments of waking, or at any time when monotonous activity (swimming, walking, mopping the floor, motorway driving) lulls the mind into a semi-unconscious state. But read the book for yourself. Every writer should have a copy.

So How Can This Help Me to Become a Writer?

The creative process is only partly under rational, conscious control. We don't fully understand how it works – and most of us feel uncomfortable with things we don't understand. Our education encourages us to be deliberate and conscious and we are expected to prepare for a writing task, for example, in an organised way. In the ideal world, so the received wisdom goes, essays, reports and projects need to be thought out in advance, developed through planning, then written in a form that is ordered and coherent.

These learned processes and procedures are central to our education system, and by the time we are adults they've become so familiar and normal that we take them for granted. Of course, many of us fall short of these standards but the point is that we are all taught, we teach each other, that thinking, planning and rationalising are the best ways of dealing with most writing tasks.

Before we go any further, please note that I am *not* arguing that planning or deliberate methods are A Bad Thing or that too much thinking makes you go creatively blind. My point is that the creative process, the creative writing process, is a human, non-magical activity like any other, but that most schooling doesn't help us develop it, particularly in the language arts. By the time we are adults, our practical understanding of creative processes is often still rudimentary and many of us have lost confidence in our own inventiveness.

Guy Claxton, Professor of Educational Psychology and author of a fascinating book, *Hare Brain, Tortoise Mind*, says:

> The study of creativity in many different areas shows that what is required...is a fluid balance between modes of mind that are effortful, purposeful, detailed and explicit on the one hand and those that are playful, patient and implicit on the other. [7]

Claxton argues that we need slower ways of learning and knowing, what he calls Tortoise Mind as opposed to Hare Brain:

> The slower ways of knowing...are not the exclusive province of special groups of people – poets, mystics or sages – nor do they appear only on special occasions. They have sometimes been talked about in rather mystifying ways, as the work of 'the muse', or as signifying great gifts.... This is a false and unhelpful impression. A 'poetic way of knowing' is not the special prerogative of those who string words together in special ways. It is accessible, and of value, to anyone. And although it cannot be trained, taught or engineered, it can be cultivated by anyone.[8]

Writing is necessarily a lonely business. You sit down at a desk or screen and just work away by yourself with only a pen or computer for company. It takes time and patience. It takes courage and intelligence. Writing uses your body and mind, your thoughts, images, ideas, emotions, in an interaction with language and culture, to produce the finished work. This complex interaction is the creative process.

I said earlier that we needed to stop pushing the river – in other words, to avoid trying to control already skilful unconscious processes with the less skilful deliberate mind. However, this metaphor implies a passivity that doesn't quite work as a guide to creative activity. Writing is more like canoeing: you need to be balanced and wide awake; you need to keep paddling strongly; and you need to understand and *to work* with the river as it takes you, as you ride it downstream.

How Do I Develop My Creativity?

- Stop thinking that creativity belongs only to special people. Write out the following line one hundred times: *We are all creative.*

- Be open to change and learning but don't be a pushover. This can be a difficult balance to maintain and your particular response to it will depend on the kind of person you are, on your experiences of life so far. Too much conformity to other people's opinions can stifle your own before they get a chance to develop. However, a knee-jerk resistance to new ways of thinking can be equally damaging. You need to challenge your own fixed ideas as well as those of others.

- Take your time. You can't hurry love, tortoises, trains or creativity.

- Remember that creativity isn't an *either/or* activity but a *both/and*. You need to develop *both* intuitive and imaginative qualities (play, relaxation, openness to new ideas and methods, inventiveness, flexibility, etc.), *and* reflective and analytical qualities (planning, evaluation, deliberation, judgement, etc.). You also need to learn to recognise the difference between these two kinds of state, to be able to switch between them and to merge the two together into an integrated creative practice.[9] If all this seems like a tall order then take heart from the fact that you're already highly skilled in at least the first three on the list. Let me demonstrate with a small but sweet thought experiment.

Try This: Creative Drifting

Look up from this page and find a clear, wordless space to stare at – the sky will do very well, or a blank wall, table or floor. Gaze at this space for a minute or two allowing your mind to drift. Sit back, relax and breathe. After a while bring your attention back to this page. Focus down onto the words. Put your analytical brain back into gear and begin to read again.

Did you feel the shift between the two kinds of consciousness? Were you aware of a reluctance to move from one particular mode to another? Or back again?

We are all used to making these mind shifts many times a day. We drift, daydream, fantasise, imagine – then we snap back to the task in hand and concentrate again: we focus, analyse, think hard. The challenging part is in merging the two modes together into an integrated creative practice. This is challenging for all writers, not just beginners and most of us get it wrong some of the time: we daydream and fantasise when it would be better to be critical and analytical; we deliberate and analyse when it would be better to let ideas develop intuitively. Creativity isn't a precise science: because it depends on interaction within complex systems (mind; language), it can't be pinned down exactly or switched on like a tap. However, it can certainly be developed, practised, learned. Remember the tennis player with his impossible return serve. The player's stroke looks 'natural' but we know that such skills and abilities depend, not on magical powers or mysterious forces, but on training, fitness and understanding. I believe strongly that it is the same with writing. There will undoubtedly be limits to learning, different for each of us, determined by genetics and other factors that we can't account for, but there is plenty of scope to go on before we reach those limits. Most tennis players are not Wimbledon champions (but can still be very good indeed if they are willing to put in the time and the training) and most writers aren't Shakespeare.

Try This: Creative Workout

- Stare out of the window. Look at the sky. (If Einstein could do it, so can you).
- Listen to music while you write. Try different kinds of music.
- Write by the light of a candle.
- Write in bed.
- Write in the bath. (Don't use a laptop.)
- Watch small children playing. Remember what it felt like to be a playful child. Practise when nobody's looking.

Let's recap what you need to do to become a good writer: read; write regularly; know your stuff; learn. These are the equivalent of the tennis player's concerns: watch a lot of tennis; play a lot of tennis; know tennis stuff (balls/racquets/pitches/rules/how other players do it/history and culture of tennis/what kind of shorts look cute); learn the arts and sciences of tennis. Understanding and developing your own creativity is part of this. You can learn to become more creative just as you can learn to become better at backhand or canoeing. Here are some writing exercises that will help:

Try This: Stretch The Imagination

Take an object – any object available to you right now, a pencil perhaps, and imagine a hundred and one other uses for it: for example: a tea stirrer; stake for a miniature vampire's heart; chimpanzee's termite gatherer. Keep going with the list – the more desperate you get for ideas the weirder your ideas may become.

Try This: Creative Mind Reading

On a bus or a train, look (discreetly) at the other passengers and give them imaginary names, jobs, lives. Choose one and imagine their thoughts as a stream of consciousness. Later, write up these thoughts into a first-person monologue.

Challenge your own stereotypes: e.g. imagine the man in the bank clerk suit as a male stripper; the little old lady as an expert in plutonium extraction; the skinhead as helplessly in love.

Try This: Make Things Speak

Take two objects – a book and a mobile phone; a computer and a pen; a table and a chair; a window and a blind; your left hand and right hand; your brain and big toe.

Now make them talk to each other. What would they say? How would they speak? If you're in a group, work with another person to develop a short dialogue. Imagine other encounters. Write down the conversation.

Further Reading

Dorothea Brande (1996) *Becoming A Writer* (London: Pan).
   Second to none on creativity. Currently out of print, but check E-bay or click on Amazon's *New & Used* for second-hand copies. Otherwise, be patient: since its first publication in the 1930, this book has been in print most of the time.
Guy Claxton (1997) *Hare Brain, Tortoise Mind* (London: Fourth Estate).
   There is a lot of good stuff in this one, although you might want to skim the detailed research.
Natalie Goldberg (1990) *Wild Mind: Living the Writer's Life* (London: Bantam Books).
   The title says it all. A creative feast.

4 The Necessity of Mess
John Singleton

Creation's Twin

In the beginning was mess, and it was called chaos. And out of it God ordered the world. Read all about it. The full story's in Genesis, the Hebrew Book of beginnings.

In the Bible account, this original primordial mess didn't just pre-date Creation, it was a precondition of Creation. Without it nothing could be made.

Such is the importance of mess.

There's another account of how mess acts as creation's twin. Science, which has its own myths, suggests that the world has emerged out of a rich chaos, or 'primal soup'. The implication of this image is that the 'mess of potage' (Shakespeare's phrase for oat soup or porridge) is full of goodness and rich nutrients waiting to be transformed (cooked) into something else. Chaos here is a figure for potentiality, promise, possibility.

Try This: Torn Texts

Tear out examples of text from a newspaper, magazine, brochure, manual, book: the more jagged and messy the pieces, the better. Cut these extracts into paragraph and sentence-sized chunks. Snip out some individual words/phrases. Casually drop them on the floor. Pick up pieces at random and arrange into a piece of writing, editing and repeating and writing-in connective stuff as you go.

The Debris of Life

Now let me talk about the chaos/mess in your life. Nothing personal. It's the same for all of us. First, there's the mess we carry around in our heads, the jumble of memories and the stuff down in the far reaches of our subconscious. Then there's the mess we are born into, what E.M. Forster famously called the 'muddle'.

This mess, and the muddle we make of it, is the chaos material out of which we spin our fictions and versions of the world. We all know this. In this sense mess is the *sine qua non* of all creative action. As does God, we start with mess; we've no choice. How we view this mess is the critical point. Most of the time, because we hate, even fear, muddle and mess, we humans are forever trying to make sense of it, get it under control, bring a bit of order back into our lives.

How do we do it?

Firstly, not everyone thinks it's all a muddle. Some think there's a secret plan at work in the world, and despite the mess already here (disease, earthquakes), and the mess we bring with us (war, environmental disaster, crime), there is an irresistible symmetry and purpose beneath. This is what holy men tell us. Others, like scientists and philosophers and investigators of all kinds, tell us different stories about the world we live in and the world that lives in us. None of them are sure they've got it 100 per cent right.

So many stories: such contrary narratives. What a muddle! Back to square one. So what do we do about it?

Well, we could choose the best story for us, a narrative that makes us comfortable and keeps the mess at bay. Or we could reject all 'stories' and take the Rhett Butler line and say we don't give a damn. Or we could say these are all cowardly pretences that turn a blind eye to the real nature of the universe, which is purposeless, unpredictable and careless of human kind. In this world we are strangers to each other and ourselves. Life is pointless; the most we can say is we exist.

Uhhm, that's existentialism for you, the Waiting-for-Godot line. We're just stuck in the mess. Tough.

The Human Endeavour

Now, those who seek order in this so-called disordered universe may be fools to try, but there is one human endeavour that recognises muddle, flux, contradiction, and, at the same time, admits the necessity of order and holds the two in gainful opposition. And that is art.

Try This: Story Mosaics

Write a story with ten short scenes. The idea is to write a mosaic of a story. Not one that is bound by cause and consequence, or which follows a strictly chronological narrative and behaves well. In your story nothing striking has to happen. Indeed your theme may be the untidiness and inconsequence of ordinary life or the arbitrary nature of events.

A Thoroughly Modern Mess

Art does, at times, alarm and upset. Writing, for instance, can persuade the reader that what they took for order and predictability and truth is, in fact, illusion and irrationality – mess in other words. Then, having led them through the turbulence of change and the anxiety of dilemma and shock, a play or novel can assuage and bring the narrative full circle with a suitable closure so we are consoled and reassured. Mess over: order restored.

Muddle, as both the indisputable subject and unavoidable context of writing, is one thing; muddle, embraced as a wilful part of the creative process itself, is another. I'm thinking here of those modernist experimenters who used chance techniques and forms of spontaneous invention as a deliberate/willed creative strategy. William Burroughs's celebrated cut-ups, Dada experiments with language, the subversive anti-grammar writings of Gertrude Stein were all acts in honour of mess and the uncertainty principle.

In some cases, these twentieth-century modernist artists were either seeking new ways of making or striking new political attitudes in their powerful protests against the dead hand of bourgeois capitalism.

Try This: Messy Business

Consider the concept 'mess'. Babies are messy almost by nature you could say. Is this the refreshing carelessness of innocence? Old people return to messiness. Is this just a measure of decline or reflective of a more relaxed attitude to life? As Freud might say, most of us spend our adult lives being anally retentive. Maybe we should be more anally relaxed? Know what I'm saying!

Take 'Mess' as a title and write a messy piece or a piece that takes a very hostile view of mess. Look at the mess in your life and evaluate its importance for you. Is a messed-up bedroom really a sign of teenage rebellion? I blame all this messanthropy on all the anti-mess products on the detergent/sanitary/household shelves of the supermarkets.

Making Mess, Making Poems

To my final point. This is about technique and how to approach the writing process.

We should start with mess and stay with it as long as possible. The mess I mean here is represented by all the initial verbal doodles, half-phrases, aide memoirs, scribblings that form the fruitful compost of the poem or short story or whatever. Mess in my view is the first and most critical phrase of composition (compostition!). I've learnt to accept reluctantly this necessary stage in my writing: reluctantly, because I like to have things ordered and coherent right from the verb go.

But what I've discovered is that the more verbal mess I create, the more likely a poem or story will emerge: I just have to be patient and wait; attend on events. When Keats advised writers against 'an irritable reaching after fact' I guess he was saying, don't get uptight, go with the flow, relinquish control, give the imagination its freedom.

I see in myself two writers now: one who is a messer, and one who is a controller. It seems to me that the first, the messer, the kid, should have his untidy turn, and then the second, the controller, the parent, can come in and clean up.

A friend of mine used to say good cooks don't bother food. It's the same with writing; let the food cook itself. In other words, don't interfere too much with the imaginative process; maintain a light touch, keep the botherer/controller at bay.

Letting the imagination take its messy unpredictable course is also a good way of getting out of trouble. Often a story or poem hits a dead end. What do you do? Give up? Yes, but only if you intend to come back later. *Or* you can go back to being a messy kid again. Chuck all your ideas up in the air, kick them around, mix them up. It might work and free up the writing. The lesson is: if your work's in trouble, get into a mess.

It's not easy letting go, 'letting your pencil go for a walk' as the painter Paul Klee used to say. Writing being the unsettling process that it is, we have the tendency to play safe, to devise elaborate plots and lengthy character studies as dependable travelling companions, or as road maps to prevent us getting lost. Well, my advice is: 'get lost' – it's the best way of finding out where you're really going.

Butterfly

Here's an instructive example of how mess morphs into something much more: a poem called *Butterfly*.

What is it with you
you flimsy, wingy thing?
got the shakes?
out of sync?
navigation on the blink?

Just what is it about
this dithering
this aerial stuttering
this er...err...erring
flight?

Is it just a nervous tic
this rapid ricocheting habit?
or some off-beat trickery?
designed to dizzy
predators
make them think you're on the piss
that something's amiss and
stop
pursuing you?
Or is this flighty fashion
just a come on?
yeah, admit it
with those gamine eyes
the velvets of your wings and thighs
your hems and frills and laciness
tarty lingerie, ma cherie
you play the flirt
i guess
it's a butterfella
and a helluva
good time you're after.

But little pleasure-seeker
your hobbled flight is over
too too soon.
Goodbye bright thing.
As you wither on the wing –
We catch our own breath faltering.

I wrote this in the summer of 2002. I must have spent at least five or six one-hour sessions scribbling in Costa Coffee with nothing happening. I had pages of notes and lists of descriptive phrases such as 'flimsy creature', 'fragile-winged', 'diaphanous', 'tapestried wings', 'damask', 'coiled antennae', 'illogical flight', 'Lepidoptera', 'Red Admiral', 'feelers', 'aerial'. And so on: little more than cliché. But this stock-taking set the poem's agenda. By this I mean it established themes like flimsiness, embroidered colouring, the insect's zany flying habits.

After this bit of route mapping I began to focus on the colouring and shape and texture of the wings and the notion of flimsy gave way to laciness which suggested lingerie and flash underwear so come-hither in the Ann Summers shop just round the corner from Costa's in Nottingham. This train of thought led me on to make-up and mascara and blusher and all the vocabulary of slap. I made lists of beauty products, splashed them like rude lipstick all over the pages of my notebook. Nothing came of this in the poem. I decided that shine and gloss was not madam butterfly's thing.

In the end, I screwed up all the verbal clutter and tossed it in the bin of oblivion. 'Velvets' was the word that eventually emerged out of all this concern with texture and colour and feel. Its soft richness, when lined up with the word 'thighs', gave me that cheap slightly sleazy-sex feeling I wanted. Actually, I don't know whether I wanted it or whether the poem gave it to me without being asked. Either way, I was glad to have something a step beyond cliché. The point is; I had to work through a lot of dross and mess to get to where the poem began to look minted and fresh.

And the end section is where the controller came in. It's a much larger observation about life, dressed up in metaphor. It's a kind of summation, a steadying of the theme after the ricocheting flights of the poem earlier on.

Looking back over pages of notes and jottings for this poem I can see a sort of pattern under the messiness. Five stages in the composition seem to have emerged.

Firstly, I started with the obvious, the familiar things. I chucked in everything, any thing that came to mind, good, bad and ugly. I censored nothing. And I knew that most of it I would never use. I remember picking up a phrase from a Robert Graves poem where he describes the 'honest idiocy' of a butterfly's flight.[1] I threw that at it. Clichés, borrowings, the lot: I dismissed nothing. The truth is, this poem, like many others, was built on the honest but dull toil of tired phrases. I now try not to be too hard on such hackneyed words – they're good for starters if nothing else. They're the plod from which the poem takes off and learns to fly.

Secondly, after a time, single words began to coalesce into phrases. I tried some odd couplings, a riff here, a riff there. More agglomerations followed as the words began to get the collaborative message. The pages were blotted with huddles of them. Lone words or images that had no partner I listed in the margin. Kept them on the sub's bench for when the going got tough or critical.

In the third phase, I decided I had too many players and one by one began to get rid of the lame and the uninspired – the litter. I gave the hard-nosed accountant/controller something to do. Redundant phrases went. He created a bit of space.

Fourthly, as a result, routes opened up, sentences grouped themselves together in another burst of congress and from then on the poem more or less wrote itself. This stage took about 15 minutes: the earlier messy stage, about a week.

Finally: a fifth phase; a final check over, last couple of lines reworked. Sorted.

Try This: Playing With Clichés

Take any object or animal that attracts you. Write down as many clichés, obvious phrases about it as possible as quickly as possible. Rework some of the clichés, substituting different words or inverting phrases. New ideas will suggest themselves, follow them relentlessly firing off as many words, images as you can pack into your notebook. I like to work in A4 size so I can sprawl across the page and leave large open spaces for later extensions to ideas already there. Work till the page looks like an ink-bomb's hit it. Now get rid of the dross. It's done its work. Time to get tough and search out the original and arresting under all the word litter. Polish and serve up.

Further Reading

Adam Phillips (1999) *The Beast in the Nursery* (London: Faber and Faber). An intriguing book to dip into. Adam Phillips is a child psychologist and has some thought-provoking things to say about mess.

William Burroughs (1987) *The Ticket That Exploded* (London: Flamingo). The best of his trilogy of experimental novels featuring his celebrated cut-up technique.

5 The Blank Screen: Developing Writing Routines and Reading Habits

Julie Armstrong

Why Do Writers Fear the Blank Screen?

Why do we go to such great lengths to avoid being alone with the screen?

There are a number of reasons but fundamentally the answer is fear. This fear is distinct from a writer's block, which tends to interrupt the process, this is the fear that stops writing before it has begun. But fear of what? Getting in touch with your thoughts and emotions? Awakening memories? Running out of ideas? Sustaining a piece of writing? Failure? Writing rubbish? Having nothing of value to say? Not making a good impression on your reader? Lack of confidence?

Why a writer fears the blank screen is most likely to be one, or all of the listed reasons. Now that we have identified a cause, what can we do about it?

Part of the Process

Firstly, don't be afraid that you are the only writer who struggles to write. It's all part of the process and it is quite natural to experience this fear and self-doubt; these feelings are inevitable. Can I do it? Who will want to read it anyway? These are questions all writers have asked themselves at some stage. Writing can indeed be a very daunting activity, but see the struggle as all part of the on-going process, with peaks and troughs along the way. Everyone fears that their creativity will vanish, you have to find a way of living with the fear: recognise it, acknowledge it, then build up a tolerance and write through it. You have to be courageous and develop a steely nerve. What matters is that you make a commitment to your work and take on board all the anxiety, fun and joy that comes with the practice of writing. If you're not on a course with creative writing assignments, then you don't have to share your work with anyone if you really don't want to. The choice is yours. And if it is rubbish, so what? Write it. It's unlikely every word you write will be rubbish. Often there will be a seed of an idea among the chaff. It is this seed that you have to nurture, to help it germinate and grow.

Writing *is* introspection. If you *really* don't want to connect with yourself, to get in touch with your inner world of emotions, thoughts, memories, ideas, then writing is probably not for you. Having made the decision that you do want to write, how do you get over the fear of the blank screen?

Confronting the Blank Screen

The blank screen is awesome, likewise the idea of making your mark on it. However, if you are to be a writer, the time comes when it's just you and the screen: you have to confront it. Some novice writers think that they should wait for divine inspiration before starting. Divine inspiration is a myth. Writers have to work at discovering ideas, even though it is tempting to find all sorts of distractions to avoid writing: you'll just have one more cup of coffee, phone a friend, go to the shops, take the dog for a walk and then you'll write. These are displacement activities: you have to overcome them.

Writing takes a great deal of time, energy, thought, and a great deal of endurance. Is it any wonder we fear writing? It is hard work. And work it is: you have to see writing in terms of work. See it as a job: a very enjoyable, but demanding one. Once you view it like this then you will realise that, as with any work, you have to put in the effort if you want the rewards. Going to work involves setting your alarm, getting yourself organised and then focusing. Adopt the same approach to your writing. Work is a daily habit. Writing is a daily habit. The trick is to work out how you structure your own habit.

Developing the Writing Habit

It can be very difficult to get in the mood but you can't always wait for the mood to be right because the few occasions when it is will not be sufficient to get the work done: some prolific writers *never* feel like writing, but they are disciplined enough to get on with it anyway and *make* the mood right.

For those studying writing at university or participating in writers' workshops, paper is most likely to be the first point of contact with your ideas. So, if the blank page scares you, scribble onto it: write a sentence: it doesn't matter what. Draw something. Annihilate the white emptiness and then write. Some writers prefer in any case to write in longhand before they write onto the screen, saying it feels more physical and connected. If you're a screen junkie, try it. Experiment and see what really works best for you.

Writing in groups often helps: perhaps, because of the sense of compulsion that study brings, there is an element of what writers call 'permission' to write: you *can* do it because someone *makes* you do it. When you are outside the group, you have to find your own way of giving yourself permission.

If you don't participate in workshops, I suggest you do. You'll meet other people who are as passionate about writing as you are, giving you the opportunity to discuss ideas and share work. This interaction will provide stimulus and help develop your self-confidence; it will act as a valuable source of inspiration and motivation. You can read more about this in a later chapter: 'Writing Together: Groups and Workshops'.

What Else Can You Do?

- Give yourself permission to be alone at some point during each day. Enjoy the freedom and peace this brings you and allow it to recharge your imagination and fire your creative energy.

- Every day set a time that suits you to write. Start with 15 minutes, then build up to 30 minutes and in no time at all, you will be writing for an hour or more and wondering where the time has gone. Remember, if you don't make the time to write, and structure your life around the practice of it, you will never be a writer. The continual act of making time to write and actually doing it will build up belief in yourself as a writer.

- Avoid distractions: if possible take the phone off the hook; don't answer the door; tell family and friends that you don't want to be disturbed, and in time they'll come to respect your writing and treat it as seriously as you do.

- Be professional: muster up as much concentration, discipline and energy as you can.

What Can You Write About?

Anything you like but make it something you care or feel strongly about, something that interests you. You need to bring passion to your subject matter. Think deeply about what fascinates you: relationships, dilemmas, loss, happiness? Maybe you don't know what you care about until you write: some writers say they write to discover what they want to write about. So, if you have no ideas, write anyway and discover what stimulates and excites you. And if all else fails, try the exercises in this book. Use them to kick start you into action.

Try This: Pictures and Postcards

Find a picture that intrigues you. Ask yourself questions about it and write down the answers:

Are there any people in the picture?

If so describe them.

Why are they there?

Who is with them? Why?

What kind of lives do they lead?

Describe the view. Use your senses.

What's going to happen next?

Try This: Objects and Owners

Select, beg, borrow something: a cup, a feather, a shell, something you find in your pocket, anything that interests you.

Describe it in detail. Imagine a character now owns this object.

The object is important to them, why? What's their emotional state? What kind of person are they? A crisis is about to take place in their life. Write about it.

Developing the Reading Habit

You can read more about this in a later chapter: 'Reading as a Writer', but it cannot be reiterated enough: writers must read.

Reading enables you to see how other writers handle specific situations that you may be having difficulty putting into words. Reading helps you develop the art of concentration: it serves as a source of inspiration; it sparks the imagination. If you're stuck, pick up a novel, or a screenplay, or a poem you know will make you want to write.

Writing Buddies

One way of overcoming the fear is to develop a relationship with a writing buddy, someone who shares your enthusiasm for writing. With this person you can discuss the trials and tribulations of writing. Receiving and giving support with a like-minded individual strengthens your resolve to write and gives you support and insight into your projects. By discussing work in progress and reading it aloud to each other, you will 'unblock' your inability to write and progress. You will also develop the art of listening, an essential skill for a writer.

Under Pressure

Sometimes writers put too much pressure on themselves: today I am going to write a short story. This pressure creates anxiety. Anxiety creates tension and stress, making it even harder to write. Simply say to yourself: today I am going to write and it doesn't matter what I write. Then write whatever's in your mind even if it's: 'I'm bored with this and can't wait until lunch time.' Then keep going, don't censor what you write; don't worry about spelling, punctuation or grammar. Just do it. You will only truly learn to write by doing it and as frequently as possible. But if you've really got a block, don't beat yourself up over it. Take a break. Give yourself a time limit. Let's say a week where you go for walks, visit friends, have days out, go and see inspiring films. After your time limit is over, tell yourself: now I *am* going to do it. Give yourself up to the act of writing and see what happens. Don't forget that first drafts are allowed to be terrible and no one need ever see them: don't get it right: get it written! You can always redraft and fix it later!

Try These: Kickstart Your Pen

- Cut out newspaper headlines. Choose one as a starting point for a piece of writing. Write for 15 minutes.

- Write down the first line of six different random books. Select your favourite and continue writing. Write for half an hour. Then rewrite the first line.

- Natalie Goldberg says she writes everything she knows about black and white for half an hour in the hope that she will be inspired. Try it.

- Write about a train or bus journey; a first kiss; a conversation. Uncover memories that you had forgotten existed.

- Examine a relationship: father, mother, son, daughter, partner, friend. Use this work as a springboard for further writing.

- What are you most afraid of? Write about it.

- Now write about one of your obsessions.

- Put on a piece of music and record your thoughts and feelings as you listen to it.

A Lifebelt for your Characters

Sometimes your work stalls because you don't know your characters well enough. Read the chapter 'Your Travelling Companions', but try this exercise about a new character, or about a pre-existing character currently giving you difficulties.

Try This: Character Questionnaire

Name
Have they a nickname?
How old are they?
Have they any siblings?
Occupation
Where do they live?
Are they in a relationship?
Does the relationship make them happy? Give reasons.
What are their hobbies?
Have they any particular dislikes?
What are their fears?
What are their ambitions? Why?
What is their favourite colour? Why?
What is their favourite food?
What country would they most like to visit?
Describe their emotional life.
Describe them physically.
What makes your character angry, happy, sad?
What is the worst thing that has ever happened to them?
What is the best thing that has ever happened to them?
What are their fantasies?
How is their life like now?
How would they like their life to be in ten years' time?

Now put this character in conflict and write about the conflict and how they resolve it, drawing on your notes from the character questionnaire.

Acknowledging difficulties is the first step to overcoming them. The second step, is writing your way through them. Good luck!

Further Reading

Maura Dooley (2000) *How Novelists Work* (London: Seren).
    The chapter about Jennifer Johnston writing her novel, *The Illusionist*,

will show you that you're not alone if you're frustrated with trying to transfer ideas to the screen. Read the book and get the energy back to confront your fears!

Stephen King (2000) *On Writing*. New English Library (London: Hodder and Stoughton).

King gives you the nuts and bolts: he helps take the fear away by demystifying the process.

Diversionary Tactics

Dear Auntie
I love writing. I'm good at it. I get excellent feedback but I can't ever seem to get round to doing any.

Some people really are too busy to write. Some people aren't, they just tell themselves they are: and some people make time for writing.

These people are lucky; the desire to write niggles them, it gets under their skin and they obsess over it like addicted gamblers rattling the dice for one last throw. Meanwhile, their washing up festers for months, their carpets decay, their cats leave home to seek refuge and food.

Which one of the three are you?

Now answer this: you are about to sit down to start writing and you glance round the room.

At this point, do you:

a. Sigh, and notice that the carpet is covered with flecks of cotton wool, which your cat (prior to leaving home) has carefully shredded and you follow the trail to the cat, feed the cat, de-flea the cat, de-flea yourself, de-flea the furniture, because, after all, a tidy room makes for a tidy mind and you can't possibly start writing until everything is in order, and before you know it you've shampooed the carpet and scrubbed down the paintwork and repapered the walls and abandoned the day's writing because there's no time anymore.

b. Play FreeCell on the computer.

   c. Realise this cotton wool incident has great potential for showing character, and write a new section about cotton wool and cats and fleas, knowing it won't fit in your story anywhere, but what the heck; it feels good writing it.

   d. Tidy the cupboard under the sink (or any other cupboard you haven't opened for over 12 months).

   e. Feel that everything is spoiled, you can't possibly write now the cotton wool incident has annoyed you, and anyway, you've got to go to the bank and that'll only leave 4 hours before you have to pick up the kids from school and you can't write anything decent in only 4 hours...

   f. Look up 'cotton wool' in a web search engine. Make notes about cotton wool, email a friend about how you're writing a novel about cotton wool, sharpen all your pencils, look up 'pencil' in a search engine, play a few hands of FreeCell, look at the time and realise you've got to go and pick up the kids from school...

   g. Do all of the above.

Or do you ignore the cat, the cotton wool, the carpet and get on with the writing?

Each one of the above – bar the getting on with the writing – is an example of a displacement activity, and displacement activities are inappropriate responses to stimuli, induced by stress, or fear. They are the strange and wild things writers do to *avoid* writing. The thing is, when you actually start writing you can wonder why on earth you spent so much time scrubbing the loo when you could have been doing this, yet, the next day, it's just as hard as it ever was to get round to switching on the computer.

There is no real answer to this other than identifying what it is you do that might be interrupting your writing activity: knowing your enemy is, after all, a good way to steer clear of being ambushed. Set yourself a time by which you must have started up the computer, or opened your notebook. Have breaks, but be careful that they don't turn into 5-hour coffee mornings.

There are other more deadly forms of displacement: maybe you spend hours browsing through websites to buy craft-of-writing texts, and, perhaps, you even read them. Maybe you spend your evenings driving between various writers' circles. Maybe you research your story so well you deserve a higher degree in its subject matter and still you keep on researching, reading, making copious notes in your journal, never moving beyond acquiring the material and onto the slog of working with what you've got...

Books are useful (otherwise we wouldn't have written this one!) but they can't do the writing for you. So, stop reading, if all you ever do is read, and put the advice into practice.

Research can be very exciting: but it is often very tempting in the first rush of ideas, to try to put in them all. Besides that, there is the vanity of creativity: many a writer has set out believing that their work will be the final say on a particular theme, so they'll research everything because their first novel, short story, play, poem will be tremendous. It will present a new angle. It will present every angle. It will be all-encompassing! Universal! But if anyone ever did manage to pull this trick off, there'd be nothing left to say in the next one. In any case, searching out more great ideas rather than working with the ones you've already got is a great way to avoid writing! Have a cut-off point at which you stop looking for new ideas, and work instead with the ones you've got. In the end, too many ideas can be as bad as too few.

All of these things are displacement activities disguised as useful writing activities. Craft-of-writing books are good, so are Writers' Circles, so is research, but not if they make you too busy to write!

The deadliest bit of displacement of them all, however, is Never Finishing, because if you finish, you might send it off somewhere, and it might get rejected and you will have failed: much nicer to be perpetually in the process of writing where you can paddle about endlessly, the possibility of success still swimming with you. This is the deadly zone where you can still hope that the story might get published, or performed...when it's ready. But if you stay here, it will never be ready.

It's hard to stop fiddling, but resist the temptation; put the manuscript away for a while. When you look at it again with fresh eyes, you might see glaring errors and plot inaccuracies that you should fix, but if all you find is your own vague sense of dissatisfaction then perhaps what needs fixing is not the writing but your self-confidence. Get some peer group appraisal or feedback from a writing tutor, or an agent or even an editor who, if you're lucky might accept it, or if you're even luckier still, will explain why it is being rejected. And remember that rejection doesn't always mean failure; it can mean the right story has hit the desk at the wrong time, and editors and agents are often too busy to send out anything other than a standard letter saying thanks but no thanks.

In the rare event of you finding your story to be absolutely perfect and brilliant and wonderful, start redrafting immediately: I'm not sure I know of any writers who ever think their work is absolutely 100 per cent perfect.

So: don't avoid writing by doing a million other things. And when you do start writing, remember to stop!

6 Dreams and Visions
Julie Armstrong

Cultivating Visions and Images

'Seeing' images and having visions is a powerful part of the visual imagination. Some writers naturally have a strong sense of the visual. Others have to work at developing this sense, much in the same way as a Zen Buddhist seeks to develop powers of concentration in order to meditate. Indeed, some writers consider writing, with its senses of heightened awareness, to be a form of meditation, something we'll return to later. For now however, since a strong visual imagination is an asset to any artist, let's explore ways to develop this, and use it in your writing.

Firstly, it is essential for all writers to develop their powers of observation. One way of doing this is to transport yourself back to childhood. Look at everything from the point of view of a child trying to capture the freshness and innocence, the fascination children have for the world around them. Try and look at things as if for the first time.

Remember, it's not what you see but how you see it.

Try This: Learning To See

- Focus on something in particular which captures your attention, a starry sky, for example. Look at it very closely then describe what you see as if from the point of view of a child.

- Choose a piece of fruit. Examine it and describe its exact colour, texture. Taste it. Now write about the experience in as much detail as you can.

- Choose a scene that delights and enthuses you in some way: a sunset, an urban setting. Study the scene: allow it to fill you with energy. Look at tones and colours, light and shade. Make a list of adjectives that capture the scene visually. Use your findings to develop a piece of writing that brings the scene alive and allows the reader to see it in visual detail.

Untangling the Mind

Many view writing as a form of meditation, not least of all Dorothea Brande, whose book, *Becoming a Writer*, is an essential read for all writers.[1] Writers, like Zen artists, strive for a contemplative way of life that prepares them for their work. The actual act of writing becomes a form of meditation; it untangles our emotions and cleanses the mind. Through writing, we cultivate qualities of absorption and self-mastery, leading to spiritual and emotional growth, qualities of value to the budding writer.

When developing our sense of the visual, the powers of meditation cannot be underestimated. Meditating allows a writer to be receptive: it helps to tune the mind and sharpen the senses. In addition, meditating develops our imagination; it also helps us gain control over thoughts and feelings and gives us a sense of order and harmony, which in turn, sets us free to write.

Try This: Learning To Meditate

- Sit in a quiet place. Relax. Close your eyes. Let your mind drift. Don't force anything but 'see' what images and visions come to you. Open your eyes. Let these images settle for a few minutes, then:

- Describe what you saw as vividly as possible. Write freely: don't concern yourself with correct grammar, spelling or punctuation that can come later.

- Now construct a context in which your vision can exist. Be as imaginative as you can, do not censor what you write, just let the words flow.

- Sit at your computer in a dreamy state. This quiet time will provide an opportunity to let in ideas. Don't worry if you're not inspired today, inspiration often comes slowly, this *dreamy* time today may result in creativity tomorrow as your visions manifest.

■ Daydream. Let thoughts and images float into your mind. Allow yourself to drift into your 'own world', your 'inner landscape'. Write descriptions of what you see, think and feel.

Don't expect instant results. Be patient. Patience is a virtue writers need.

Other Ways to Cultivate the Visual Imagination

The writer Penelope Fitzgerald has said that her work often begins with a persistent idea or image. She speaks of one image, in particular, which inspired her. On a visit to Cambridge, she saw cows under willow trees. It was a very windy day, and it seemed to her that they were almost dancing in the wind. She was so captivated by this one image that she started a piece of writing.[2]

Try This: Starting Points

Collect written images from your daily life in your journal in much the same way as an artist collects drawings in a sketchbook. Be alert. A writer is never off duty. What do you see that captures your attention? A V of geese flying through the sky? Capture the image in your journal. Be precise and specific with language.

Look for images on journeys. Take a train or bus journey. Gaze out of the window. Visit art galleries. Jot down anything interesting that catches your eye. Make sketches of images you find stimulating. Put two different images together and try to connect them in a piece of writing.

Now for Something Different...

Engage with activity that gives you the opportunity to connect with your unconscious mind, usually something physical and repetitive like walking, cycling, swimming. Allow yourself to relax as you perform these activities. Absorb what you see. Be receptive to whatever images come into your mind. Can you make any connection between a good writing session and a particular activity, be it swimming or visiting an art gallery? Did you write more easily after taking a bus or train journey? Be sensitive to connections and engage in the type of activity that results in your most fluent writing.

The Reality of Dreams

Most writers are also dreamers. It is a question of entering these *dreams* and transforming them into writing. When we engage with images, visions and dreams we are connecting with the unconscious mind. Dreaming is accepted as a plunge into the unconscious. Freud believed the unconscious to be the 'true' reality. Jung saw dreams as a way in which the conscious and the unconscious engaged in dialogue with each other. He believed that dreams are creative symbols. Like visions and images, dreams can be very useful to the writer: they can often be a trigger for the imagination and ultimately a focal point for writing; it is a question of knowing how to realise their potential.

Making the Most of Your Dreams

In the early 1980s, Stephen King made a trip to England. He fell asleep on the flight and had a dream about a popular writer falling into the hands of a psychotic fan living on an isolated farm, and wrote the dream down on an airline napkin. Later, in a London hotel, he could not sleep. He got up and went downstairs to ask the concierge if there was a quiet place where he could write. The concierge took him to a desk on a second-floor landing where King filled 16 pages of a notebook.

He says that the *actual* story did not exist at this point. However, knowing the story wasn't essential. He had located the fossil. The rest, he knew, would consist of careful excavation.[3]

Get into the habit of recording your dreams over a period of time, especially any recurring dreams. Always keep a notebook by your bed to write about your dreams upon waking. This way the dream will be captured when it is most vital. Dreams have a tendency to lose their potency as the day moves on, or it may be that we simply begin to forget them.

Dream Time

Some writers prefer writing deep into the night because it is a time when they have access to their fantasy lives more easily, perhaps because they are close to sleep. Blurring the edges between dreaming and waking can be an important part of the writing process.

Others prefer to rise early in the morning: Barbara Trapido often sets her alarm for 4 a.m[4] and Dorothea Brande stipulates it in a chapter titled 'Harnessing the Unconscious':

> If you are to have the full benefit of the richness of the unconscious you must learn to write easily and smoothly when the unconscious is in the ascendant.

Again, this is a time when you are close to your dream world: it is a time of quiet and solitude; the space between sleep and the full waking state. So try it one dawn: rise early and before engaging in conversation with anyone (if they're also up and about), write freely and uncritically. Write for as long as you are able. Write about anything at all.

Making Your Dreams *Real*

Writers make things up. We tell ourselves stories and fabricate our dreams. It is important to realise that we can make our dreams *real* through writing.

Try This: Wish Fulfilment

What do you wish were true about you? Would you like to have won the lottery? Do you wish you had been a famous film or pop star? Write it down as if you were telling it to someone else.

If you were granted one wish, what would it be? To fly to the moon? To sail round the world? Live the wish in your head and then write about it.

The Dream Nightmare

And then I woke up and it was all a dream...

You've probably already been told it's inadvisable to finish a story like this: you might even have witnessed a weeping writing tutor pummelling a desk and howling, 'Never ever, ever finish a story with this!' but have you ever considered why not?

So discuss it!

As with all rules, it's there to be broken by a skilled writer who can make it work without leaving readers feeling cheated: but it's a dangerous game to play, perhaps because reading is in itself a kind of dream into which we are swept, willingly suspending our disbelief as we go.

There are, however, plenty of examples of narratives that use dream as a catalyst: a character's strange dreams can hook the reader, or further the plot. The atmosphere of dreams can be very unsettling: film narratives such as *Solaris* use the strange disconnected quality of dream as nervous characters begin to question the reality around them.[5] And *The Matrix* is built upon the premise that the world we know is a computer-generated dream.[6]

Using dreams in stories is not a new idea: Jacob, clad in an amazing coat, was a dreaming protagonist long ago. Perhaps we like using dreams because it parallels the creative process, something Sigmund Freud discussed:

> Storytellers are valuable allies, and their testimony is to be rated high, for they usually know many things between heaven and earth that our academic wisdom does not even dream of. In psychic knowledge they are far ahead of us, ordinary people, because they draw from sources that we have not yet made accessible to science.[7]

Further Reading

John Gardner (1991) *The Art of Fiction: Notes on Craft to a Young Writer* (London: Vintage Books).
Although there isn't a specific chapter dedicated to writers and dreaming, the index reveals a wealth of comment and advice for dreamers to be found throughout.

Sigmund Freud, trans. Helen M. Downey (1993) *Delusion and Dream in Wilhelm Jensen's Gradiva* (Los Angeles: Sun and Moon Classics).
This is a great little novel dealing in dream and memory, with a commentary by Sigmund himself examining how writers use dream, and how creative writing assists in dream analysis.

I Might Fail...

Dear Auntie
I know I should send work out, but
I'm terrified of failure!

Like acting, writing is a business where 'failure' is an everyday part of the process. Actors audition for parts, and most are rejected, not necessarily because they are terrible, but because they are not what the casting director is looking for at that particular moment. It's the same with writing: your story's brilliant, but it might garner enough rejection slips to wallpaper your living room, and don't forget that editors often don't have time to do more than send out the standard 'thanks but no thanks' pre-printed letter. The sad fact is that agents, magazines, publishing houses, or theatres will reject good pieces of writing: not every good piece will make it into print, but don't let the fear of this prevent you from ever getting to that stage. Don't take rejection slips personally; they're part of the job. Don't rely on just one piece of work: keep writing, keep finishing things, keep sending them out: if they didn't like the last story maybe the next one will be more to their taste, and carrying on writing will keep your mind occupied since nothing is more agonising than waiting for the acceptance letter that raves about your worth, your achievement, your genius...Beware: like kettles, watched letterboxes never boil!

II
Journey Essentials

7 Journals and Notebooks
Robert Graham

One of the virtues of Kate Atkinson's award-winning first novel, *Behind the Scenes at the Museum* was the level of specific detail about the 1960s. Atkinson was able to include details such as the fact that schoolgirls back then wore a particular kind of blouse for games, one covered with pin-prick air-vents that was manufactured by a company called Aertex. It so happens that Atkinson's impressive range of historical data was thanks to the journals she had kept while growing up.

Why Journal?

Nicola Ward Jouve speaks of the journal as 'the beginning of a voice of my own' and a place where a person can find 'a sense of self'.[1] Both of these observations, but particularly the first, hint at the most useful function of the journal: it's a place where you can develop your writing. The writer's journal has been described both as a nursery for creativity and as a creative midwife. But even more fundamentally than that, keeping a journal is an effective way of ensuring that your ideas don't get lost. Here's some advice from a Writing student:

> One of my tutor's sayings inspired me to search for a thrown-away idea and create something new from it: 'The best plays I have written are the ones I have forgotten.' In my case, it was true for stories.

Hallie and Whit Burnett concur with this, with the additional wisdom that recording something at the time it happens captures a certain freshness:

For the writer, first impressions are to be seized upon, and the act of writing in a journal often ensures that these impressions are permanently recorded.[2]

In her books on writing – *Writing Down The Bones* and *Wild Mind*, for instance, Natalie Goldberg promotes the idea of *writing practice*, something the writer should do every day in order to keep writing-fit. This is another good purpose for your journal.

In *Writing Fiction: A Guide To Narrative Craft*, Janet Burroway offers yet another purpose for the writer's journal: 'A major advantage of keeping a journal regularly is that it will put you in the habit of observing in words.'[3]

Here's an example of a writer doing just that:

Feb. 20th, I must canter my wits if I can. Perhaps some character sketches. Snow:
She came in wrapped in a dark fur coat; which being taken off, she appeared in nondescript grey stockinette & jay blue stripes. Her eyes too are jay blue, but have an anguished, starved look, as of a cat that has climbed on to a chimney piece & looks down at a dog. (Virginia Woolf, *A Writer's Diary*)[4]

Of course, a writer's journal may just be a bolthole, a place to wrestle with your demons and insecurities:

November 4, 1959: paralysis again. How I waste my days. I feel a terrific blocking and chilling go through me like anaesthesia. I wonder, will I ever be rid of Johnny Panic? Ten years from my successful *Seventeen* [publication], and a cold voice says: what have you done, what have you done? (From the journals of Sylvia Plath)[5]

Try This: Character Sketch

Use your journal to write a character sketch. Just for now, don't try to create a character from the ether. Instead, write a description of someone you have encountered in the course of your day. (Flannery O'Connor said, 'The writer should never be ashamed of staring. There is nothing that does not require his attention.') Try to find the telling details. Are the shoes particularly well polished, or not? Is there a moustache which disguises bad teeth? I know a man who, when he's talking to you, repeatedly plucks at the front of his shirt, tugging it upwards and outwards. (Is it to disguise his paunch?)

Write for five minutes.

Forms of Journal

You could use a hardback A4 pad with blank pages. However, an A4 ring-binder with plastic envelopes, a cardboard box, a cardboard envelope or a filing cabinet would all work as well. Here's another student on her approach to the journal:

> My journal is largely an assortment of bus tickets and scraps of newspaper with characters scribbled on them. If a person catches my attention, then they must, surely, be worth writing about:
>
> *Too-much-make-up lays her head on her companion's shoulder. She grins up at him cheekily and pretends to bite his fingers off.*

A journal can take many forms. For instance, in a 2003 interview you can find at the *Guardian Unlimited*[6] website, Richard Ford, author of the Pulitzer Prize-winning *Independence Day* describes what is effectively his journalling procedure. He speaks of collecting in a large cardboard box all of the notes he has made, on anything that came to hand, towards his third novel about Frank Bascombe (the protagonist of *Independence Day* and its predecessor, *The Sportswriter*). He describes the next stage as transcribing these notes and collating them in files organised around characters, themes and settings for the developing novel. That may sound reasonable not to say predictable. However, you may find it refreshing to have learned that one of the finest novelists alive develops his fiction in big cardboard boxes.

Possible Purposes of Journal

Just about the most useful book on the writer's journal is *The New Diary* by Tristine Rainer.[7] If you want an exhaustive inventory of the possible purposes of a writer's journal, read her book. (You should read it anyway.) To whet your appetite, here's a list extracted from *The New Diary*:

- Repository for thoughts, feelings and ideas which would otherwise be lost
- Recording dreams – also daydreams

- Spontaneous writing
- Note-making
- Recording overheard dialogue
- Descriptive writing
- Overcoming writer's block
- Creative project journal
- Diary (record of daily events etc.)
- Paste in photo, clippings, letters, quotes, drawings, doodles, dried flowers, business cards, labels
- Exaggerate
- Pray
- Express love, anger, sorrow, grief, ecstasy, joy, conflict etc.
- Write to your future self, your past self
- A place for the writer to work out

Jennifer Moon, in *Learning Journals*, a text that is aimed more at academic than creative writing, suggests some other activities you can try in your journal. She talks about meditating on something (her example is a shell): 'An object can focus attention and provide a starting point.' She suggests asking yourself questions, making lists, and concept mapping (also known as mind-mapping or making spider diagrams): 'A concept map encapsulates an idea and the themes radiate from the main idea.'[8] For example:

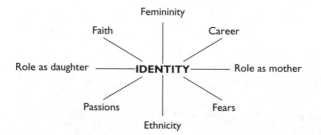

Try This: Daily Work-Out

In *Becoming A Writer* (which by the way is for many writers the most helpful book ever published on writing) Dorothea Brande advocates a particular discipline for the writer. But before passing it on, I should summarise something that is key to this text, and to the writer's life.

Brande posits the theory that our mind is split in two. One side, the unconscious mind, is the home of all creativity, while the other, the conscious mind, is where our critical senses reside. She emphasises the importance of using the unconscious to write and the conscious to redraft. Very briefly, the unconscious mind is best tapped when we are closest to being unconscious: the early moments of waking, or at any time when monotonous activity (swimming, walking, mopping the floor, motorway driving) lulls the mind into a semi-unconscious state. But read the book for yourself. Every writer should have a copy.

Here she is on the values of making an appointment with yourself to write each morning, early:

'If you are to have the full benefit of the richness of the unconscious you must learn to write easily and smoothly when the unconscious is in the ascendant.

'The best way to do this is to rise half an hour, or a full hour, earlier than you customarily rise. Just as soon as you can – and without talking, without reading the morning's paper, without picking up the book you laid aside last night – begin to write. Write anything that comes into your head: last night's dream, if you are able to remember it; the activities of the day before; a conversation, real or imaginary; an examination of conscience. Write any sort of early morning reverie, rapidly and uncritically. The excellence or ultimate worth of what you write is of no importance yet. As a matter of fact, you will find more value in this material than you expect, but your primary purpose now is not to bring forward, but to write any words at all which are not pure nonsense.'[9]

Try this for a week; then make it a habit for life.

Your Journal

It's all subjective and highly personal of course. However, you're reading this book, so you are in the market for some advice. I would say a bare minimum in terms of notebooks and journals would be the following:

As we've seen already, your journal doesn't need to be a book – it might be a drawer or a shoebox. The novelist Paul Magrs recommends exercise books:

> I always carry one with me and each of them soon gets filled up with what I'm thinking about or descriptions of scenes I've witnessed or made up: irresistible snatches of dialogue from bus stops and shops. Little drawings, too. The books are my place to file things away.[10]

My preference is for something more appealing to the senses than an exercise book, so I would say go to a good stationers or bookshop and buy yourself an attractive A5 or A4 hardback journal. (Have you noticed? Writers are often stationery junkies who get excited by a visit to Paperchase or Ryman's.) The more you like the look and feel of your journal, the more likely you are to want to use it, so choose carefully. Maybe the cover is a Degas reproduction. Maybe it feels soft, but not shiny. When it comes to the inside, you might think about opting for blank rather than lined pages. This frees you up to write in any direction you want, to doodle or draw and it's ideal for mind-maps and spider diagrams. Think about the quality and feel of the paper. I have some notepads at home with terribly flimsy paper and some which are more sumptuous and there's no doubt which I prefer.

So what do you write in your journal? Most of the available options have been mentioned already, but let's take a flash through mine. This particular one is A5 and has a pretend photograph of Mickey Mouse driving in his car and whistling. The photograph looks as though it has been pasted onto a map of Los Angeles. Don't ask me why.

The first page contains two ideas for a novel that I'm writing; I haven't used either yet. There are then a few pages of notes for a radio play about Billy Fury (which I have yet to write). Sometimes there is a page or more describing what I can see around me. Often this is when I am somewhere new. The point of it is more to practise writing than to record the experience. Nicola Ward Jouve speaks of the journal as:

> a writerly gymnastics. It's like being a dancer or a musician. Unless you practise, you don't develop the muscles, or the suppleness, or the nimbleness of fingers.[11]

Anaïs Nin argues for the same thing, but adds a motivating reason for being 'writing-fit':

> Writing…as one practises the piano every day keeps one nimble, and then when the great moments of inspiration come, one is in good form, supple and smooth.[12]

Quite often, my journal contains pieces of fiction that end up in a novel I am writing. Here's a cast list for the last one. Here's something I was told:

> Three-year-old to mother returning from hospital after an operation: 'Are you dead, Mummy?'

A lot of sentences begin with 'How about'. Some notes on the film *Toto Le Heros*. Sometimes I have stuck in a Post-It note or notes made on scraps of paper. Here's a list of chapters with word-counts from a novel I was working on – very important to fiction writers. A list of possible titles. Some notes on the film *Don't Look Now*. (Both the films I've mentioned became points of reference for my novel.) Sometimes there will be notes I've made about a piece that I have tabled at my writers' group. Part of a song lyric I was writing. Sketches for the staging of a play I was putting on. And notes on this very book, reader!

The important thing to remember about your journal is that anything can happen there. It's a place of freedom, as Hallie and Whit Burnett contend:

> …being private, [it] permits us to draw no morals, obey no rules, censure no extravagances. We write for ourselves only and need show no one what we have written.[13]

Your Notebook

Some writers take their journal everywhere with them. Because it won't fit in a pocket and I don't always have a bag to put it in, I mostly keep my journal at home. Instead, I always carry a notebook that's small enough to slide into one of my pockets. I have three different specimens on the desk in front of me now. One is paisley patterned and covered in stiff card; the second is Moleskine (a cult notebook amongst writers), black, with an elasticated strap to keep it closed and a cotton bookmark; the third kind is spiral-bound and plastic-covered, again with an elasticised strap. All of them would fit in the back pocket of your Levis.

Let's start with the flowery paisley one. At the back are several pages where I have noted down vocabulary while reading, words that I admire but tend not to use. I write them down and then make a point of using them in my writing. 'Fathom (v.)', 'dawdle', 'pzazz' and 'sprightly' are all down here. From time to time, I will keep a notebook by my bed solely for the purpose of recording words I find that I don't use and would like to.

At the front of the paisley notebook are pages of notes from a holiday in Israel:

> Israelis blare their car-horns at the drop of a hat. Honk at cyclists – every last, damn one! Different honks: warning; greeting; leching.

One section of these notes recorded an Arab teenager at the Dead Sea who approached women bathers of various ages and offered to cover them in Dead Sea mud, which is good for the skin. I was struck by how few of the women he approached refused the offer. These notes became 'Mud', a short story I wrote on my return. (Paul Magrs: 'Think of your notebooks as a way of capturing the things that go through your head.'[14])

Ideas for many stories that were never written are here, along with some that have been. A list of things men talk about ended up merged with notes (under the heading 'Carry On Bowling'), a record of conversational snippets I eavesdropped on during a bowling match in my local park. The result was a story called 'The Urban Spacemen', which is about the daft things men talk about, bowling, aliens and John Major.

In the Moleskine I find notes I made on a documentary about British showbiz in the 60s and 70s. (I was writing a novel partly set in that world.) There are the addresses of a number of little magazines to which I was planning to submit my work. And, further on, notes I made on Jonathan Franzen's *The Corrections*, speculations about what worked in it and why. (You have to work these things out so that you can emulate them!)

The third notebook, the plastic-covered one, contains a list of things I had observed people doing at the beach – looking for crabs, taking photographs, drawing their names on the sand, inspecting flotsam. One page is given over to a possible title for the showbiz novel I just mentioned. Another page has this overheard conversation:

> I've just been watching this programme about The Beatles.
> Have you heard of them?

I revised this to suit its new context and used it in the novel I've just been talking about. There's a page that says 'Fray Bentos', because for an instant I remembered that in the 1960s people used to eat that brand of corned beef, and I didn't want the memory to slip past. Another page just says 'stodgy burghers' – presumably a term I came across and planned to use.

Try This: Using A Notebook

- Go out and buy yourself a notebook that will fit in your pocket.

- Carry it with you everywhere you go for one week.

- Record any interesting conversations you overhear. If this doesn't seem to be happening for you, go and sit in a busy café and make it happen.

- Jot down any memory that pops into your head during the course of the week.

- Write down any brainwaves you have before you forget them. Most of the ideas for writing that you have in your life won't arrive when you're sitting at your desk. Don't let them escape.

- If after a week you haven't recorded anything you regard as valuable, give up using a notebook, give up writing as well. (You won't have to; a week should convert you.)

Further Reading

Dorothea Brande (1934) *Becoming A Writer* (New York: Harcourt, Brace).
   I first came across this book when the scriptwriter Paul Abbott (author of, among many television series, *Cracker, Clocking Off* and *State Of Play*) recommended it to me. In my view this is the one book on writing that all writers should have. It doesn't tell you much about craft or technique,

but it tells you everything you need to know about harnessing your creativity, about how your creativity operates. It has been in print, uninterrupted, since 1934, which should tell you something.

Tristine Rainer (1979) *The New Diary* (New York: J.P. Tarcher). This is the only book I know of on the subject of journal and diary writing. It isn't aimed especially at writers – maybe there's a gap in the market for a text on this subject that is. Meanwhile, I can't imagine anyone coming up with a more exhaustive list of things to do with your journal.

8 Reading as a Writer
Heather Leach

Friday morning. April. It's raining outside and I'm staring through the window thinking of Einstein. Nothing's happening out there apart from clouds: nature grey in tooth and claw. The notes I've prepared in researching this chapter are lying expectantly on the desk close to my elbow. I've put in the title: *Reading as a Writer* at the top of the page and now I'm peering at the blank whiteness on the screen waiting for words to miraculously appear. You have to have a beginning: you have to find a door in the page's wall. I wait, my mind tracing the flat, wordless space, searching for an edge, a recess, a movable brick. Still nothing. Then my daughter comes in with a cup of coffee. She leans forward and reads the title: *'What's the difference?'* she says. *'Why can't writers just read like everybody else?'*

And that's it: abracadabra; the page swings open.

Why *can't* writers read like normal people? It's a good question that raises a number of others: are there special ways of reading? Are there particular things that writers ought to read? And don't all writers read as a matter of course? Why do we need a chapter about reading at all? As you might expect, in a book that explores creative practice, there are no absolutely right answers to these questions, no one-size-fits-all solutions. In chapter 1 I argued that the second commandment for beginner writers, for all writers, is that we need to be readers. This chapter will unpack some of the pleasures and pains of reading in more depth, and will offer guidance and practical exercises to help you deepen and extend your own reading as a writer. There are as many different kinds of reader as there are writer and while I hope I can speak directly to you, to your particular experience, it is up to you to nip and tuck these ideas for yourself; to custom-read this chapter, for your own purposes, to make this writing into reading that can fit *you*.

Reading for Pleasure

The starting point for all of us, whatever our education or experience, has to be reading for pleasure. If you don't enjoy reading at all, if you've never enjoyed it and if you don't intend to put your heart into reading as well as writing, then stop now. Put this book down right this minute and go and become brilliant at whatever it is you *do* enjoy. Astro-physics; cat-breeding; tantric sex; it'll probably pay you more than writing anyway and life's far too short to put years of effort into something you don't like. Let me repeat Stephen King's words, quoted in the first chapter: *Reading is the creative centre of the writer's life.* You have to read and you have to learn to love to read. There's no getting round this one. Honest. Reading needs to become necessary to you, as addictive as tobacco or beer.

For many people, this is easy: they've already joined the Obsessive Book Club. But for others, reading may have become associated with a whole lot of other issues: serious study; homework: *Lit-er-rich-oo-er*; none of which seem like much fun. Pleasure cannot be forced and many people have been put off reading as children after being urged to read 'good' books by well-meaning adults. This kind of hierarchical categorising is a big turn-off. Reading difficult or classical texts simply because they are difficult or classical is nothing to do with reading for pleasure and will almost certainly not help in your development as a writer, although it might help when you want to impress others about your qualifications as a culture snob. Reading is alleged to:

- help you pass exams
- enable you to make intelligent conversation
- give you a leg-up into the intellectual classes
- make you a better person.

Such things may happen because of reading or they may not, but these are side-effects, off-shoots, ephemera. One of the key elements in reading for pleasure is freedom – *you* choose what you read, you and nobody else. If you're someone who has been put off then I suggest some mild therapeutic rebellion to clear the decks:

Try This: Do Bad Things To Books

Many people make books into gods, fetishes. Libraries become silent, holy places. Boxes of dusty paperbacks are transported from house to house, never to be read again, but never given away for someone else to read either. Believe me I know. It's not surprising: books *are* wonderful, but every once in a while I think it's important to rebel against too much literary holiness and to remind yourself that books are simply things:

Bad things to try (only on your own books of course...)

■ Write on books. Comment in the margins. Answer back.

■ Cut up books and make up your own stories or poems using the bits you've cut out.

■ Tear a book apart. As you read it, rip out a chapter at a time and throw it away (this is really naughty).

Now you've left all that *ought* and *should* luggage behind, you can begin again, as a free reader. If you want to be a writer, you need to learn to love reading because you can't help it, not because someone else tells you it's a good thing. There's no getting away from this one, so settle down to it and make the choice. It may take time but sooner or later, reading will hook you in like a drug; reading will make you love it – like love itself.

Reading to Learn/Learning to Read

Pleasure can't be forced but it can certainly be learned. Writers need to extend and develop their reading, to learn to read much more widely and deeply than the average punter: not because it's good for you, but because you cannot learn to be a writer without, at the same time, learning to be an intelligent, self-aware, reader. Jonathan Franzen says that reading teaches us how to be alone: through reading we slowly become persons, selves: we make up our inner, *imagined* lives from the books we read, from the feelings and thoughts we have about them.[1] In today's manic, digital world of noise and chatty togetherness, silence and solitariness becomes scarier and harder to find. This inner space is like the Tardis in Dr Who: small and insignificant from the outside: huge and complex on the inside. Reading alone, buried in a book, you are building your own version of the Tardis, a reflective mind space essential for the writer. You can *learn* to love reading.

Get Stuck In

Find a writer you like – Roald Dahl maybe, Tolkein or J.K.Rowling – and read as much of their work as you can get hold of: find out about them; look them up on a website; read their autobiography if there is one. This is how most addictive readers begin: a particular genre, style or voice hooks them in. For me, at 9 or 10, it was Enid Blyton. I read so many and got so desperate for my regular fix, that I used to hang around the library door, checking people coming in to see if they were bringing back a Blyton I hadn't read. The library staff got so irritated they suggested I tried something more worthwhile but by some miracle I was already impervious to literary do-gooding. Translate this into the grown-up world and simply read whatever appeals to you: love stories; science-fiction; horror; magic; rap-style poetry; nineteenth-century novels; chick-lit. Read until you've had enough, read until you're sick: no shame, no blame.

Don't Get Stuck

Those first great loves are wonderful, never to be repeated or forgotten, but you do need to find new styles, new forms, new books to fall for. Readers who want to be writers can't afford to be monogamous. There's a big world of books out there and life is short: time to kiss goodbye and move on. Let me repeat: this is not because the literary Thought Police have decreed that this is A Good (cultured/clever/posh) Thing, but because if you are to develop your own writing voice you need to have read a wide range of other voices. Chefs eat widely; writers read widely. The point is to become addicted to *reading itself.*

Read Harder

(Easy isn't always better – but it is sometimes.)
   Here's a quiz:

1. You're on a beach; the sun is beating down; somebody just out of sight is trickling sand over your lightly tanned toes; the ice in your drink is slowly, deliciously, melting. Is this the right time to tackle James Joyce's *Ulysses*?
   Yes   No   YOU CANNOT BE SERIOUS!

2. You have broken both your arms falling over the edge of the Karaoke platform (believe me, this really did happen to someone I know), and you are lying in bed next morning, your two plaster casts at right angles to the duvet making you look like a cruel cartoon, when a friend offers to read to you to take your mind off your troubles. Do you choose Franz Kafka's 'Metamorphosis', in which the main character wakes up one morning to find he has been changed overnight into a giant beetle stuck on its back?
   Y☐   N☐   YCBS☐

OK, you get the point. There are times and circumstances when you just want to read something easy and relaxing; holiday reading, one of those stories that slips down like strawberry ice cream or strong lager. There are other times, harder times, when you might want to go back, to re-read: *Harry Potter* maybe; *Jane Eyre*; Maya Angelou's poems. What it is doesn't matter: at difficult periods in our lives we may need to return to stories that are familiar, retracing old safe ground in order to make sense of the world just as small children like books to be read over and over.

But at other times, particularly when in training as writers, when we have emotional space and enough of our faculties (and arms) to get by, then we need to push beyond the limits of habit and safety, to read with more attention and effort. If you are not already an experienced and confident reader, then this will be hard at first. You will try things that don't immediately appeal: you will struggle with unfamiliar ideas, strange voices. You may feel awkward and wrong-footed, floundering in what feels like an alien language, deliberately designed to confuse and exclude you. This is painful and you might be tempted to give up, to blame the writing or the writer: *it's rubbish; incomprehensible; pretentious; deliberately obscure.*

What helps here, I think, is to remember that reading is a process of self-development, of *learning*. Learning – real learning – is not a passive business: you can't become a tennis player by watching Wimbledon on telly. I know, I've tried it – it didn't work. And you can't develop as a reader or a writer without pushing beyond your comfort zone. If *everything* you read is easy, accessible, straightforward and familiar, you're not doing it right. The learning thing, I mean. Let's recap: everyone is free to read whatever they find easiest, safest, simplest: Mills and Boon; the *Sun*; Shakespeare's sonnets; text messages; and nothing else for the rest of their lives if they so choose. But only if they don't want to be writers, which I assume you still do, otherwise you wouldn't have come this far. This doesn't mean that everything difficult or challenging is good, but how will you be able to tell the difference between brilliance and bullshit if your experience is limited?

Remember that you don't have to *like* everything you read. Even if something is well written, it may not be your thing. When you're reading for pleasure, when you've given the writing a fair-enough chance, you've really tried and you still don't like it, then put it down, take it back to the library, throw it through the window. There are plenty of other books out there. However when you're reading *as a writer*, it pays not to give up too soon: remember that some good things take time to get into, so challenge your own reading boundaries. Nothing is easier than to criticise a piece of writing or a writer – what is hard is to say *why* you think something is bad or *why* you don't like it. Sometimes, if we're honest, we may get it wrong. Some people quickly categorise work as pretentious and overblown, for example, but which actually includes words that are appropriate but that the reader neither understands, nor is prepared to look up. This is a case *of bad reading* rather than bad writing.

On the other hand there is a lot of bad writing; when you're reading as a writer, you can learn a great deal from it. For instance:

- People can be bad writers and still get published. This is annoying but encouraging.

- That it's a lot easier to recognise other people's weaknesses and faults than your own.

- Even really good writers can write bad stuff.

Try This: Bad Reading And Bad Writing

For many of us, the pressure (outward or inward) to be good readers/ writers is inhibiting. You can often learn a lot more by trying to be bad. Just remember not to get stuck there.

- Find a really bad poem

- Read the poems aloud in a group and – when everybody has stopped laughing – identify exactly what it is that makes this writing bad. Make lists of bad qualities. At this point you may want to revise your judgements: one person's bad is another's good; some writing is so bad it becomes good.

- Now, using the lists from everybody's reading, try to write the worst poem you possibly can.

- Pass it round and read out in the group.

- Now write a really good quality version.

This also works well with genre writing: Fantasy; Horror; Sci-Fi. Or you can have a go at writing the worst TV drama sex scene you possibly can.

Reading the Process: Work Out How It Was Done

Most of us are taught at school, college or university to read as critics, and it is sometimes difficult to get out of the habit. Reading, as a writer, is not the same as reading as a critic. Before we move onto some practical examples and exercises, I'd like to examine what I mean by these two approaches to reading, and to point out some of the differences between them.

For a start, the critic looks at the piece of writing *as a whole, finished and complete*: here is a story; a poem; a novel, says the critic, it exists in the world, a solid *thing*, almost as natural as rock. I say *almost* because, of course, the critic knows full well, that this book, poem (or, as the critics might say, *text*, but we're not being critics), was written by a real person and that there once was a time when it didn't exist. But the critical reader likes to *discuss* the book as if it has always been in the world, to speak of it as if it were a natural object. The key point here is that nobody seems to have to do any actual *work*: the *process* of writing: the *making* of a story or poem is largely irrelevant.

Many beginners imagine that a piece of writing that reads fluently, naturally, is *actually* natural: that it arrived fully formed, out of the creative ether, on the page. This is another version of the writer-as-God theory – no work needed, just the odd miracle. In the real world you make a tentative beginning, either in your notebook or on the screen, and when you read it back it's often a mess. Not only are there a couple of spelling mistakes plus the odd 'at the end-of-the-day, life's-a-bitch' clichés, but the rhythm and pace are all wrong and the whole thing is vague, unfocused: it doesn't quite say what you meant it to say. This is, sadly, where some people stop. '*I can't write*,' they say, '*it's crap. I'm no good. Time to give up.*'

Others, with tougher egos, but also taken in by the writing-should-be-as-simple-as-breathing theory, decide that, so what if it is crap: crap is what came out and, as nature is truth, the world can take it or leave it.

Neither approach helps: the first is clearly dead in the water and the second is likely to lead to terminal disappointment as most people who are not your mother, your lover or who owe you money, will take you at your word and leave it, thanks very much. What *does* help is to think of your first draft, however confused, clunky and awkward, as exactly that: a first draft; a bald and scrawny duckling, ugly as hell but it's your baby and it needs you.

The good thing about reading as a writer is that you can have double vision: you can read like normal people – following the story, poem, idea, as a continuous drama or dream. But you can also learn to look beneath the surface of the print for traces of *the making* process, the writer at work. When reading as writers, it helps to deconstruct the writing: to examine its elements, structures, interconnections, not only in terms of its meanings and contexts; but also in terms of its *form*: we need to look at how it *works*. A word of warning: we can never *completely* understand a piece of writing: there will always be some parts that are beyond deconstruction, beyond rational description, and a good thing too.

Writing is not rocket-science: it's much more complex than that. Fiction, poetry and so on are made out of the writer's consciousness interacting with culture, time and place. And when we bring *our* consciousness, as readers, to bear, we begin to change a piece of writing simply by reading it. Any creative process involves intuition, emotion, play, all of which, by their nature, are beyond final and complete analysis. But, hey, we don't need to *know* everything. There is much we *can* learn, much that is useful: skills and processes, techniques, methods, *know-how*.

Read to Find Out How It Was Done

Most of us, by the time we get into double figures, are unconscious readers. By unconscious, I mean that we take it for granted: we rarely need to laboriously spell out a word to ourselves, or to mouth the letters until their collective shape/sounds coagulate into a word. By the time we are 10 or 11, we have forgotten those eureka moments, when the meaning suddenly emerged out of incomprehension, and we found ourselves actually reading. Now that we are skilled readers, this process is so fast and seamless, that the words become image, sound, idea, emotion without us noticing: words strung together in a sentence become a story, a voice. (Some people may have a disability, say dyslexia, which interferes with their reading abilities: others may have simply missed the early reading boat for a variety of reasons. I suggest, that in either of these two situations, you seek extra support. For anybody else who still finds reading a chore, and isn't willing to learn to love it, I refer you back to the first page of this chapter.)

This seamlessness is what most prose writers are trying to achieve: writing that is apparently effortless – almost transparent – so that the reader slips through the words, like Alice through the looking glass, to the world beyond. As writers, we need to reverse this process: first we read the story, the poem, like normal readers, but then we need to step back, to refocus and let the detail of the writing, its patterns and shapes, come into view. There are many ways you can do this and no absolutely right way. Here are some suggestions:

- Take two pages of any piece of creative writing: fiction, poetry, script.

- Look at the title. What kind of expectations does it raise? Does it draw you or repel you? Without reading any further, make a note or two about what kind of writing you think the title indicates.

- Read the first line. First lines are crucial: they set the tone; introduce a voice; give a taste of what's to come. If you only read this
  one line, what could you guess about the rest of the writing?
  About the writer? Is it blatant or subtle in its attempt to seduce
  you? The first line may be the only thing a prospective reader will
  read before they put the book down or take it to the cash till.
  How does this one work? Do you trust or resist it? Does it make
  you want to read on? Again: make a note of your responses.

- Now read the piece through. Were your original expectations
  confirmed or challenged?

- Now go back and look closely at the first paragraph. Pick out the
  words that have the strongest impact on you. If you are in any
  doubt use a good dictionary to be sure you fully understand what
  the words mean. Ask:
  – why is this word striking?
  – why this particular word in this place?
  – how does the word work with the others around it?

- Identify metaphors and similes. These dry, rather grammatical,
  terms often make the heart sink. I've watched it happen – simply
  saying the words themselves – *metaphor; simile* – can reduce a
  normally cheerful group of people to anxious, shifty-eyed shadows
  of their former selves, muttering stuff about *a metaphor is a figure
  of...while a simile uses like...* . Sad. Reading as a writer is not
  about naming and defining every grammatical term, but recognising
  a good image when we see one, and learning to use our own to
  good effect. Are these images clichéd or fresh? Do they fit with
  the tone of the piece?

- Read for the beat. We *all* have a sense of rhythm. Even if you
  can't sing or dance, you can recognise music and movement when
  you hear or see it. The more music and dance you have experienced
  for yourself, the better you will know how to appreciate and
  practise it. The feeling for rhythm, pace and pattern in language
  is also mainly learned through experience – which for writers
  means (you guessed it) reading and writing practice. Writing has
  music in it – all kinds of music: slow or speedy; classic and jazz;
  rap and rock. You need to read for the beat. Listen for the beat of
  language. Read a couple of sentences in the piece of writing – first
  silently, then aloud. What is the difference? Did you stumble over
  either reading? Were there any awkward parts? Imagine these

sentences as songs you have to learn. Practise reading them two or three times. Work out where to put the right emphasis and inflection. Now read aloud again. Can you hear it?

■ Pattern and structure. Look at the way the writing is ordered. Does it move along with an obvious narrative line: a story or argument that unfolds – beginning, middle, ending – as you read? Or does it jump from one voice, idea or description to another, so that you are not quite sure where it's going? Is this writing that carries you along with it like a boat on a river? Or is it more like a puzzle, a maze?

■ Imagine the beginning before the beginning. The Zen buddhists have koans (and a koan, so I'm told, is a puzzle meant to drive you so crazy trying to solve it that you give up the struggle and become sane), a famous one being: *What did your face look like before your mother and father were born?* Now, imagine your chosen piece of writing when it was nothing at all, not even a thought. Think of those very first notes: words scribbled on a scrap of paper; two or three ideas still unconnected in the writer's head; a voice whispering or screaming in the writer's ear; a door, half-open; a face. Imagine what these notes might have been and write them down.

Try This: Reading Into Writing

Read the poem 'Full Moon and Little Frieda' by Ted Hughes.[2]

■ This one small event (a father walking with his small daughter along a lane in the evening) has long gone, but Hughes has tried to hold it still, the way we would all like to do with perfect moments. Try to recreate the moment: read over the poem line by line, and as you read, close your eyes and try to see/feel/hear what they experienced. Deliberately conjure up the sights and sounds Hughes describes in as much detail as you can. Don't skim: focus your inner attention; be precise and slow; see it, hear it, smell it, feel it.

■ Rewrite the scene in prose, or as a monologue, using the first person. Extend and elaborate the scene; add things Hughes doesn't mention, e.g. the smell of the cowshit; the sound of insects. Use your own imagery to describe these things: focus that inner attention to enable you to go into the scene again and find the right image for your additions. Learn from the precision of Hughes's imagery.

■ Write your own 'special moment' poem or prose piece. This moment should be in a contemporary setting, and should use appropriate contemporary imagery. You are not trying to create a 'poetic' pastoral piece of work. However, you should still aim for precision, honesty and freshness through your own way of seeing things. Try to use as many of the senses as you can.

Reading Myths: True or False

1. *You have to be highly intelligent and thrillingly attractive to be a big reader.*
True: but this question puts the cart before the horse: if you become a big reader you will develop into a highly intelligent and thrillingly attractive person. I should know.

2. *If you read a lot of other people's work then you won't be able to write in your own original voice.*
False: The opposite is true: if you currently read very little, then what you once read when you were younger will probably have the greatest influence. Many beginner poets, for example, find themselves using archaic diction and syntax which *feels* original and natural, but which demonstrates that they are still strongly (and unconsciously) under the influence of the nineteenth-century poets they studied at school. If you read only one writer or form, then you are likely to be strongly influenced by that style or form. There is no way to avoid any kind of influence, and anyway what's so good about unsullied individuality? We are all part of a complex culture and by the time we are adults we have already been influenced, like it or not, by a vast range of voices: how else would we learn? If, through reading, you absorb a wide range of forms, genres and styles; 'high' and 'low' literature, then you will eventually be much better equipped to speak in your own voice, to write what you like.

3. *Scriptwriters don't need to read as long as they watch films/stage plays/television.*

False: By the final edit or performance, a film or stage script is the work of many: director, producers, actors, technicians and so on. and so what you see on stage or screen is a long way from the writer's initial work. The skeleton of the script may be clearly visible beneath the body of the performance and you may get good ideas and inspiration by simply watching but it will be difficult to distinguish (and therefore learn from), the writer's particular part. If you really want to learn how to do it yourself you need to go to the source: the script itself. Here you will see the initial design, structure, raw materials and layout. Here you will learn how words can be turned into visions: how bones become flesh.

Further Reading

A. Manguel (1997) *A History of Reading* (London: Flamingo).
   Much more than a history, this book is a feast of fact and fiction about reading, libraries, books and readers. Not at all dusty, one to dip into on a lazy afternoon in between novels.
Ruth Padel (2002) *52 Ways of Looking at a Poem: How Reading Modern Poetry Can Change Your Life* (London: Chatto and Windus).
   A creative course book on how to read poetry, this book is based on Ruth Padel's popular newspaper column. There are 52 poems and 52 readings. Illuminating rather than prescriptive.
Francis Spufford (2000) *The Child That Books Built* (London: Faber)
   The title speaks for itself. A beautifully written autobiography of reading. Makes you want to write your own.

9 Looking Your Words in the Face: Reflection

Robert Graham and Heather Leach

This chapter looks at what we mean by reflection and why we think it's important for writers.

We've already learned that writers are readers who write, but perhaps that should be developed further: writers are readers who think carefully about *what* and *how* and *why* they write.

What Is Reflection?

The swiftest source to hand, the dictionary in Microsoft Word, offers eight interpretations of the word 'reflection'. This is the one that comes closest to our meaning:

> Careful thought, especially the process of reconsidering previous actions, events or decisions.

Reflective thinking means stopping and considering what you're doing. It's an opportunity to compare where you are now with where you have come from, a way of discovering how you are changing as a writer and of deciding where you want to go next. Of course, all of us think most of the time about what we are doing – thoughts come and go: some deliberate, some spontaneous. The problem with thought is that it is ephemeral and easily forgotten, which is why we believe that reflection in this context means *reflective writing*. Work of this kind enables you to record, order and shape your thoughts into useful insights and meanings. In this chapter we will suggest a number of ways that you might go about this.

Writers Reflect on their Work

In an essay called 'I Am A...Genius!' the American short story writer Thom Jones talks about the occasion when, after decades of struggle, he sold three stories in the same afternoon – to *Harper's*, *Esquire* and the *New Yorker* – which, in poker terms, is like finding yourself holding a royal flush.

> After getting lost and being found time and again, the writers who don't quit discover the ecstasy within the process of the work itself.[1] They discover the sublime joy of seeing things come together to produce an artistic whole. You read books and love them and someday hope to have the talent and vision to write your own.[2]

Jones is using the space to reflect on the joys as well as the struggle. It's always worth recording the good moments – and, as he says, there will almost certainly be some, if you stick at it.

Next, here's Bobbie Ann Mason commenting on the way she approaches characters:

> I wrote a novel (it was never published) about a twelve-year-old girl, a sort of female Huck Finn. When I was in graduate school I had a wonderful teacher who said, 'in the future you're going to see a shift, where the hero instead of trying to get out of society is trying to get in'. I didn't know what to make of that, but I thought about it when I started writing about characters who had never been at the centre, who had never had the advantage of being able to criticise society enough to leave it.[3]

In completing a novel, reflection may require that you examine the structure and form you're using. It may be a matter of contemplating the narrative choices. Will closing the distance between narrator and story improve the reader's relationship with the fiction? Have you balanced exposition and dramatisation? How well judged is the variety of tone, or the handling of time? (Linear? Fragmented?) This ruminating may be at surface level or structural level – Thomas McCormack's dermal and internal flaws (see chapter 19. 'Cut It Out, Put It In: Revision'). Perhaps you will feel the need to express yourself about the attendant anxieties: is this going anywhere? Am I committing myself to a very long-haul journey for good reasons?

Maybe the rationale of reflection is as simple as this: in the short term, in order to complete a piece of writing, you need to examine your creative processes, your handling of craft; in the longer term, studying the experiences and approaches involved in producing each successive work will make you a more informed craftsperson – and therefore a better one.

About two and a half thousand years ago, the Greek philosopher Socrates proposed that the unexamined life was not worth living, the implication perhaps being that by examining your life, you may live it better. A good enough reason maybe, but what we're talking about here is not an examination of your whole life but of your life and work as a writer in order to help you write better. All writers worth the name reflect on their work in some way or other and they're not the only ones doing it.

If you went through the British secondary education system any time after the late 1980s, you will have been prompted to reflect on your learning as part of your Record of Achievement. If you're a student in higher education now, you will be asked to reflect in a Personal Development Plan. If you work for any largish organisation, you and your line-manager will reflect when you have your annual appraisal. If you're a parent, you, your child and your child's teacher are reflecting at parents' evenings. Most of us have already had some relevant experience although we may not have developed a focused approach to writing about our own work.

For the first exercise in this chapter, you won't need to be an expert in reflective writing; but it will help that you already know how to redraft. (See chapter 19, 'Revision'.)

Try This: Reading Yourself

Take a draft of a recent piece of writing, ask yourself a series of questions about it, and write down your answers.

- Why did I want to write this piece in the first place? Where did it come from? Where did I get the idea?

- Has the original idea changed? In what ways?

- Why am I writing in this form (short story / novel / script / poem, etc.)? What effect would a change of form make? What would I gain or lose?

- Which books / texts / films, etc. have influenced or inspired me in this writing? In which ways?

- What problems have occurred in writing it? How have I resolved them? What problems remain?

Why Reflect?

Writing can be a lonely business. We spend many solitary hours a week at the blank screen, and as many hours again buried in a book. As a writer, you need someone to discuss your writing with and that person will often end up being yourself. (Is it any wonder that the writer Jack Nicholson played in *The Shining* flipped?)

It helps you to look back and remember and it helps you look ahead and dream. It gives you a sense of continuity and authenticity in a hard world. In other words, it makes you real to yourself as a writer, helps you make yourself up as a writer as you go along.

Good reflective writing is a way of thinking; it's a dialogue with yourself. As you reflect, you will find out what you think about your own work, but also about your reading. Reflection makes you write about your writing and reading experiences and thus discover your opinions. The process makes them real and builds interconnections: thought is ephemeral and often vague – writing is more solid and usable. As E.M. Forster said, 'How do I know what I think until I see what I say?'

Reflection is a way of developing your writing. In that sense it's connected with the writer's journal. The journal is often the place where you record thoughts and experiences, where you work out ideas, but a formal piece of reflective writing is more polished, more shaped.

Reflective writing is complementary. It goes alongside the creative work. A finished piece of reflection is arguably creative writing in its own right. If you go about it right, reflection will help you read and write better. You will learn to be a more self-conscious, more self-critical writer than you might otherwise have been, and you will have a better understanding of the context into which your writing may fit.

Writing a Reflection

Let's unpack the term a little more and look at some of the details.

To produce worthwhile reflective writing, you will need particular disciplines. You will need to be self-critical and self-aware. Self-criticism does not mean negativity but having a willingness to look carefully at your writing with an open and honest frame of mind: to learn to see what the writing says to you. At a fundamental level, you will need to be able to read as a writer. (See chapter 8, 'Reading as a Writer'.)

Reflection involves examining the process of writing and finding ways to express an understanding of that process. Here you will explore the experiences that have informed the writing – including, if you are in a class, the stimulus you may have been given to work from.

You might think about what your intentions were at the outset, how well you have fulfilled them and how they may have changed during redrafting. You may discuss any problems encountered and the strategies that were employed to overcome them.

At the moment of finishing it, most writers think a first draft is good – which may be followed quickly by the feeling that it is useless. But how can you revise a draft unless you read it from a critical perspective? In redrafting, you must make decisions about what's good and what needs to change, but the one thing you should avoid is making value judgements about the overall quality of the finished work. You can be fairly certain that you will either overrate or underrate its worth; you aren't in a position to see the wood for the trees.

By now you've got some idea of what reflection is and why you should engage in it. You've read three examples of writers reflecting, you've been given some indication of how you might reflect on your own work and, with the last exercise, you've made a start on it. In a moment, you'll get a chance to work on a more substantial piece of reflection. First, let's look at some useful ways to get going (and some potential pitfalls).

Possible Approaches

- Write down the inspirations for this piece of work – where the ideas came from.

- Write a short commentary on any books or films that may have influenced you – in what ways?

- Write about what you originally intended.

- Write about the problems you've come up against and how you've dealt with them.

- Explain why you chose this particular genre or form: script/ poetry/short story, etc. Justify your reasons: narrative/aesthetic / structural, etc.

- Discuss the elements of craft you've studied (dialogue/narrative structure/pace). How have you applied them in this piece, and what have you learned as a result?

- Describe how the piece has been redrafted and for what reasons.

- If anyone has already read the work or it has been discussed in a writers' workshop, write about the ways that the response has influenced your redrafting.

- Write about yourself as a writer in this place and time: why do you want to write? What kind of writer are you? Would you like to be? What is your philosophy of writing; your manifesto?

Possible Pitfalls

- Retelling the story is pointless and won't make very interesting reading, especially where the audience for your reflection has access to the creative work.

- It may be unhelpful to have too much self-consciousness; you need to strike the balance between self-awareness and overemphasis on inner motivations and emotions. What is important is that the reflective process is meant to help you write better. Keep your eye on the work itself.

- When you read a reflective chapter or article that a writer has constructed for publication, all nicely turned out and tidied up, bear in mind that this is just another narrative. As with recording history, in writing there is no objective truth – only subjective versions of it.

Try This: Reflective Writing

For this exercise, write a 1000-word piece of reflection, with the focus on your growth as a writer over the past year (or an appropriate period for you).

Use the above list as a way in. You might begin by listing what you want to include as a spider diagram, or mind-map.

Forget about being comprehensive; instead aim to be heterogeneous. Choose the themes or factors that appeal to you at this moment and then mix the ingredients together as you might when baking a cake. It will help if you can construct a narrative or a line of argument that is cohesive and includes transitions where sharp changes of subject matter occur.

Finally, to give you a model of a learner writer's reflection, we've included two thoughtful and detailed pieces, in the Appendix, 'Self-assessment/Annotated Bibliography and Reflection' which we hope will inspire you to begin writing your own.

Further Reading

Will Blythe (ed.) (1998) *Why I Write: Thoughts on the Craft of Fiction* (London: Little, Brown).
Essays reflecting not only on craft but also on the writer's life. The Thom Jones chapter we've quoted is worth reading in full if you need encouragement for the long journey you're on. There's a characteristically quirky piece from Amy Hempel. (Track down her story 'In The Cemetery Where Al Jolson Is Buried'.) Other contributors include Mary Gaitskill, Pat Conroy and Jayne Anne Philips.
Bonnie Lyons and Bill Oliver (eds) (1998) *Passion and Craft: Conversations With Notable Writers* (Urbana and Chicago: University of Illinois Press).
Substantial, informed interviews on the craft of fiction with a dozen contemporary American fiction writers, including Richard Ford, Bobbie Ann Mason, and Tobias Wolff.

Writer's Block

Dear Auntie,
I can't write anymore. Can you help?

Writer's Block is a disturbing condition that afflicts most writers at some point in their careers. Don't be embarrassed; we've all been there, apologising to our keyboards, muttering things like: 'This has never happened to me before.' Relax. Allow yourself to daydream. If lazing in a hot bubble bath with a glass of wine does it for you, then lock the bathroom door and laze and drift and drink, pen and paper nearby. Or perhaps you get ideas looking at paintings or photographs; so, go to an art gallery, go the library and browse through the coffee-table photography books you've been meaning to look at for ages. Or even, dare I suggest it, read other people's writing. Choose an author whose work you admire, whose work first made you want to be a writer. Capture the desire again. Try doodling with a pencil if you usually type: try typing if you usually write by hand. Put on music: because they are written to follow a narrative, film soundtracks can be very effective for evoking new images and stories.

Perhaps you have a story already but you just can't do a thing with it. Perhaps your angle is wrong. Try changing the point of view: make a third-person narrator into a first-person narrator. Or maybe the tense is wrong: if you're using the past tense try shifting a paragraph into the present tense to see if it makes a difference.

Maybe you've worked too hard on the story: perhaps you need to take some time out and watch some films, read some poetry, listen to some new music and let your subconscious simmer for a few days. Remember that if you're boring yourself the likelihood is that you're boring your reader.

Sometimes problems stem not from a lack of ideas, but from the stern internal editor rejecting ideas before you've had a chance to explore them and plant them. Ideas are like seeds; if you throw them away too soon, they don't get a chance to germinate, and while you may find they sprout into thin weedy useless little things, they might not; they might just put out strong fresh roots and shoots and flourish and grow into mighty oaks.

Sometimes writers think they're blocked because the work is hard. Well, wake up and smell the ribbon ink: writing *is* hard! Very hard! If it were easy everyone would have written *War and Peace* by now. Sit back down and just do it! It won't get any less hard if you put it off for another day. A walk round the block can help, but only if you then go back to the desk!

10 Writing Together: Groups and Workshops

Heather Leach

There are more writing workshops, classes and courses now than ever before. Wherever you live, you're almost sure to find a writing group, if not within spitting distance, at least a bus ride away. Many universities and colleges have writing options and an increasing number are offering half or even full degree courses in Creative Writing.

Before we go any further, reflect for a moment on whether, in your view, this is a good or a bad thing. It's important that you get this straight because there are plenty of people out there ready to tell you that such activities are a waste of time, that real writers would rather eat concrete than join a group. Writing, goes the argument, is a lonely game and you can only learn to write through a long solitary process: the group is at best a distraction, at worst, a destroyer of talent, goes the story. I hope, after reading chapter 3 on creativity that you'll recognise some of this as romantic snobbery.

On the other hand let's not be under any delusions: it *is* absolutely necessary for writers to sit down alone in a room and struggle with words for hours at a time. After all, here I am, doing exactly that. Without long periods of writing alone, nothing at all would be produced. That's the job. But the *cult*, the *ideology* of solitariness is a different thing entirely. Writers do not *need* to be lonely, palely loitering creatures, in fact the majority of them are not and never were. Even the most unashamed romantics, Keats, Coleridge and Wordsworth, spent plenty of time talking to others; reading each others' drafts; discussing ideas in person and by letter. Mary Shelley describes how she began writing *Frankenstein* after a group of her friends agreed that they would each write a story and read it to each other as they went along.

Ernest Hemingway is reported to have said that 'the best way to become a writer is just to go off and write', but as John Gardner points out:

> His own way of doing it was to go to Paris where many of the great writers were and to study with the greatest theorist of the time and one of the shrewdest writers, Gertrude Stein. Joseph Conrad, though we tend to think of him as a solitary genius, worked in close community with Ford Madox Ford, H.G.Wells, Henry James and Stephen Crane.[1]

Writers have *always* been helped and encouraged by others. If you read the biographies and letters of famous and not-so-famous writers, you will find details of introductions, meetings and conversations; of friendships and collaborations between writers; of writerly social gatherings, readings and festivals. Past and present literary landscapes are criss-crossed by informal networks – literary groups, university societies, family and friendship connections. This is fine if you live in the kind of small but perfectly formed world where such networks and connections are possible, but there are plenty of places where the likelihood of meeting another writer down the chip shop, or even someone who knows a writer's Uncle Tarquin twice removed, is as remote as the likelihood of meeting Elvis, dead or alive. Writers' groups and courses offer *everybody* the opportunity to gain from the skill and experience of other writers and give you a helpful leg-up into the writing world.

Stephen King comments that the main benefit of writing courses and groups is that they take writing seriously:

> ...for aspiring writers who have been looked upon with pitying condescension by their friends and relatives ('You better not quit your day job just yet!' is a popular line, usually delivered with a hideous Bob's-yer-uncle grin), this is a wonderful thing. In writing classes, it is entirely permissible to spend large chunks of your time off in your own little dream world.[2]

Writer's courses and groups give you ideas, feedback, time to write and motivation, but above all, they give you *permission* to be a writer. Visual artists, musicians, dancers, actors all study on courses – and so do bricklayers, physicists, airline pilots and TV gardeners. It's the modern day equivalent of the old boys' and girls' network, except that it's no longer open only to the few who know the network password.

It must be obvious by now that I am strongly in favour of open courses and classes for would-be writers, which is not really surprising since I teach on one, but that doesn't mean that I think that they are *all* useful *all* the time, or that they will supply a quick-fix solution to the problem of how to become a good writer.

In the next section of this chapter I will look at the pros and cons of writing workshops, at their potential as both creative opportunity and dangerous territory, and will suggest ways that you can get the best (and the worst) out of them.

Writing Workshops: The Pros

■ *Practice in reading as a writer*
Most good writing classes include a space for writing activity using examples from published work as a stimulus. You get an opportunity to close-read and discuss a piece of writing in the group and then to write in response. You may get something to read that you really like and which stimulates your imagination – great. On the other hand, you may hate what you're given by the class tutor or leader: like Stephen King you might be put off by a high literary style, or irritated by what seem to be clichéd characters and simplistic plots. Which is also great. Learning from what you *don't* like, *and being able to articulate why*, is a crucial step on the way to finding out what you want to write for yourself. The more widely you read, the greater the range of choice. Also, trying to write in the manner of a writer you think is pants or pretentious may help you gain a little more respect for what they are trying to do, as well as teaching you some useful tricks and techniques. The most important thing they'll teach you, though, is how *not* to write.

■ *Writing to order*
Some workshops allow you time to practise writing on the spot: 10 minutes on an opening paragraph; 5 minutes on a quick-fire dialogue; half-an-hour for a poem with a formal structure. This is a real bonus for many writers. At least you get a start: even if you throw away most of what you produce in those short bursts, it's good practice. Also, for increasing numbers of people, this is the only time they get the chance to use an actual pen or pencil. Which is sadly archaic but strangely moving.

■ *Talking about writing*
This is a rare and precious thing. Let's face it, there aren't many places where it is possible. There you are in the pub having a quiet

drink with a friend or two, or waiting with the other parents in the school playground, and you start to tell them about your recent painful struggle to create a dramatic beginning for a story, or a punchy but plausible confrontational dialogue between two characters in a script. What happens next is interesting but painful. Awkwardness; incomprehension; kindly concern. Occasionally, if you've hit on a group of people who are very kind or very drunk, they'll comment on how brave or clever you must be to be a writer. They might even adopt you as their literary mascot: 'Here's our writer,' they'll say, patronisingly, when they see you coming: 'Written a best seller yet? Ha Ha Ha!' Normal people don't care *how* books are written: they don't want to know about the nuts and bolts; they just want to read the damn things. The best people to talk to about writing are other writers and the workshop gives you just that.

■ *Motivation*
Most writing workshops expect you to produce regular drafts of work in progress which will then be read and discussed by members of the group. The need to get something, *anything*, written by a particular date and time is a powerful motivator. I should know – the editors of this book are expecting the draft of this chapter by last week – which is motivating me bigtime. Writing is hard work and very few of us work hard unless we have to. Deadlines are the writer's friend.

■ *Your first readers*
The people in the workshop are, ideally, not your close friends, lovers or relations but other writers who are willing to give you honest feedback in exchange for the same from you. If you're lucky, they'll tell you what they really think and feel about your writing. They may not be experts; they may not be clever or literary or even kind. They're readers. Give them respect and attention. Listen when they speak. Carefully.

■ *Confidence*
I said earlier that being in a group gives you *permission*: the best groups also give you confidence. This is not the same as praise, which we all need, but which can be both addictive and misleading. A group of attentive, honest and interested readers can help you to recognise your weaknesses and to build on your strengths. A group's intelligent support can help give you faith – faith in your ability to work and to keep on working as a writer.

Writing Workshops: The Cons

■ *Literary snobbery*
Watch out for workshop members or leaders who value only one kind of writing. I don't mean specialised groups, say for poetry or fiction, which may be useful but those groups where writing is considered to be good only if it fits a certain set of rules. Remember that thrillers, literary novels, experimental fiction, autobiographies and so on are sold in the same bookshops and manage to live tolerantly together side by side on the library shelves.[3]

It can work the other way: watch out for groups that only value 'straight' narrative styles or which insist on realistic or socially meaningful stories. If you're a writer interested in experimentation, then look for a group with an open mind. The key to a good workshop, in my view, is that it will allow for a range of forms and genres, and will help writers to develop the best that they can do in whatever form they choose. However, keep in mind that genre writers also need to read widely and to practise a range of forms in order to develop an understanding of how to write well. Junk writing is junk writing however posh or popular it is.

■ *Too much praise*
We all need it but sometimes we need other things more. Too much praise bad: too little praise also bad. Praise is like sugar or alcohol: a lot rots your teeth or makes you fall over, but life without it would be dull, dull, dull. It is often praise that started us on this writing business in the first place: a doting family member who commented on the beautiful sadness of our poem about the pet ex-gerbil cruelly murdered by the cat; the thrilling laugh-out-loud appreciation of a mate at our equally cruel parody of the headmaster's assembly talk; even a brief positive comment by a teacher in the margin of an assignment can be enough to make the beginnings of a writer.

Praise in workshops can be very motivating, but just like sugar and alcohol, it can also be addictive. Praise can become so important to you that you begin to write simply in order to please others. And sometimes, if you don't get enough, you stop writing. David Foster Wallace says there's a point when you discover a tricky thing about writing:

[A] certain amount of vanity is necessary to be able to do it at all, but any vanity above that certain amount is lethal. At some point you find that 90-plus percent of the stuff you're writing is motivated and informed by the need to be liked. This results in shitty fiction. And the shitty work must get fed to the waste basket, less because of any sort of artistic integrity than simply because shitty work will cause you to be disliked.[4]

We all need to give and receive praise; we wouldn't be human otherwise. However, workshops at their best are not mutual back-slapping societies, but places where work in progress is looked at honestly and realistically. Expect your work to be given truthfulness and respect and give the same in return. Then let it go.

■ *Not writing but talking*
You can make friends for life in writing workshops. You can fall in love in writing workshops. You can impress people with your charm, wit and cleverness and be thrilled by other people's warmth, style and experience. Great. But be aware that too much talking, even talking about writing, can become a substitute for the actual writing itself. For some people, and I have to sadly admit that I am one of them, there is nothing easier than getting carried away on brilliant descriptions of a project, only to find that later, in the quiet dull silence of your own company, the idea disappears like smoke, like the ghost of a ghost. If you're a good talker, fine – plenty of writers have been talkers and plenty haven't; there are no rules – but in a workshop, the main emphasis of attention needs to focus on words on the page, words actually written. Dreams, ideas, plans are not writing. Only writing is writing.

Workshop Practice

The major value of a writer's workshop is to have your work read and discussed by the other members of the group and to read and discuss the work of others in their turn. There are many ways of organising and running sessions, some of which may depend on the size of the group, but in my experience there are key elements that make for successful and productive workshops.

■ *Establish workshop guidelines*
Groups of any kind work best when all the members have a stake in the process. The group leader or facilitator (if the group hasn't got one of these – try giving the job to a different person each session) should begin by asking people to set their own rules of engagement. These might be

practical – who goes first; how much time each person can have, and so on. But they should also cover commitment, style and attitude. For instance, mine would be: everyone presents work; everyone reads; respect for each person; honest but fair criticism; aim to bring out the best.

It is better if the group develops this kind of democratic and open participation naturally rather than through a set of rules but there are some things that help:

- Limiting the size of groups: between 6 and 12 is ideal but not always possible. You could split into smaller groups for discussions but this can be logistically difficult.

- The group leader/facilitator making a deliberate but gentle effort to encourage all to be involved – not just at the beginning, but throughout.

- Occasionally meeting outside formal settings – e.g. having coffee together, going on visits and readings.

- *Start small*
In the beginning group members can be encouraged to share their work in groups of two or three to get them going. By keeping the feedback informal and low key, people build confidence and avoid too much nerve-racking exposure too soon. A variation on this can be to ask a member of each small group to tell the larger group about one or all of the pieces of writing.

- *Everybody gains by commenting on other people's work*
You may feel that the main value of the workshop is to see what people think of *your* writing and that therefore your feedback on other's work is primarily for *their* benefit. But you also learn a great deal by looking carefully at a piece of work-in-progress, even if it is nothing like your own. People who keep silent, make no comment and don't submit work are acting as an *audience* rather than as fellow writers, which can be experienced by others as intimidating or freeloading. On the other hand, participation does not mean domination. If you're the kind of person who has a lot to say, learning when to shut up can be hard but useful. Listening is a vital skill for writers. The key point is that a group is a group: one jumps; all jump.

- *Everybody should present work to be read*
This is so obvious it shouldn't need elaborating. Make sure everybody regularly gets a slot by agreeing a timetable in advance and setting

clear deadlines. In larger groups, this may mean that people may only get one or two chances a term to have their work discussed, but as long as they get careful responses this will be more than enough. Some people may be nervous about presenting their work, but like parachute jumping, if they won't jump, it's kinder to push them. In my experience, people feel much better after having their work discussed, whereas people who cop out feel even more anxious. Face the fear.

■ *Reading aloud?*
Some people like to read their work and others hate it. I don't think it is essential and in any group larger than 4 or 5 it can take up so much time that there's little left for discussion. If drafts are distributed and read in advance there is no need for reading. However, monologues, performance work, scripts may benefit from by being read aloud or informally performed.

■ *Writers keep quiet*
This can be difficult to get going but, once established, works well for both writers and readers. The idea is that the writer whose work is being discussed keeps quiet while the discussion is going on, simply listening and observing. It helps if you sit back a little from the group, perhaps imagining yourself as a fly on the light bulb or someone having an out of the body experience gazing down curiously while the workshop surgeons do an operating job on your draft. It can be frustrating but instructive to hear people misunderstanding your plots or falling in love with insignificant characters. The temptation, which should be resisted, is to jump in and put them right: *no, this is what I meant, no you're reading that wrong*…and so on. Let your work speak for itself and listen to the responses. You can take it away afterwards and rewrite it in any way you want. Try not to take the comments too personally: this is only a draft after all, not finished work – and the next draft you write may be the one to blow their heads off. Keeping quiet also lets the writer off the hook, focusing on the work itself, which for many people can be a relief. Which leads neatly on to the next point.

■ *Talk about the work not the person*
Readers should aim to discuss the work as if the writer wasn't there. This may feel awkward and artificial at first, but once established, it works well. It stops readers giving the writer too much personal attention; it keeps attention on the work itself. This means that

readers can say something is good or not so good without seeming to flatter or blame the writer personally: it is the draft that is being discussed, and drafts can be changed more easily than personalities. Just as writers will find it difficult to keep quiet, many readers find it difficult to avoid using personal names and pronouns or asking the writer direct questions: *What did you mean by this word, Gemma?...Is this about your mother?...* which can be distracting and embarrassing. It helps if readers use a more objective language in discussion: *the* characters; *I don't understand what this word means*, as well as avoiding pointed discussion about the personal life of the writer unless information is volunteered. This practice models the usual relationship between published writers and readers and reinforces the experience of *writing as a process.*

■ *Writer talks back*
At the end of the discussion the writer could be given a minute or two to respond to any absolutely burning questions, but this has not been a trial, so the writer has no need to defend themselves or their work.

■ *Readers try to be truthful*
In this postmodern age, so many of us mean different things by *truth* that I'm tempted to put speech marks around the word. What I mean is that you should tell the writer what you think and feel about their work-in-progress as honestly as you can. This sounds simple and easy but it isn't. For example, you may not be sure what you think or feel; and you may not be confident about your opinions. This is understandable, particularly if you have not read much in the form or genre of the draft work: if someone submits a sci-fi story, for example, and you haven't read a word of the stuff, then you may think you haven't anything worth saying. You may even hate sci-fi; or romantic love stories; or poetry; or scripts about murder; or anything with religion in it...there's always something more to hate.

Another barrier to a truthful response is that you may not warm to the writer or you may warm to them a lot and want them to notice you or like you or go out with you after the workshop. Good news can often be harder to speak than bad: particularly within English culture, it can be toe-curlingly embarrassing to tell someone to their face how much you loved something they've written. All these difficulties and issues stand in the way of an honest response, which is why talking about the work itself and not the person helps. It also helps to remember that you are here, not as an expert, but as an ordinary *reader* and you are giving a *reader's* response; a thoughtful, self-aware reader who is open to learning. There's not a lot you can do about liking or not liking people – we are all human – but be aware of the pressures on you to fudge and flatter. Truthfulness doesn't need to be blunt or over-effusive. The point is to be helpful – to find the work's best potential and to bring that out. It may be just one well-placed word, one image, one idea. Find it and praise it.

■ *What kind of responses?*
David Kaplan suggests that a writer ideally needs two good readers:

> ...a 'line' reader and a 'concept' reader. They aren't usually the same person. A concept reader focuses on the Big Picture. She can tell you what is and isn't working in your story. She can make suggestions for scene changes, for adding or dropping characters, for changing middles and ends and beginnings. Concept readers Think Big. Line readers concentrate on the details: They go over your work...word by word, line by line. They do what a good copy editor at a publishing house does. You're lucky if you have a reader like this.[5]

The workshop as a whole should pay attention to the work's *big stuff* (themes, story, plot, genre, form, structures, etc.); the *middle-sized* stuff (character, setting, point of view, voice, pace, etc.); and the *small stuff* (vocabulary, sentence structures, imagery, etc.). It may be up to the workshop leader to draw out discussion of elements that haven't been covered. Punctuation and spelling come last. Of course, these must be impeccable on the final draft – but we're a long way from that.

Structured Workshops

Once a group has gained experience and most people are confident about taking part as writers and readers, then you can decide whether you want to structure the process. This doesn't mean that the actual discussion of the work needs to be formal or solemn – just that people give more time and detailed attention to each piece of writing. It is difficult to give honest and realistic feedback off the top of your head and workshops which over-rely on spontaneity tend to favour already confident speakers. This is not only unfair to the others but doesn't necessarily produce the most intelligent and creative discussion.

These kinds of workshops may take place over a period: say 4 weeks for a group of 12, with each person getting one workshop of 30 minutes each. The above guidelines apply, but there are some added processes that enrich the experience.

Distribute Work in Advance

Ideally, work should be given to the other members of the group a week before to give them time to read it at least twice and to prepare a thoughtful response.

Writers Ask for Specific Help

Writers should prepare information and questions and attach them to the work. When you give your work to a workshop group you are effectively getting the chance to find out what a group of captive but willing readers think. This is valuable and rare, so make the most of it by asking them to think about the things you want to know the answers to. One way of organising this is to have prepared a cover sheet that all of the group can use and which each person can adapt for their own purposes. I've reproduced one at the end of this chapter, which developed out of one writing workshop.

Readers Give a Written Response to the Questions

It goes without saying that everybody in the group should read the draft carefully and respond to the questions in as much detail as possible, using specific examples from the work. Having to write responses is useful for a number of reasons:

- The writer gets the benefit of all viewpoints, including those of people who may be reticent about *speaking* in groups.

- Written comments may be more considered than spoken ones.

- The effort of paying attention to specific questions and writing down their responses gives everybody in the group good practice in using a critical and creative vocabulary.

- Having to prepare a written response means that readers come to the workshop better able to take part in a discussion.

- The writer can take away the responses and reflect on them later – it can often be hard to take in what is being said in the more heated atmosphere of the workshop.

After the Workshop: What Happens Next?

At the end of the workshop you, the writer, are left with a piece of your own writing plus a lot of feedback. Now you have to go off on your own and look at your work again in light of all this and this can be difficult. People may have given you contradictory opinions; you may not have agreed with some of them; you may think some are not well founded or that the people who made them lack experience, critical ability or experimental courage. Fine. You don't need to change a single thing if you don't want to and you certainly don't need to incorporate everybody's opinions.

Think of the workshop as a driving lesson: you get lots of good ideas and advice but once you're on your own in the car with your hands on the wheel, you're in charge. It helps to read the feedback and then to digest it. Take it in, learn what you can, then let it go. You're alone in front of the page again. Time just to write.

Further Reading

John Gardner (1999) *On Becoming a Novelist* (London: Norton).
  This excellent book includes a substantial section on workshops and classes, which (as long as you ignore the unquestioned assumption that beginner writers are predominantly male and young), is inspirational and useful.
Paul Hyland (1993) *Getting Into Poetry* (Newcastle-upon-Tyne: Bloodaxe).
  If you want to write poetry, this is a very good place to start.

No More Ideas...

Dear Auntie,
What if I have no more ideas? All my best ideas have gone into the first project and I know I'll never have ideas this good again ever, ever, ever! I've read there are a finite number of stories. Surely they've all been used up by now. Why am I a writer? Why am I doing this? No one will read anything I write. I'm nothing. AaaAAAaAaaargh!!

(*Writer tempestuously screws up paper, aims at bin, throws and misses.*)

Calm down. Think back to when you were starting this project. It's likely you thought you'd never think of an idea, and then, bam, from apparently nowhere, you had an idea, which led to another and another, and before you knew it, you were flying...Writing at the end of a project can be different from the writing we do at the beginning. The beginning is characterised by blank pages and pencil-chewing and writing and daydreaming, the middle by planning and writing, the end by redrafting and fine-tuning. So remember how it was at the beginning: you probably had the same panic. The blank page can be a very frightening place; it is wide open and so full of possibility that there is no focus; so draw something on it. Blot its whiteness with doodles. Scrawl random words over it and play with them, putting them into sentences. Have fun and the ideas will start to sneak up on you before you know it.

There are finite combinations of story structures. But you are a unique person. Find your angle on a story. No one will ever tell the story quite the way that you tell it; take comfort; lots of tales are retellings. You are a writer presumably because you enjoy it. You are doing this because it gives you satisfaction. And there is no guarantee that anyone will ever read you, but if they never do, this does not mean you are nothing. So, you could either give up now, or come to terms with the fact that it's a hard, hard slog, and then roll up your sleeves and get on with it. No one promised it would be easy. There are few rose gardens out there, but when you find them, they smell very sweet indeed.

III
Keeping Going

Basics: Layout for Fiction

Roughly every decade, the conventions about layout for fiction shift. At the time of writing, here's my understanding of the current view of how to lay out your short story or novel.

- Make sure your work is double-spaced.

- Use one side of the paper only and number your pages.

- The first line of your story is not indented.

- Thereafter, every first line of each new paragraph should be indented.

- When you go to a new scene or section, press return on your keyboard twice to leave one line's worth of white space. But do *not* do this after a paragraph in other circumstances – the extra space indicates a break between scenes.

- Each new speaker requires a new paragraph (new speaker, new paragraph). Malcolm Bradbury, amongst others, abandoned this convention in 1970s novels such as *The History Man*. Personally, I think life is too short and too fast for readers to have to stop and work out which character is speaking.

- Each suggested shift of focus (from one character to another) needs a new paragraph. New person, new paragraph: help the reader easily understand who is acting or speaking.

11 Narrators: Whose Story Is It Anyway?

Robert Graham

'Nothing,' Ethan Canin says, 'is as important as a likeable narrator. Nothing holds a story together better.'[1] If the narrative is the end product of the fiction-writing process, the starting point is the narrator. The reader of a novel or short story is entering into a relationship with the narrator.

In the matter of narrators Rimmon-Kenan differentiates between narrators who participate in the narrative, and those who don't.[2] As an example of the latter, the realist novels of the nineteenth century employ what David Lodge, in his essay, '*Middlemarch* and the idea of the classic realist text',[3] refers to as 'the convention of the omniscient and obtrusive narrator'. It's a matter for debate whether such a convention has fallen out of fashion in contemporary fiction, but my advice would be to avoid it. While Margaret Atwood, Angela Carter and Salman Rushdie all successfully use an ironic version of the omniscient narrator, in general I would say that this approach is for the experienced writer. Instead, why not plump for having a narrator who participates in the narrative, as exemplified in this extract from Sarah Waters's *Fingersmith*:

> We were all more or less thieves, at Lant Street. But we were that kind of thief that rather eased the dodgy deed along, than did it.[4]

Sue Trinder isn't a narrator sitting in an armchair telling you about the action, she is immersed in it.

Examples of such narrators include Pip in *Great Expectations* and Holden Caulfield in *The Catcher In The Rye*: they play a central role in the story they narrate; they are protagonist-narrators – they narrate their own story. Those, such as Lockwood in *Wuthering*

Heights, whose role is subsidiary, are described as witness-narrators in that they narrate someone else's story. Thus, Sue Trinder in *Fingersmith* is a protagonist-narrator. Sue is present for nearly everything that happens in the course of her narrative and involved in it up to her neck:

> I felt them do it and began to struggle again. I was not thinking now of Gentleman and Maud. I was thinking of myself. I was growing horribly afraid. My stomach ached from the nurse's fingers. My mouth was cut by the spoon. I had an idea that, once they got me into a room, they would kill me.

Point of View

The handling of point of view (or POV) is key to the way a narrative will function. Your choice of point of view will affect the way your story is told and the way in which it is perceived. So what *is* point of view? It's simply the perspective from which the story is told. *Great Expectations* is told from Pip's perspective, *The Catcher In The Rye* from Holden Caulfield's. In these two novels, these are your point of view characters. As it happens, both are first-person narratives – throughout, it's 'I did this' and 'I said that' but your point of view character might just as well be written in the third person: 'She did this' and 'She said that'. First-person singular and third-person singular narratives are most common, but Jay McInerney's *Bright Lights, Big City* uses the second-person singular:

> You are not the kind of guy who would be at a place like this at this time of the morning. But here you are, and you cannot say that the terrain is entirely unfamiliar, although the details are fuzzy.[5]

And Jeffrey Eugenides's *The Virgin Suicides* is, uniquely, first-person plural. The book is narrated by a group of teenage boys in a suburban neighbourhood:

> We saw the gangly paramedic with the Wyatt Earp moustache come out first – the one we'd called 'Sheriff' when we got to know him through these domestic tragedies…[6]

Some of the advantages of multiple points of view are discussed later in this chapter. First, though, let's stick with single viewpoint matters.

The advantage of having a single narrator is that he or she becomes, in Oakley Hall's term, the 'central authority'.[7] Hall's belief is that since Henry James, the establishment of a central authority is, 'the chief means to believability'. The contemporary reader is perhaps less likely than the nineteenth-century reader to accept the author as the central authority. Perhaps the difference between a central authority and the intrusive narrator of the classic realist text is worth briefly noting: it's the difference between a point of view character – the one through whom we *experience* the narrative – and an omniscient narrator – the one who *recounts* the narrative. Showing versus Telling again. Nevertheless, the narrator as central authority only succeeds if the chosen narrator – however unsympathetic he or she may be – compels the reader.

Which Viewpoint?

I'm going to stick my neck out here and disregard much of the available advice about the various points of view. The distance from which a narrative is pitched is more significant than the choice of viewpoint – as you are about to see. Arguably more important than your choice of point of view is whether or not you opt for single or multiple points of view. In the meantime, here are your POV choices:

- First person (I saw the dog). Arguably invites more direct engagement from the reader. The main shortcoming with this point of view is that the novel or short story is going to be limited to what the POV character is present for, and it's difficult for one character to witness everything that may need to happen in a novel. It's also easy in first person to slip into internal monologue mode. The other shortcoming, arguably, is that there will be a tendency to tell.

- Limited third person (she, he saw the dog). To my mind, this POV has many of the same advantages and limitations as first person. It is, however, more flexible in that you can adjust your focus, edging, for instance, away from limited third person to detached third person and even to omniscient third person. According to Orson Scott Card, 'the overwhelming majority of fiction published today uses the third-person narrator'.[8]

- Detached third person. This is a little more remote from the narrator, a little less subjective. If limited third person is looking from within the POV character, detached is looking over his or her shoulder. This is the point of view most conducive to what David Lodge calls 'staying on the surface', and you are less likely to slip into telling when using detached third person.

- Second person (you saw the dog). This addresses readers as though they were the point of view character – and is thus very similar in effect and limitations to first person and limited third person.

- First person plural (we saw the dog), which, as I've mentioned, has only ever been used in Jeffrey Eugenides's *The Virgin Suicides*.

Try This: POV Shift

Pick a novel or short story you like and rewrite a page of it, changing the point of view: if it's first person, change it to third and so on.

How does the change affect the piece?

Single Viewpoint

There are problems with the single viewpoint narratives and the use of the protagonist narrator. One of them is the drift towards the monolithic: the reader will have to spend 80,000 words or so in the company of the narrator, and with one narrator, this will be unbroken time. First-person narrative, and especially single viewpoint first-person narrative, is a limiting form. Writing in his preface to *The Ambassadors*, Henry James says 'the first person, in a long piece, is a form foredoomed to looseness'.[9]

Certainly, it often feels as if in choosing that form, the novelist is giving himself enough rope with which to hang himself. It allows for self-indulgence, and to some extent it has a tendency to work against dramatising: it is easy for the first-person narrator to tell the reader about events he ought to be showing. In the same preface, James writes of a further problem with the form, the problem of the monolithic, of the potential for dullness: 'the question of how to keep my form amusing while sticking so close to my central figure and constantly taking its pattern from him had to be faced'.

Multiple Points of View

This narrative strategy has several advantages. The move from single to multiple viewpoints affords the possibility of a quilted text such as that outlined later in this chapter. A shift in viewpoint is change, and narrative tension, narrative itself, is all about change. But that is not the only advantage of deploying more than one point of view.

Deploying two viewpoint characters means that the single viewpoint character doesn't have to witness everything. However, a drawback to having two viewpoint characters is the commonly held opinion that in a dual viewpoint novel the reader will always prefer one viewpoint to the other. For example, in Carol Shields's *The Republic Of Love*, which looks at a love affair from both points of view, I preferred the sections narrated by Tom, the easygoing disc jockey, to those of Fay, the more highly strung folklorist. Maybe there's an argument for saying then that if you're not using single viewpoint, more than two point of view characters are preferable.

Presentational Fiction

'In a good presentational story,' Scott Card says, 'the audience will forgive a certain shallowness of story because they so enjoy the writer's style and attitude.'[10] *The Catcher In The Rye* is very much a piece of presentational fiction, where the narrator addresses the reader directly:

> I'm not going to tell you my whole goddam autobiography or anything. I'll just tell you about this madman stuff that happened to me around last Christmas just before I got pretty run-down and had to come out here and take it easy.[11]

The voice, the style, are very much more important than the story. A narrator who wasn't opinionated would effectively neuter a presentational style. Apart from giving a potent view of the narrator, the fact that the narrator has strong opinions and expresses them also delineates his presence.

In *Catcher*, I believe it is fair to say that the narrator's voice and strong opinions are more significant as characterising devices than his actions. In the course of the novel, Holden Caulfield doesn't really do all that much, but he expresses a good many extreme opinions and does so in an idiomatic and stylised way:

The reason he fixed himself up to look good was because he was madly in love with himself. He thought he was the handsomest guy in the Western Hemisphere. He was pretty handsome too – I'll admit it. But he was mostly the kind of hand-some guy that if your parents saw his picture in your Year Book, they'd right away say, 'Who's *this* boy?' I mean he was mostly a Year Book kind of handsome guy.[12]

If, like me, you feel you are less skilled in the creation of plot, you may aspire to a presentational style and voice in the hope of winning over just the kind of reader that Card has described: one who is willing to forgive your shortcomings.

Try This: Presentational Versus Representational

Rewrite the first two pages of *The Catcher In The Rye* so that Holden never addresses the reader directly. This alters it from presentational to repre-sentational fiction.

When you've finished, compare the two versions and try to say what the effects of making the change are.

Further Reading

Anne Lamott (1995) *Bird By Bird – Some Instructions on Writing and Life* (New York: Anchor Books, 1995), p 49.
   This is one of the most enjoyable books on the writing life. Sure, there's good advice, but I recommend it mainly because Anne Lamott's world-view is very engaging and she makes you feel good about being a writer.
Jay McInerney (1985) *Bright Lights, Big City* (London: Jonathan Cape).
   You shouldn't need me to recommend *The Catcher In The Rye*: reading it should be a writer's reflex action, so instead I'm sending you in the direction of *Bright Lights, Big City*, the progenitor of a Hollywood subgenre: the yuppie nightmare. The second-person narrative here is a virtuoso performance. Major laughs, too.

Style: Syntax

According to the dictionary in the word-processing software we all use, syntax is 'the ordering of and relationship between the words and other structural elements in sentences and phrases'. Here are a couple of suggestions regarding your use of syntax.

Group Related Parts of a Clause Together

Words that connect with one another to form meaning work best when keeping each other company – for instance, the subject and verb of a clause. Compare:

a. Stephen Spielberg's influence in late twentieth-century Hollywood was almost unrivalled.

b. In late twentieth-century Hollywood, Stephen Spielberg's influence was almost unrivalled.

The Sentence Ending Packs the Most Punch

This one's easy: push the information you want to emphasise as far back in the sentence as you can. Compare:

a. Neil Finn would sell more records and play to bigger crowds if he still traded as Crowded House.

b. If he still traded as Crowded House, Neil Finn would sell more records and play to bigger crowds.

If you want to get serious about improving your written expression, take a look at Strunk and White's classic, *The Elements of Style*, which you can find on-line at: http://www.bartleby.com/141/

12 Your Travelling Companions: Characters

Robert Graham

You can't have credible action without characters (although you can have characters without action). However, it may be oversimplifying to see the two as a hierarchy. As Henry James has pointed out, the relationship between character and action is too interdependent for that:

> What is character but the determination of incident? What is incident but the illustration of character?[1]

Where Do Characters Come From?

For my money, characters that aren't drawn from life won't be fully realised. We all know enough interesting people to prompt a lifetime's worth of characters for our writing, but you don't need to use that uncle with the allotment in all his complex glory: you might just use the fact that he lives for his allotment. Then you might add in a characteristic you've noted in one of your neighbours – that she will often lock her front door on leaving the house, then go back to check that she really has locked it. Your characters, therefore, will often be a conflation of two or three of your family and friends. Here's a student writer explaining how she gets characters off the ground:

> I often write about people I know, or at least use elements of them for characters, and far from finding it restrictive, I feel that it is a strong and familiar

way to kick start my writing. For example: 'Julie Sanderson remembers little of her childhood but the smell of popcorn and petrol. She grew up on a travelling fair.'

There's no rule, however, that characters *have* to be based on people we know well. It could be that you develop an intriguing character inspired by somebody you observed for five minutes on a bus. Here's another student reflecting on the creation of convincing characters:

> I have begun to take more notice of people that I see in the street. I take notice of their appearance, their clothes, the way they talk and act. I have also found that through observing people I have developed skills with dialogue. Perhaps I have developed the nosy side of my personality where I have been listening to what people have said or commented on and quite often this has helped me with character development.

Observation is key in this: your characters have to have some basis in reality (and this is where carrying your journal at all times will help you). I would be reluctant to use a character with no recognisable elements of truth about them.

Try This: Visualisation

It's important to visualise characters and settings to make fiction, and that's the purpose of this exercise. I picked it up from the novelist Lesley Glaister, who suggests using a character you're already working with, but if you're between characters at present then imagine from scratch.

Shut your eyes. Clear a space inside your mind. Inside your head, put a chair in space. Move around it. Touch it. Get to know it. Colours? Texture? Strain to visualise it. Open your eyes. Jot down the details.

Shut your eyes again. Look to see if you've missed anything. Look around the chair to see where it is located. See what's there. Anything incongruous? Time of day? Atmosphere? Write that down.

Shut your eyes again. Go back to place and check it over again. Have a character enter that space. Have this person look around. Is it strange? Familiar? Will the person sit on the chair or not? If so, watch the movement. Study character. Height. Age. Colouring. Clothing. The way a character moves and sits down will tell you a bit about them. What about attitude? Are they happy, fearful, peaceful? Write it all down.

Close your eyes again. See the space. See the character. Look into their eyes. Look at the hands.

Now, be that person. Sink into the body and feel what it's like to be there. Different body. Different weight, etc.

Write in the voice of this character.

Start with, for example, 'God I hate it here' or, 'One thing I would love to do is . . . ' If you're stuck, go back to the chair in the space and visualise.

Flat and Round Characters

There are many more aspects to a real person than a fictional one, however multifaceted you've written them. Some fictional characters, however, are less complex than others. It was E.M.Forster who first distinguished between flat and round characters, but Wellek and Warren have expanded on these concepts:

'Flat' characterisation . . . presents a single trait, seen as the dominant or socially most obvious trait. . . . 'Round' characterisation . . . requires space and emphasis; is obviously useable for characters focal for point of view or interest.[2]

In Will Ferguson's novel, *Happiness*, Edwin Vincent de Valu is a clear example of a rounded character. Being the point of view character obviously helps; it offers the 'space and emphasis' to which Wellek and Warren refer. Edwin is disorganised, not terribly competent, ambitious, intelligent and critical of the world of publishing in which he is employed. He is a comic character, but he certainly has tragic undertones. His wife, Jenni, is a useful example of a flat character. If we set aside the fact that she is stupid, she really only has two 'character-indicators': she is shallow and very enthusiastic about sex. The best example of the former characteristic, is the way she adopts a magazine article ('Better Living Thru Post-It Notes') and makes it a philosophy of life:

Yellow Post-It Notes were everywhere: in the kitchen, in the dining room, even, no doubt, in the washroom. There were Post-It Notes on the lampshade ('Energy consumption! Think about the big blue planet!'), above the dishwasher ('Clean dishes! Clean mind!'), and on front of the fridge ('Better health and a more beautiful body').[3]

Jenni is a pretty flat character, but the flattest I know of is the chauffeur in Richard Brautigan's *Dreaming of Babylon*, whose one characteristic is the back of his neck, which appears to threaten C. Card, the novel's hapless private eye protagonist.

Unlike a major character – who says and does and changes enough to appear rounded – a flat character is no more than her character-indicators. This is fine. You will hope to create characters as rich and complex as Madame Bovary, but you will find that you have room for, and need of, characters who would not be out of place in the *Mister Men* books. Dickens's novels are full of them: Tiny Tim in *A Christmas Carol* and Joe Gargary in *Great Expectations*, for instance.

Saying, Doing, Appearing

There are a number of ways of creating character.

In Maggie O'Farrell's novel, *My Lover's Lover*, the reader gets an initial idea of what the character Marcus is like from descriptions of his physical appearance:

> The curve of his bicep is a pale, milky white, his forearms a deep brown. His fingers are stained with green ink.[4]

But he is also characterised by the things he does, in this case, with Lily, whom he has only just met:

> He moves nearer and, without speaking, slides one arm around her shoulders and the other around her waist. The length of his body rests against hers. He bends his head and presses his lips to the dip just below her cheekbone.[5]

We now know that Marcus is decisive, forceful and, depending on your viewpoint, forward. We know it and, more importantly, we worked it out for ourselves; nobody told us. We were *shown*.

The way characters look and what they do is informative to the reader, but so too is what they say. A little later, Marcus holds a piece of paper out for Lily and says:

> 'Do you want it?'
> They look at it together, a tiny runway on his outstretched hand. She keeps her face serious. 'Not really.'
> 'How about if I write my phone number on it?'

Now we know that Marcus is quirky and a bit of a tease. And again, we have reached these conclusions by inferring. O'Farrell hasn't said that Marcus is a tease, or eccentric.

In the case of Marcus, we come to understand his character not only through what he says, but also through what he doesn't say. When Lily moves into his flat, into what has been his girlfriend Sinead's room, he is so reticent about her that Lily comes to the conclusion that Sinead has died. And from this we may deduce not that Lily is slow, but that Marcus is manipulative.

As we've just seen, the best ways of creating characters are showing what they say and do; but it doesn't hurt to let us in on how they appear. A few tips on the latter, though: it's generally a good idea to describe a character's appearance on the hoof. Incorporate description into action or dialogue. Fiction more often than not resembles a movie rather a photograph; it's a moving picture and if you stop to describe things, your readers may lose interest. A head to toe description of a character's appearance is unnecessary: let the reader fill in from some choice pointers, and if you give details of appearance, do it early on in the narrative, before the reader has had time to imagine Freddie having dark hair, when on p. 341 you suddenly announce his hair is red. Readers find this very disturbing!

Characterisation by Association

Characters aren't defined just by what they do and say: the setting in which we find them may say a great deal about who they are. This is what the novelist Jane Rogers describes as conveying character by association with 'place, mood or occupation'.[6] It can work in several ways. At its most literal, characterisation by association may be as functional as the relationship between character and setting. If we meet a character lying in a hospice bed, she is defined as a dying character because she is in a hospice – nobody says she is dying.

If setting is the stage in the theatre of fiction, then I suppose what characters wear is their costume. This too is a means of characterisation. In Michael Frayn's novel *Spies*, Stephen Wheatley, the young protagonist, is presented to us wearing a 'too-short grey flannel school shirt hanging out of too-long grey flannel school shorts' and an elastic belt 'striped like the hatband of an old-fashioned boater, and fastened with a metal snake curled into the shape of an S'.[7] His clothes tell us at the very least that he is a schoolboy from another era.

At a slightly more sophisticated level, the physical objects associated with a character may have connotations that are helpful to the reader. Which brings us back again to Henry James.

Solidity of Specification

Writing of Henry James, Scholes and Kellog famously coined a term, which well describes the aspect of fiction writing I want to discuss next:

> the air of reality (solidity of specification) seems to me to be the supreme virtue of a novel – the merit on which all its other merits helplessly and submissively depend.[8]

Solidity of specification: I take this to mean that specification creates solidity and naming the names – 'a *Finding Nemo* bag', not just 'a bag' – is a priority when you're writing. Why? Because a plain bag is nothing in particular and a piece of Disney merchandising says something about both character and setting. To Jane Rogers's list of 'place, mood or occupation' I might add that character may be conveyed by association with mode of transport. Or record collection, choice of shop, taste in coffee. And, speaking of record collections, Nick Hornby's work illustrates the power of solidity of specification. In the space of one page in *About a Boy*, Hornby manages to specify the following: Laura Nyro's *Gonna Take a Miracle*, afternoon reruns of *The Rockford Files*, *Countdown*, Nirvana. If you just flick through the book at random, you might find, amongst many, many other specifications, Snoop Doggy Dogg, *The Simpsons*, Bruce Springsteen, shaved parmesan, flavoured condoms, *polenta*, Nottingham Forest, *Pinky & Perky*, Mozart and Joni Mitchell. All of these specific details function as little jewels embedded in the narrative; little jewels which light up for the reader. Solidity of specification does what it says on the packet: it makes the world of the story *solid*. 'Amy drove her car to the shop', tells us nothing much. 'Amy drove her MX5 to Harvey Nicholls', tells us quite a bit about Amy.

Try This: Data

In *On Writing*, the novelist George V. Higgins puts the case for research in action writing. He contends that the novelist should have as much data to hand as the best feature writer.

Think of someone you know well. You will know a fair amount about this person's tastes: the cereal boxes in the kitchen cupboard; the designer labels in the wardrobe; the TV set; the music system, and so on. You may not use all these details, but you need to know them. This exercise won't produce a fully formed character for you, but it will get a character started. It's an easy way of focusing on your character's tastes.

- Your character is at a supermarket checkout. List ten things in his or her trolley.

- List ten books on your character's bookshelves.

- List ten records in your character's collection. (Are they CDs, LPs, 78s?)

- Log your character's broadcasting week. Which radio and TV programmes does she listen to or watch?

- List your character's five favourite shops.

Double the Effect

What a viewpoint character notices about other characters almost doubles the effect. It amounts to a list of connotations about the characters in question, but it also reveals something about the viewpoint character. In this passage from *Nice Work* by David Lodge, Vic Wilcox, the managing director of an engineering firm, is accompanying Dr Robyn Penrose, a Women's Studies lecturer, to the car park:

> Wilcox shook his head impatiently. 'Where's your car?'
> 'The red Renault over there.'
> 'Why did you buy a foreign car?' he said.
> 'I didn't buy it, my parents gave it to me, when they changed it.'
> 'Why did they buy it, then?'
> 'I don't know. Mummy liked it, I suppose. It's a good little car.'
> 'So's the Metro. Why not buy a Metro if you want a small car? Or a Mini? If everybody who bought a foreign car in the last ten years had bought a British one instead, there wouldn't be seventeen per cent unemployment in this area.' [9]

Here we clearly learn as much about Vic as we do about Robyn. We already know that he opts for a Jaguar rather than a German make for his company car, and thus, cars here become a means of characterising.

Change

One of the fundamentals of storytelling is that there must be change. Often, the change has to do with action, with what happens. But sometimes, change may be about perception. Somebody whom the author has presented as unsympathetic may later be presented as more appealing. Usually this will be to do with the perceptions of the viewpoint character altering.

In David Park's novella, *The Big Snow*, Detective Sergeant Gracey is initially presented as a thug, a man who goes about his duties as a policeman in ways that would not generally impress Amnesty International. Early in the narrative, through the eyes of the tyro Detective Constable Swift, we see Gracey interacting with a criminal in the toilet of a pub:

> Through the gap he saw Brown on his knees, his long thin fingers holding on to the rim of the wash basin, an open razor glinting like a grin in the grime on the floor, his eyes fixed on Gracey staring back at him as he raised his wooden truncheon high in the air above his head, then without breaking their locked gaze brought it drumming down on Brown's hand.[10]

Later, when Swift has been showing too much initiative, Gracey lays into him:

> 'Swift, from the moment I met you, I could see you were a snotty-nosed little twat with your education and your head full of half-baked ideas from too many films and detective books. A regular little Sherlock Holmes who thinks on the basis of five minutes in the job he's got it cracked.'[11]

During the early and middle stages of the narrative, Gracey is portrayed in the least sympathetic light, but as the final stage begins, Swift and Gracey have a punch-up and come to some kind of understanding. Thereafter, they work on the murder case as a team, and the reader begins to see that Gracey may not be so villainous after all. Due to changes in the presentation of a character, the reader's perceptions have altered, and this is good. Readers like change. They also like a villain who has some charm.

Pitfalls

It's all subjective, horses for courses and so on. The particular course that Yours Truly trots round is dramatic fiction, where exposition is execrable and introspection is invidious. Allowing for the fact that I'm speaking from a rather extremist perspective, allow me to suggest a couple of things in the area of characterisation that I think it's good to avoid.

You think, to a greater or lesser extent, all the time. It's desirable in a human being, but in a character in fiction, I would argue, it's a turn-off for the reader. When marking student writing, I always respond badly to internal monologue. As Rob Watson puts it,

> introspective writing…may strike you as more literary and less reliant on the disciplines of form (easier, too, since you just have to open up and let it fall), but few novelists have done it well. Most introspective stuff is miserably inept.[12]

Such writing feels claustrophobic and it isn't dramatic: no other characters are involved, nobody acts and nobody speaks. Maybe human beings and characters in fiction are really not that different: aren't you interested in what other people say and do, and not particularly energised by what they're thinking about?

The other thing to avoid wherever possible in characterisation is simply telling the reader about a character. Say you're introducing us early on in your novel or short story to the narrator's family:

> Mother had been born to a rich family in Sydney and lived at home until she ran away at the age of sixteen with my father, Peter. My Dad, the son of a storekeeper from Alice Springs, was not an ambitious man. He was happy to sit on the porch all day listening to early Birthday Party records and smoking dope, which irritated my mother no end…

This isn't terribly dramatic or engaging, especially on the first page of a novel. I would never argue that it is possible to avoid telling the reader things; I'd just recommend trying your best to do so. The reader wants to be intrigued and to be put to work. When you explain, you are handing it to the reader on a plate and you don't want to do that.

Finally

It might be foolhardy, but I'm inclined to think that writing character is fairly straightforward. If you stick to what a character says and does, your fiction will stand a good chance of being readable. A word of warning, though: you won't get far in the task of characterising on that alone. Before you write a word, you need to know your character in detail.

Robert McKee, the screenwriting guru, has ten commandments for writers, one of which is that the author should know his world as God knows his. You can't spend too much time preparing characters before you begin to write. The creators of Alan Partridge spent hours and hours developing the finer details of Partridge's life. It's crucial to them to know that he wears Pringle sweaters and drives a Lexus. It may even be important to know things about your character that never get mentioned in the fiction. Hemingway had a theory that what you knew about a story but omitted made the story stronger, whereas that which you omitted because you simply didn't know it weakened the story.

Further Reading

John McGahern (2002) *That They Might See The Rising Sun* (London: Faber & Faber).
   Turn to page 23 and read the story of John Quinn, as recounted by other characters in this masterful novel. It won't take you long; it lasts 14 pages. Quinn is a monster, but a human monster. You can learn a couple of important things here. The first flies in the face of most of the chapter you have just read: all you really need when it comes to creating memorable characters is to keep your eyes and ears open. Does McGahern use characterisation exercises? Probably not. The second lesson is that rounded, convincing characters are complicated. John Quinn is a thug who abuses the women in his life, but at the same time, his kids think the world of him. It's the Tony Soprano lesson: a villain has to have his redeeming features.
John Gardner (1991) *The Art of Fiction: Notes on Craft for Young Writers* (New York: Vintage).
   This is essential, which is why we've put it in *A Writer's Bookshelf*. Read it yourself and find out why.

The Trouble with Adjectives...

Dear Auntie,
I love adjectives. I want to use them, but they seem to have a bad reputation.

In controlled numbers, adjectives are harmless little things, and may even be beneficial to your text, but occasionally they proliferate and all balance is lost; the outrageous, rampant result is a gruesome and vile pest infestation. Always keep adjectives under control by only using those you need. De-tox your work every so often, and you'll find that your paragraphs are neater, and your sentences clearer. In severe cases, an astonishing condition called Purple Prose results. It is not incurable, but can be painful to deal with. To treat: rinse work well. Shaking it firmly will then loosen unnecessary adjectives. If all else fails, it may be kinder in the long run to put the gorgeous golden garlanded text down and start again with a piece of clean white paper.

13 Setting

Helen Newall

If narrative is a journey, character being the driver, and plot the vehicle, then setting is the scenery along the way. The big mistake, however, is to think that it's merely the backdrop: if you use it well, setting can powerfully amplify theme, show character, advance the narrative. It creates atmosphere; it is the world in which your characters exist; and in some cases, it's the story itself. Some writers have even gone so far as to say that they treat landscape as another character.

Whether you're writing from memory, or from your imagination, places need to be as vivid as possible as you write, otherwise, how will you convey them to your readers? Because part of the pleasure in a text concerns not just the unfolding of events, but the evocation of the environment in which events occur, it's worth spending as much time knowing your setting as you would one of your characters. Just as in a journal you note remarkable characters or images, 'collect' places. Read and think about how other writers use environments.

Graham Swift's novel *Waterland* is a haunting portrayal of the East Anglian fens. The carefree atmosphere of Gerald Durrell's *My Family and Other Animals* depends not just on the comic portrayal of his mother and siblings, but on his fond evocation of long ago Corfu summers bejewelled with insects and animals.[1]

Try This: Remembered Places

Sit for a few moments recalling a childhood memory. Think beyond the action to the environment. Is the setting a room or a landscape? Think about colours, smells, sounds and textures. Write down as much as you can remember without stopping. Later, if you have time and opportunity, you could speak to relatives about this place: there might even be photographs. Seek them out. The new perceptions gained may add valuable information to your sense of this place.

Use the writing to frame a short evocative piece recounting the memory: now use it as the setting for a fictional event with a cast of invented characters.

Circuits of Connection

The pleasure in a text's sense of place often occurs because, just beneath the surface, there's an intrinsic connection between events and setting: just as it's risky for a writer to ignore setting altogether, it's a waste for a writer not to exploit the potential of such connections. Think of them as circuits conveying power, and you'll see how setting can light up characters, or illuminate actions.

Consider Thomas Hardy's *Tess of the D'Urbervilles*: when Tess's fortunes are high, Hardy presents her in a rural idyll, milking cows in lush summery meads: however, after she is rejected by her husband, we see Tess picking turnips in the bleak desolation of Flintcomb Ash. Even the name of the place is telling.

The panoramic opening to Alan Paton's *Cry, The Beloved Country* is an elegiac foundation for the rest of the novel. It sets the tone. The prose has the lyric rhythm of a song, and is structured almost in contrasting verses. The early paragraphs present the riches of the landscape: the voice says (or sings):

> Stand unshod upon it, for the ground is holy, being even as it came from the Creator. Keep it, guard it, care for it, for it keeps men, guards men, cares for men.[2]

But the latter paragraphs detail the decay, which was the daily lot of a disenfranchised people.

> Stand shod upon it, for it is coarse and sharp, and the stones cut under feet. It is not kept, or guarded, or cared for, it no longer keeps men, guards men, cares for men.

In the final paragraph we learn that:

> The men are away, the young men and the girls are away. The soil cannot keep them anymore.

And the song has become a haunting lament, and a powerful cry for justice.

Try This: The Great Outdoors

Go to a park, a street, the countryside: for as long as possible write down everything you see, hear, smell, taste, feel. Note the changes: perhaps the street grows busier; cloud shadows might darken a hillside; a park lake might gleam as the sun lowers. If possible, make several visits and observe how differing weather changes the mood of a place.

A story may emerge from this writing. If not, use it as the setting for a scene on which you are already working.

The Secret Unity of Words and Place

Unity of Place usually refers to the playwriting notion that too many scene changes are disruptive. While the setting potential of the novel is generally wider than it is for the stage, the concept is useful as a guiding principle when applied to more abstract systems of imagery.

Take, for example, E. Annie Proulx's novel *The Shipping News*. The protagonist, Quolye, has moved from a disastrous and tragic relationship in New York to the remote coastal wilderness of Newfoundland. Sense of place is evident beyond descriptions of the setting: it is evoked in the field of Proulx's descriptive devices. At the start of the book, when Quoyle receives the awful news of his wife's fatal car crash, Proulx depicts it thus:

> Quoyle gasped, the phone to his ear, loss flooding in like the sea gushing into a broken hull.[3]

There are any number of images Proulx could have used, but the one chosen concerns the sea and a stricken ship; it reflects the nautical landscape of Newfoundland and the broken and sinking state of Quoyle's mind.

When Quolye and his kids stay in a run-down motel, Proulx describes it thus:

> Room 999 was ten feet from the highway, fronted by a plate glass window. Every set of headlights veered into the parking lot, the glare sliding over the walls of the room like raw eggs in oil.[4]

We have been given enough to imagine the unsettling movement of light down the walls, the tawdry greasiness of the motel, and perhaps queasily, the half-cooked breakfast that awaits them. All very suitable: all very complementary. To have described the Newfoundland sky as being the colour of television, as William Gibson does at the start of *Neuromancer*, might have been accurate, but inappropriate, however brilliant a comparator it is for Gibson's fictional world of virtual realities and computer hacking.[5] This agreement is part of the grammar of sense of place. Writers exploit it.

Similarly, in Anne Michaels's *Fugitive Pieces*, the chance discovery of a photograph precipitates the devastating revelation of a family secret, after which the narrator notes that:

> The snow gradually disappeared from under the trees, leaving wet shadows. Detritus hidden all winter lay strewn across lawns and floating in gutters.[6]

And it seems that after the silence of snow, all things hidden are suddenly, painfully exposed.

The more you look for these examples, the more you'll find. It's unlikely that your readers will consciously note every example, but there will be an unconscious acknowledgement as layer upon layer is laid down, deepening the sense of place. Perhaps discovering examples is like snow melting, revealing a writer's secrets, but the magic is not lost if you start making the connections work for your own writing.

The Pathetic Fallacy

This is John Ruskin's famous phrase for the poetic convention whereby inanimate things are imbued with human emotion (from 'pathos' for emotion, and 'fallacy' because it doesn't really rain when we're sad; sometimes it just feels that way).

Ernest Hemingway once said:

> Remember to get the weather in your god damned book – weather is very important.[7]

It is the texture that brings setting to life, and it can either contrast or complement the action. A word of caution, however (with which Ruskin would whole-heartedly agree): it doesn't do to use the pathetic fallacy in the vocabulary of setting. Rain falling 'like heaven's tears' tends to sound overblown, and if your daffodils are 'happily fluttering', and your fluffy bunnies hopping joyfully, your story has crash-landed in the Greetings Card Land. Get out now!

The fact remains: you can make the weather do whatever your story needs: the funeral scene might gain more pathos if everyone huddles under black umbrellas, or perhaps, what is required is spring sunlight to conflict with the sombre anguish of the mourners.

It's no accident that it rains in films: pavements become beautifully shiny and reflective, rain is dynamic, it makes noise, and characters behave in interesting active ways, rushing to get inside, papers or coats shielding their heads.

The same principle is true of prose: the action of L.P. Hartley's *The Go Between* occurs in the oppressive heat of an Edwardian summer. As the heat builds, so does a secret and illicit passion, until it is certain that violent storms of many kinds are imminent, and, as the heat breaks, the circuits of connection between setting and plot are the lightning strikes that destroy so many lives.

Sense of Pace

The trouble with sense of place is that it's tempting to achieve it by dropping in chunks of description, but if it doesn't actually bring a narrative to a dead stop, description certainly slows down the pace, so care is advised. Incorporate description into action and dialogue: keep the action moving. Conscious use of pace, however, is a vital part of a writer's arsenal: Umberto Eco, author of *The Name of the Rose*, notes thus:

> There is no doubt that at times an abundance of description, a mass of particulars in the narration, may serve less as a representational device than as a strategy for slowing down the reading time, until the reader drops into the rhythm that the author believes necessary to the enjoyment of the text.[8]

If you want to slow the action, perhaps one character is waiting anxiously for another to make a decision, then the inclusion of a visual detail, just as a character might be seeing it, might help you make the moment stand still. For example:

> 'Did you do it?' she asked.
>
> A gull hung in the air, keening into the wind, and for a moment, the expanses of sea glittering behind him seemed so brilliant that she had to close her eyes. She

could imagine him shaking his head. She was sure that as the gull screamed, he shook his head. She opened her eyes, and he opened his mouth to speak…

The moment of resolution is delayed to maximise suspense. Let's hope the answer lives up to the build up of tension or there's the danger of a terrible moment of bathos.

In contrast, if your character is too rushed to notice scenery, then it's likely that the narrative pace won't have time to stand and stare either: generally, when there's too much setting, the narrative is static, besides which, given too much description, readers have no imaginative leap to make; it's all been done for them.

If in doubt, imagine the setting as directions for the journey the reader will make through your narrative: given too few details, the reader may miss a vital turning because the route is unmarked, the landmarks are not distinguished, the writing is bland: too many and the description of the route becomes cluttered, and noting all the various landmarks becomes a laborious and complicated task.

Try This: Street Building

This exercise concerns itself with a place that doesn't exist. Use the cues to imagine a street. If you can get someone to read the cues to you while you sit with eyes closed, so good. If not, think about them as you read them, then daydream for a few moments.

The street is cobbled.
It is dusk.
The wrought iron gas lamps are beginning to glow.
A neon sign in a café window flashes pink and blue.
Snow falls.
There's a car parked by the door of the café.
Someone runs into the street, shouting.
No one in the café notices.
The Someone runs passed, chased by a pack of dogs.

Rewrite the above, adding to the action, and the environment. Note when changes in pace occur and when emphasis on the types of visual detail might therefore be shifted.

A Place to Practise

Some writers start from somewhere that inspires them and find a narrative in it; others create characters and plot and then build suitable environments around them. Louise Erdrich (*Love Medicine*) begins with landscape, and says of her response to it:

> It has a lot to do with where I grew up. I set myself back in that pure, empty landscape when I am working on something…[because] there's nothing like it…it's the space where everything comes from.[9]

If this doesn't sound familiar, don't panic. Perhaps your characters drive the first draft: the second draft can then be about interweaving the setting. You have to find your own way of working: do whatever works for you, but as you draft, open yourself up to the possibilities of character influencing setting, and vice versa. Each new draft is about adjusting the balance between aspects of character, plot, setting, till they seem holistic and inseparable, but they don't often start out that way: when you read a novel you're watching the polished performance; you're not seeing the moments when the writer got it wrong and had to start again.

Try This: Chicken or Egg?

Images 1: clip out pictures of places from magazines. Imagine what kind of a character that place would be if it were personified.

Images 2: use a character already under development, or clip out a magazine picture of an anonymous person: imagine who this character might be; where are favourite places? If this character were a room, a car, a landscape, what would he or she be like?

Visual Writing

Having chosen somewhere to locate a story, budding screenwriters may think that, having labelled the setting for each scene, they need not weave setting through their narratives to the same degree as fiction writers do, after all, the camera will fill in the rest; but consider the fact that before they are filmed, all screenplays are read, and to get filmed they have to be a damn fine read. Jane

Campion's award-winning screenplay *The Piano* is a wonderfully dark and lyrical read: the prose is visual but spare: it gives just enough for the reader (and the camera) to fill in the scene.[10] Perhaps the most famous image is the piano abandoned on the wild beach, but having given us this, she merges visual and environmental details into the action descriptors:

> 31. EXT. BUSH AND CLIFF ABOVE BEACH. DUSK
> Again ADA stops to look at her piano from the cliff top. The sky is darkening and the air is full of bird calls. She turns from the cliff top, her face grimly set. She walks past BAINES, oblivious of his curiosity.[11]

The darkening sky and the birdcalls are the details that bring the printed information to visual life. They are the keys which can unlock for the reader the power of the mind's eye, making the scene more vivid and immediate, and since the darkening reflects Ada's mood, this immediacy concerns character as much as environment.

Similarly, in *Apocalypse Now*, Francis Ford Coppola's 1979 masterpiece about the Vietnam War, the link between narrative and setting is inextricable, something of powerful relevance to *all* writers, so prose writers take note. The visual detail of the screen is impossible to give in full in prose, prose can suggest, rather as Campion does in her screenplay.

Based on Joseph Conrad's 1902 novel, *Heart of Darkness*, the film is a quest narrative: the protagonist, Willard, must travel up the Mekong River to find and 'terminate with extreme prejudice' the renegade Colonel Kurtz, but, as with all good quests, the journey itself is as important and transformative as the final goal.

As Willard journeys, the river changes from a wide, open place where the American Army controls and surfs and destroys at whim, to a narrower, more winding course through a darker, more thickly tangled jungle, which the Army finds harder, if not impossible, to deal with: although the weapons with which Willard's boat-crew are attacked grow more primitive, they are picked off one by one. At one point, contrasting with the American air superiority seen earlier, the boat passes under the crashed wreckage of an American bomber still smoking in the trees. Upstream, it seems, things are darker, less sure, more mysterious, and as in all good forest myths, the advice is not to get out of the boat.

As he gets physically closer to the mysterious Kurtz, Willard tries to understand him by reading his file, and ponders on what Kurtz has done to so enrage High Command (and this is where the narrative of setting comes into its own, since sitting in a boat reading classified papers isn't exactly active stuff). Yet the closer he gets, the more intangible and atavistic everyone's motives become. When Willard finally reaches his destination he explores Kurtz's camp in an overgrown temple ruin. At one moment, the camera pans over a desk showing that Kurtz has a copy of James Frazer's *The Golden Bough*, a book that seeks to collect together world stories and mythologies to thereby find a source which will show how the primitive mind operates, and what Frazer offers is that to become the god, you kill the god. [12]

Willard is seeking the source of the river, and the heart of darkness: and in the very end the only way he can fully know Kurtz is by becoming him. The setting *is* the story because travelling upriver has become a metaphor for this journey into the brutal and primeval darkness of the human psyche.

Try This: *Apocalypse Now*

Film narratives have much to teach all writers, so prose writers: try this too! A good technique, if you have time, is to watch a film twice, making notes the second time around.

Compare and contrast the visual details of the US Army Camp where Willard receives his mission and Kurtz's jungle camp. Notice how in the ordered Army camp, the camera frames straight lines. How is this contrasted in the jungle camp? What rituals are evident in each place?

Write the scenes as if you have been commissioned to write the book of the film; can you show in your prose how each setting reflects a different state of mind? Consider also the pace of the action and how this affects your treatment of place.

Words: The Building Bricks of Place

If all this seems hard, then remember that even the best writers work at it: Ernest Hemingway, whose prose seems effortless, wrote:

> What I've been doing is trying to do country so you don't remember the words after you read it but actually have the Country. It is hard because to do it you have to see the country all complete all the time you write and not just have a romantic feeling about it. [13]

Bear in mind that unless you're writing autobiography in the strictest sense, you need not be true to how the place really is: if need be, let details shift to accommodate the narrative you're weaving, but if you use a famous place, get the salient details right: there's nothing more annoying to a reader than an error that breaks the frame (and nothing more annoying to a writer than receiving endless pedantic readers' letters about it!).

The setting for a sustained piece of writing should lodge itself in your mind as clearly as if it were a memory of an actual place, even if it does not in fact exist. It is built, developed, landscaped, changed, rather in the manner of a virtual make-over, according to the demands of characters and plot. And if there is a secret, it is to see the setting so vividly that you can run the film in your head, without giving it all to the reader: offer instead tantalising descriptors which suggest, and your readers will fill in the rest, and think you've told them more than you have. This is the ultimate circuit of connection; between writer and reader, and it is the most powerful of all.

Further Reading

Larry W. Phillips (ed.) (1999) *Ernest Hemingway on Writing* (New York: Touchstone, Simon and Schuster).
   A book to dip into again and again, and, with chapters such as 'What Writing is and What Writing Does'; 'Advice to Writers', and 'Knowing What to Leave Out', who could fail to learn something from it?
Francis Ford Coppola (1979) *Apocalypse Now.*
   Look at screenplays if you can get hold of them, but bear in mind that this one was filmed in rather unconventional circumstances. A good technique is to watch films with the sound turned down; you'll be surprised about how much more you notice about setting (and character and structure and so on for that matter) when you're not swept into the story by the music and dialogue!

14 White Space: Page Design

Robert Graham

Page design amounts largely to the use of white space and I regard it as an important element in the reader's perception of the fiction. Mike Sharples, in *How We Write*, argues that page design,

> assists in the communication of information…Each choice we, as writers, make in laying out text…on the page generates multiple meanings for its readers.[1]

White space can be used to make the page accessible and inviting to the reader. Sharples articulates this inclination nicely:

> In a novel, the writer's implicit contract with the reader is that, in general, the writer will make it as easy as possible for the reader to keep moving from one word and sentence to the next.[2]

With this in mind, both at the composing and the revising stages, it may be helpful to use short paragraphs and speeches in dialogue that are generally no longer than a line or two. It's also useful – indeed, it's currently a convention of fiction writing – to use extra spacing to show that a scene is over. As Sharples says, white space can be used to 'indicate breaks in meaning [and] signal the macro-structure to the reader'.

In its day, Fay Weldon's use of the page, particularly in her novel *Puffball*, was innovative. She was influenced in this by her background in advertising, where the most effective work carries a minimal amount of text (see for instance almost any print advertisement for Volkswagen cars).

The logic behind this awareness of white space is that we live in a visual society. Just as description in nearly all contemporary fiction acknowledges the fact that most readers will know what most things look like, so I think intelligent use of white space acknowledges that contemporary readers aren't nearly as text-friendly as their nineteenth-century forebears. As Sharples writes, 'research suggests that readers prefer text to be set in a more open manner'. However, it is perhaps Weldon herself who best theorises this approach:

> Designers and topographers actually teach you to look upon the page. Words are given resonance by their positions, they must be displayed properly. If you wish to give something emphasis, you surround it by space.[3]

If you want proof that the way you fill your page has an effect on your readers, compare these two pages. (The passages were whole pages in their original context.) The first is from William Golding's *The Spire*:

> ...In this dark and wet, it took Jocelin all this will to remember that something important was being done; and when a workman fell through the hole above the crossways, and left a scream scored all the way down the air which was so thick it seemed to keep the scream as something mercilessly engraved there, he did not wonder that no miracle interposed between the body and the logical slab of stone received it. Father Anselm said nothing in chapter; but he saw from the Sacrist's indignant stare how this death had been added to some account that one day would be presented. A dark night had not descended on the cathedral, but a mid-day without sun and therefore blasphemously without hope. There was hysteria in the laughter of the choir boys when the chancellor, tottering at the end of their procession from the vestry, turned left as he had done for half his life, instead of right to go into the Lady Chapel. Despite this laughter, these sniggers, the services went on, and business was done; but as in the burden of some overwhelming weight. Chapter was testy, song school was dull or fretful and full of coughing, and the boys quarrelled without knowing why. Little boys cried for no reason...[4]

The second passage is from Melissa Bank's *The Girl's Guide to Hunting and Fishing*:

> Bella says, 'We are just here until my stepfather sells the house.'
> 'How is Alberto?' Jamie asks Bella.
> I ask Yves, 'What do you do?'
> Bella stops talking and turns to listen.
> 'What do I do?' Yves says. 'Take pictures. Write novels. Play the piano.'
> I say, 'I didn't see a piano.'
> He tells me that Europeans are different from Americans – not so single-minded about careers. 'The most important thing to is to live freely.'
> I say, 'Live free or die, I guess.'
>
> ...

Back at the house, I smoke a cigarette on the veranda before going to bed.

Yves comes out. 'Jane?' he says, and kisses my cheek so slowly it's like his lips are melting onto my skin. 'Good night.'

In the bedroom I ask Jamie, 'What's going on?'

'What do you mean?' He's almost asleep.

'Well, something is.'

He doesn't answer. I wonder if it is because he doesn't know.[5]

Let's be clear: I'm not talking about the comparative quality of the prose or of the narrative in these two pages – and obviously I deliberately chose them to support my case, but you tell me: which one is more inviting, more reader friendly?

Some basic strategies will maximise white space on a page; dialogue, for one. Golding uses none, while Bank uses quite a bit. The length of the speeches is a factor too: the longest in the Bank extract is only two lines and most are one line or half a line. Paragraphing is important. Golding has only one, which in fact runs on to almost a further page in length, whereas Bank has many. Not only that; the longest paragraph on her page is three lines. Finally, you can see from the Bank excerpt that page-breaks (an extra space dividing two paragraphs, which denotes a change of scene or a break between sections) also add to the volume of white space on a page.

Try This: Page Design

Examine the first draft of a piece of fiction you have written.

- Dialogue. Look for ways to tighten up dialogue. Is there superfluous material here that should go? Speeches that ought to be shorter?

- Paragraphs. Check that you have taken a new paragraph for each new speaker. Look carefully at any paragraphs that are half a page or more in length – see if you can't split them in two (or three).

- Scenes or sections. Have you left a page-break where one scene or section ends and another begins?

Style: Plain and Simple

In life and in several aspects of Creative Writing, less is more, plain and simple are best. Certainly this is the case with style. In *The English Style Book*, Robert Clark argues for simplicity in written expression: 'Look closely at the sentences of most distinguished writers and you will invariably find that the words chosen and the syntax used are fundamentally simple'.[1]

Anton Chekhov was arguably the greatest influence on twentieth-century short-story writing; one of the ways in which he shaped the way modernist and postmodernist authors wrote was in his approach to style. Here he is advising a peer, in a letter of 1899:

> You understand it at once when I say, 'The man sat on the grass'; you understand it because it is clear and makes no demands on the attention.
>
> On the other hand, it is not easily understood, and it is difficult for the mind, if I write, 'A tall, narrow-chested, middle-sized man, with a red beard, sat on the green grass, already trampled by pedestrians, sat silently, shyly, and timidly looked about him.'
>
> That is not immediately grasped by the mind, whereas good writing should be grasped at once – in a second.[2]

Chekhov is widely thought to know what he was talking about.

15 Your Vehicle: Plot
Robert Graham

Yes, you're on a journey as a writer, but don't forget that you want to send your readers on a trip, too. Plot is the vehicle in which you shunt them down the road.

For most authors plots are difficult, and it would be nice to think that you could write fiction that relied on voice or characterisation alone. Sadly, that isn't possible and a plot of some kind is a necessity. How do you come by one? The same way as every other writer – by, in Anne Lamott's phrase, 'flail[ing] around, *kvetching* and growing despondent, on the way to finding a plot and structure that work'.[1]

Maybe a good place to begin is with what Robert McKee calls 'the inciting incident'.[2] *The Joy Luck Club*'s inciting incident is the death of the central narrator's mother. Perhaps your protagonist's husband has been abducted. Or son arrested on drugs charges. Or the protagonist has just been unfaithful to his wife. Coming up with an inciting incident is not a bad way to start planning your plot.

But you might think about establishing the characters and the setting before going to the inciting incident – showing the *status quo* here. If somebody is going to be abducted, the impact of the abduction on readers will be greater if they know and liked the person(s) who are left behind. If you want to maximise reader involvement, you will introduce characters and setting in a dramatic fashion before getting to the real meat of the narrative. In short, you need to hook the reader right from the start. Just about any James Bond film you care to name does this in what is often called the pre-title sequence, a brief, cliffhanger episode which hauls viewers to the edges of their seats, but is self-contained, unconnected to the rest of the film.

The Hook

If you look at how other writers snare the reader early in their narratives, you will see something similar. Perhaps the best hook you could find in a short story is Russell Hoban's masterly opening sentence in 'Telling Stories':

I wonder if this happens to a lot of men?[3]

This raises, in a gently confessional tone, an engaging reader-question. The initial sentence of Richard Ford's novel *Wildlife* has the strength of being very definite. It is also a sentence packed with information:

In the fall of 1960, when I was sixteen and my father was for a time not working, my mother met a man named Warren Miller and fell in love with him.[4]

We know right away that this story is going to be told from the first-person point of view, which, for most readers, is appealing. Arguably, there's a greater sense of immediacy with this point of view because the reader experiences the action through the channel of the narrator, where, as is the case in *Wildlife*, the narrator is involved in it. Thus, the first sentence of the novel introduces us to the narrator. It also tells us his age. It tells us when these events occurred. It gives us an efficient synopsis of the novel. It introduces us to the four main characters. In addition, the first sentence establishes a simple hook, one which will keep the reader engaged for some time: if the narrator's mother falls in love with Warren Miller when the father is away, what was the outcome? Did the family break up, or did it stay together? And, either way, what was the effect on the narrator?

Ansen Dibell argues that every effective opening to a novel does three things:

The chief of these is to get the story going and show what kind of story it's going to be. The second is to introduce and characterise the protagonist. The third is to engage the reader's interest.[5]

I believe that Richard Ford's short, clever opening to *Wildlife* fulfils this dictum.

So, let's say you now have an opening hook, closely followed by an inciting incident. That might take you through the first 10 per cent of your story. Somehow or other, flailing and *kvetching*, you now need to gestate a plot that builds on what you've achieved so far. That last sentence contains two crucial notions. One is that you have to gestate your plot. You need to live with it. You need to let the plot thicken. Partly, that is as passive as it sounds: you live with it and listen to what it tells you. But it can also be active, as Patricia Highsmith shows us here:

> When I am thickening my plots, I like to think 'What if...What *if*...' Thus my imagination can move from the likely, which everyone can think of, to the unlikely but possible, my preferred plot.[6]

The second crucial notion in that sentence is flailing and *kvetching*, Anne Lamott's memorable phrase. I've no idea what *kvetching* means. But I know I flail and *kvetch* all over the place when I work on my plots – and so will you.

Try This: The Simple Linear Plot

A person or persons has a wish, desire, need or objective. The fulfilment of this wish, desire or need, the gaining of this objective, meets an impediment. The impediment is overcome. The objective is gained or the wish is granted.

   NB This will only work if the writer can interest the reader in the central character and the character's sense of purpose.

Variations:

A. The pursued aim is either unattainable or, when attained, not worth-while.
B. The protagonist fails to overcome the impediment – to comic effect.
C. The impediment is established and nothing progresses until the very end of the story. (The plot put off.)[7]

You'll need at least two characters – three would be better. If you've no character notes lying around, use one of the writing exercises in chapter 12, 'Your Travelling Companions: Characters' to generate some. Put that together with the above and you should be able to write the first draft of a workable short story. Don't try to write it all in one sitting. Instead, spend time letting the ideas gestate. Take them for a walk. Daydream about them in your bath. Do the housework with them.

Steadily Rising Conflict

One of the ways in which you may ensure that your plot is an engaging experience for the reader is by trying to create steadily rising conflict – a concept which has been helpfully explained by James N. Frey:

> conflict which fails to rise is *static* – any kind of conflict which is unchanging. Conflict which rises too quickly is *jumping* – it leaps from one level of intensity to another without adequate motivation or transitional stages. What the dramatist wants is slowly rising conflict which reveals more facets of character because the characters will react differently at each stage of the conflict. As the character responds to rising conflict, he changes, showing all of his colours. Conflict proves character.[8]

Frey suggests that a rising conflict should take place in what he calls a 'crucible – the container that holds the characters together as things heat up'.[9] In John Fowles' novel *The Collector*, the crucible that holds the characters together is the cellar in which one holds the other captive. Similarly in Jan Martel's *Life of Pi*, Pi and a Royal Bengal tiger are adrift in a lifeboat – their crucible.

Steadily rising conflict is not, in my view, well served by an authorial presence.[10] As David Lodge explains:

> The intrusive authorial voice … detracts from realistic illusion and reduces the emotional intensity of the experience being represented, by calling attention to the art of narrating. It also claims a kind of authority, a God-like omniscience, which our sceptical and relativistic age is reluctant to grant to anyone.[11]

Nor is steadily rising conflict well served by lengthy passages inside this or that character's head, by exposition or (much) flashback. Narrative tension is, however, served by starting chapters *in medias res*;[12] by brevity and economy; by straightforwardness; by description being incorporated into action and dialogue; by dialogue that builds tension and advances the narrative; by sharp beginnings that hook the reader and endings that resolve the conflict and don't outstay their welcome; and by much redrafting – genius, as Wilde said, is an infinite capacity for detail.

Steadily rising conflict is easier to achieve if the second of Robert McKee's Ten Commandments is followed, the one about not making life easy for your protagonist.[13] This – giving your protagonist a hard time – is, in a sense, most of what any plot concerns. It seems self-evident that in a story, things will often go gradually from bad to worse and that in so doing they should raise the tension for readers. I don't foresee much future for a plot where things just keep getting better and better.

Further Reading

James N. Frey (1988) *How to Write a Damn Good Novel* (London: Macmillan).
For all that it has a tacky title, this is a very helpful book. It's a particular kind of novel that he theorises, the dramatic novel. Frey covers much of the necessary ground in quite a short space and usefully summarises essential things, such as Aristotle's *The Poetics*, probably the earliest advice on writing. He has memorable chapter titles like *The Three Greatest Rules of Dramatic Writing: Conflict! Conflict! Conflict!* I found it more useful than many texts on writing.

Joyce Carol Oates (2001) *Middle Age: A Romance* (London: Fourth Estate).
Because she appears to publish a book of one kind or another about once a month, Joyce Carol Oates is sometimes regarded satirically by other writers. It's only envy. *Middle Age* adopts a highly structured approach to the multiple-viewpoint novel: there are three major sections to the book, each consisting of five chapters, each of which is written from the point of view of one of the five main characters. In each section we meet these characters in the same order. What holds the whole together is that the book traces the effects of the death of Adam Berendt, a mysterious bohemian sculptor, on each of five of his friends. We read on because the multiple narratives promise to unravel the mystery of who Berendt was. That and the fact that everything that happens has been catalysed by his death cements the narratives together and stops the novel being nothing more than a series of linked short stories.

Scaffolding

Dear Auntie,
Help! I'm writing a short story and I've got lots happening, and plenty of ideas, but I can't seem to organise them. What is the best structure to use?

Hey! There's no magical one-size-fits-all structure: the best structure for any piece of writing is the one that enables you to complete it: because form and narrative are often intertwined, different narratives need different structures. If you're not sure what I mean, go away and watch *Donnie Darko, Memento,* or *Run, Lola, Run*[1] or read Kurt Vonnegut's novel *Slaughterhouse 5,* or Martin Amis's *Time's Arrow.*[2] In each case the structure *is* the story.

These structures almost certainly didn't arrive fully formed with the first idea; their writers worked at them, and remember that this is often the conscious activity that feels like you're squeezing stones for drops of blood. See chapter 3, 'Creativity', for more on this.

So, if you race through writing first drafts consisting of the first three paragraphs or, in the case of a novel, the opening chapters, but then grind to an ignominious halt, the fuel of inspiration has run out. But don't throw it away to start on another inspired fuel-injected project: time to start planning. Writing on into the narrative interior is often only possible when an appropriate structure is assembled.

There is, you see, the order of events along the usual yesterday-today-tomorrow trajectory of a protagonist's existence. And then there's the best order in which to reveal these events to the reader or audience, and that might be different: it might be tomorrow-today-yesterday. The best structure is, therefore, the one that can accommodate the work, allowing it to continue and finish without the text feeling like a square peg is being beaten with a really big old red croquet mallet into a round hole.

If you haven't already done so, read chapter 15, 'Your Vehicle: Plot'.

Style: Verbs (and Adverbs)

Just about any text on the craft of writing will advise you to write with verbs and nouns, and avoid using adverbs and also adjectives too heavily (see Auntie's advice in 'The Trouble With Adjectives'). One reason for this is that if you find a verb that accurately conveys what you want to say, you won't need to qualify it with an adverb. Compare the two phrases here:

a. Noah looked at the screen studiously.
b. Noah studied the screen.

If you want to write in a direct, clean and concise style, adverbs are often superfluous to requirements. Not everyone wants to write like Ernest Hemingway or Raymond Carver, though – but that's another story.

16 Scriptwriting For Nervous Beginners

Helen Newall

There are many other books out there which deal extensively and exclusively with the intricacies of writing for screen, stage, radio, and television (which in itself is a wild zoo of vastly different script animals), so for more specific advice use the Further Reading section. In the meantime, this will deal with the *process* of writing any script, something which seems to mystify many people.

Do Scriptwriters Just Do the Dialogue, or Do They Write All the Script?

No, writers do not just do the dialogue: and yes, they write the stage directions as well. At the outset, when wrestling with an embryo script, dialogue is often the last thing on your mind: not many scriptwriters I know sit down thinking, today I think I'll write a play, and, flexing their fingers, type at the top of the page...

ACT ONE: SCENE ONE

...and having typed, sit, fingers drumming, waiting for inspiration to strike (I think I might naïvely have done this the first time I ever tried writing a script, but it soon became apparent as I worried about what the virtually non-existent characters might be saying in Act I, Scene i that my story wasn't at all ready to be spoken).

A script is much more than what characters say: if in doubt, watch a film with the sound turned down and it's likely that you'll still be able to follow most of the story, because a large percentage of the narrative information is carried in images and visual action. This is what you have to find: the action, often visual, that carries and fleshes out the abstract summaries of your story.

I Have No Idea Where to Begin

Fear not: here are a few brief and loose guidelines to phases of the scriptwriting process: just as with fiction, these are not the unbreakable rules of How It Should Be Done, and they are more or less applicable to screenwriting, stage writing and radio drama, or fiction writing for that matter: many writing skills are transferable. A screenwriting book may unblock something for the fiction writer, and vice versa; and writing poetry may illuminate your screenwriting. The trick is to keep an open mind: try the phases till you work out a process that works best for you.

The phases are bordered with permeable membranes; that is to say, who can really tell when one phase in the process ends and another begins? Often different phases are simultaneous, so if you have the desire to write a scene while you're still planning the structure, then write the scene: what have you got to lose?

How to Begin

Just as with fiction, or poetry, there is often a giddy untidy mix of exploratory writing in journals or on the backs of envelopes or in the inside covers of library books; and planning that feels difficult; and drafting, and manic redrafting; and scribbling genius things down at midnight, and crossing them out again at dawn.

So begin by finding a story. Think of a narrative: a chain reaction of events – with a beginning, middle and end – that happens over a period of time to a character. Ha! More easily said than done, but take heart: just as with short stories and novels, it takes time; stories rarely descend fully formed in a flash of lightning to the accompaniment of the Hallelujah Chorus (however hard we all wish they did!). Instead, you pace about the room, or round the block: you mull over possibilities; you play the 'what if' game: what if a man has a dog he hates? What if he tries to get rid of the dog, but the dog loves the man so it keeps coming back? What if, one day, it doesn't come back, and the man misses the bad breath and the dog hairs and the whining, and sets out on a quest to find the dog and bring it home?

These 'what if' doodlings in your head, in your journal, on the backs of toilet doors may either lead you somewhere, or they may turn out to be dead-ends: in the case of the former, fantastic! And as for the latter: well...fantastic! The trick is to keep coming up with ideas: they're not dead in the water till you've satisfied yourself that they don't work. Perhaps they simply don't inspire you at this particular moment, but don't discount them; they may be the stepping-stone to another, better idea. A thrifty writer never throws anything away; ideas, like elastic bands, might just come in useful one day...and if they don't, you can flick them at your scriptwriting tutors.

The joy of the 'what if' structure is that the story is already active; it is already a chain reaction of events: perhaps not a particularly brilliant one, but it is from the outset more than the phrase, 'I think I'll write about a man and his loyal dog'. Wanting to write *about* something, whether it be an emotion, a woman who has a secret, a town that is about to suffer a natural disaster, is a long way from *the chain reaction of events told over a period of time*, which is the essence of most scripts.

When scribbling down potential 'what if' stories, use the third person and the present tense: this allows you to put yourself into the position of the audience, or camera, receiving the story. While with prose we can creep inside a character's head and admire the interior first-person view, stories told on stage and screen tend to be external affairs, unless voiceover is used, and some scriptwriting gurus strongly advise avoiding voiceovers if at all possible. Radio drama is a different kettle of fish as far as interior monologues are concerned, and you'll hear them quite often, but it's still best to use the third person as you plan, until you start trying out your character's voice.

Try This: What If...

Write as many 'what if' chains as you can; see where they lead you. If you can, work with a partner: you can bounce ideas off each other, helping each other to keep the chain going without veering off into the surreal (although, come to think of it, why not?).

Don't let your internal editor cramp your style: if ideas feel silly, enjoy the silliness. The point is to keep them coming because you might just find, among the silt, a golden nugget: experienced writers know that it's not *what* you say, but the *way* that you say it that counts. The most rubbish seeming idea might actually be priceless in the hands of a writer who believes in it, and sees its potential.

So, now in your journal you have a what-if paragraph or three. You need to fashion them into a rough paragraph story by answering the 'what if?' with a flow of definite actions.

What if a man finds a dog he hates? What if he tries to get rid of the dog?

becomes:

A man finds a dog he hates, but feeds it and looks after it and takes it for walks, but decides to get rid of the dog...

Eventually you'll end up with a rough chain of sequential events.

The Middle of the Process

After a few minutes, or maybe a decade, you have a story. Now all you have to do is start thinking about *how* you're going to tell it. It is at this point that you might want to invest in a block of card index files and an elastic band (didn't I say they always come in handy?).

To tell the story in a script, the abstract concepts need to be made visual and concrete (this concept is true of radio drama too): which character actions will represent a man hating a dog? So rewrite the paragraph in visual, concrete terms. Your original concepts will shift from:

For many weeks, although the man hates the dog, he takes it for walks.

And become units of action:

He strides over a hillside, calling to the dog, and kicking out at it as it passes him.

Nothing to it? Ha! Prepare to bite your pencil: this can be a very frustrating time. It may take days or weeks, but it's worth spending time and energy on these early phases: although you're not yet writing the working script, this is a vital part of the process.

Now write each unit, or each link in the chain, onto a separate card. You can now add other bits of information you need to feed into the story on more cards. There might be, for example, things you need to plant for a later pay-off. It's also easy to take away units of action that you find you no longer need. Each unit should be offering a new piece of information about character or plot. There's little, if any, dialogue yet, but then again, as we've already seen, the dialogue shouldn't be the whole story.

Laying and relaying out the cards in different configurations can solve problems beyond the scope of the cut and paste function of your computer. Numbers written in pencil in a corner can help you here, because what tends to happen is that once you've slogged for weeks and eventually found the elusive yet perfect order of events for thirty or more cards, a child comes along and helpfully shuffles them for you.

Since the cards are portable, writing becomes a game of patience you can play in a doctor's waiting room, on a bus, in the bath. Beware however: shuffling and reshuffling, seeking the perfect narrative, can become an endless displacement activity: at some point you need to launch into the next phase.

The End of the Process

Now you can start moving into layout, working out scenes, defining the visual action – see also chapter 18, 'It's Showtime: Immediacy' – and putting words into your characters' mouths. If you've been using your journal, capturing inflections of speech, listening to how people *really* speak, as opposed to how we *think* they speak, then drawing your characters through what they say and how they say it becomes less daunting. More specific craft of writing texts can deal with conventions of dialogue particular to screen, stage and radio scripts, but it is worth mentioning here that often less is more: so after you've written what needs to be said, edit. We tend to speak in the same way that water runs downhill, taking the easiest route. So, 'No, I will not throw a stick so that you can chase it, you horrible smelly dog' is more likely to be 'Get lost!' (Now read chapter 17, 'Dialogue in Prose Fiction'.)

And finally: a word on layout. Beware that when you start to format the work, you're using working layout as opposed to published script layout: they can differ considerably. Using the correct layout is a good hint to a reader (who might produce your work) that you know what you're doing. The reading given at the end of this will guide you.

Which Medium? Which Story?

Not all narratives are simultaneously suitable for screen and stage and radio and TV without adaptation. If your story is long and involved, crossing continents and spanning several decades, and involves a cast of several principal characters and hundreds of extras, and fires, storms and floods, then it's problematic if you want to write it for a theatre stage...but not impossible. Experience is the key, however. The stage tends to suit stories set in a small number of locations. It is a symbolic medium in that it can suggest location without needing to fully represent it, although it can and does do this too; film, with its bigger budgets and the verisimilitude of its presentation, can flit all over the place, and gives us the illusion of reality; while radio, it seems, relying as it does on the imagination of the listener, can suggest any location it wants and get away with it: they have the best sets on radio.

The best way to get a feel for the kinds of narrative found in each medium, is to experience them – lots of them. Go to the theatre; listen to radio drama; watch films. But read too. Scripts are available, and since the production involved in taking a story from page to stage is so collaborative, it's often easier to understand the writer's part in the work by reading rather then watching a play or film.

Try This: Similarities and Differences

Compare and contrast stage, screen and radio as media for drama. Think about:

Production budgets
The numbers of people involved in production
The cost of a ticket
The audiences: who are they? How captive are they?
Audience numbers?

Popularity of the medium
Marketing
Buildings
The writer's status
The medium's cultural status

Writing a Blueprint

The script is never the finished work of art; it is the blueprint, or the assembly instructions for the actors, the director and the designers. Each time a theatre company puts on a production of a particular play, it is never exactly the same as the previous production; and it's never *exactly* the same as the playwright envisaged it during the writing process: often, because designers are better at designing than writers are, and actors are better at acting than writers are, the production is more than the writer ever imagined. In other words, the finished script is only the beginning of a collaborative creative process. James Schamus, who wrote *The Ice Storm*, says of film writing:

> A shooting script, at the end of the day, is simply a series of suggestions to the director, cast, and crew about how to use their time and spend the film's budget. The more coherent those suggestions, the better. Best of all is when they serve merely as a pretext and foundation for the collective experience of surprise and discovery that makes filmmaking so much fun – and films so different from their scripts.[1]

Experiment

As you watch more and more plays and listen to radio dramas and read scripts, you'll get a feel for the 'vocabulary' of a medium. This doesn't mean that you should always write what you've seen or heard. Try writing what you'd like to see. Read your work aloud. Get friends to read it out. Push the possibilities, and have fun.

Try This: Alphabet Scripts

ALICE has a secret: BEN wants to know the secret: CHRIS is not sure what the secret is but doesn't want BEN to know. You work out the secret if you have to. You worry about the reasons. But don't worry too much;

this is about playing, and therefore don't worry too much about having to explain your premise to an audience, simply imagine that this is an excerpt from the middle of something. Now let the characters loose and let them talk to each other, the only rule being that when each character speaks, the first word of each new speech must be the next letter of the alphabet...

ALICE: As I was saying...
CHRIS: Before you start nagging again ...
BEN: Chris! Let her speak. I want to know!
ALICE: Don't interrupt! Why does everyone always interrupt?

Yes, it's tricky. Yes, it may take some time, but have fun; it's like a crossword puzzle, but then again, isn't all writing a form of problem solving? What the alphabet rule does is disrupt the fixed patterns of call and response we can all slip into when writing dialogue; it forces your characters to use unpredictable and unexpected speech patterns. It doesn't necessarily make great theatre or cinema, and I'm not saying you should use this technique in a finished piece: use it as a way of flexing your writing muscles.

Further Reading

Syd Field (2003) *The Definitive Guide to Screenwriting* (London: Ebury Press).
   The first must-have of screenwriting.
Robert McKee (1997) *Story: Substance, Structure, Style and the Principles of Screenwriting* (London: Regan Books).
   The other must-have of screenwriting, and what these texts offer in terms of character, structure, dialogue, etc. is worth noting for fiction writing.
Sheila Yeger (1990) *The Sound of One Hand Clapping: A Guide to Writing for the Theatre* (Oxford: Amber Lane Press).
   A good entry point into writing for the stage. Plenty of guidance and wisdom.
www.irdp.co.uk
   Independent Radio Drama Productions website: all you ever wanted to know about writing drama for radio but weren't aware that you needed to know. Detailed and essential.

Basics: Speech Marks

Like everything else in life, punctuating direct speech is easy when you know how. You may have to excuse me teaching my granny how to suck eggs here, but the fact is that year in, year out I come across many students who get the punctuation of direct speech wrong.

Here are a few pointers, based on the elements that tend to get confused. (Please note that the guidelines on single speech marks are contemporary conventions.)

1. Put the dialogue (that which is directly spoken) inside *single* speech marks:
   WRONG: "Given a choice, I prefer white chocolate"
   RIGHT: 'Given a choice, I prefer white chocolate'
   Double speech marks are used for quotations within dialogue.

2. Place any punctuation of the dialogue *inside* (not outside) the speech marks:
   WRONG: 'Given a choice, I prefer white chocolate',
   RIGHT: 'Given a choice, I prefer white chocolate,'

3. Consider the speech tag a part of the same sentence which includes it and the dialogue:
   WRONG: 'Given a choice, I prefer white chocolate.' She said.
   RIGHT: 'Given a choice, I prefer white chocolate,' she said.

Style: Directness

Concision is key to good style. So, too, is directness. In narrative writing, in order to intrigue, you will often want to keep your reader in the dark. However, when you do want the reader to understand something, you shouldn't leave anything to chance. You want the information you wish to transmit to travel as directly as possible from your mind to the reader's. Here are a few suggestions.

Write with Verbs and Nouns

This means as far as possible avoiding adjectives and, especially, adverbs. It has to do with hitting the nail on the head first time, so that the reader accesses the information immediately. Compare these two expressions of the same information:

a. Selina walked angrily out of the room.
b. Selina stormed out of the room.

Which is more direct?

Avoid Qualifying Phrases

Part of the secret to direct communication is getting it right first time. Compare the following versions:

a. The Beatles came out of Liverpool and conquered the world, having first become the most popular band in Merseyside and then in Britain.
b. The Beatles came out of Liverpool and conquered the world.

In other words, make your point and leave it alone. Get it right first time.

17 Dialogue in Prose Fiction

John Singleton

Dialogue Is an Unnatural Practice

Sometimes you hear writers praised by reviewers for their 'natural' dialogue. Such and such has a 'real ear for dialogue/ordinary speech/ conversation,' they write approvingly, as if the ability to capture actual speech is a gift. It's not. It's a misunderstanding of the true nature of dialogue.

Fictional dialogue for the most part is very unnaturalistic, full of contrivance and artfulness. It has to be to avoid all the defects of ordinary everyday conversation. I say 'defects' simply because what is acceptable in the oral is not in the literary. Just eavesdrop on any conversation in a pub or café and you'll see the obviousness of what I'm saying.

Literary dialogue is shorn of all the hesitations, repetitions, fractured grammar, fragments, uhhms and errs and all the other unofficial alphabet of sounds and additives that feature in daily conversation. Such dialogue is crafted. It is cleaned up and shaped and articulate. Only when characters are inarticulate or under great emotional stress does written speech begin to take on the rawness of the 'natural'.

It's not that dialogue in novels and scripts shouldn't be naturalistic, if by naturalistic is meant it *sounds like* the real talk of actual characters. And that's the trick: making the artificial and crafted appear natural and unforced; hiding the art in artlessness. Even those writers who believe in *actualité*, who write it as it is, do, nevertheless, manage to subtly shape their dialogue, creating underlying rhythms and patterns and echoes.

In this sense I'm being unfair to the critic who recognises and praises a writer's *ear* for dialogue. It is absolutely essential for a writer to have such an 'ear', by which I mean having a feeling for the tune and melodies of conversation. It's easy to write tuneless and flat dialogue, but the best is full of the music and expressiveness of the spoken language.

Dialogue Is More Than Just Me and You

Like all utterance, dialogue is expressive of both the individual's personality and the social context in which they operate. I remember once an old Potteries' man describing his thirst to me with the phrase: 'I'm so parched I could go licket mop stick.' The expression here is graphic and so indicative – of character, regional distinction (note the dialect omission of the *and* between 'go' and 'lick' so typical of a local grammar), class (my middle-class business-man father would never have used such a phrase), and of a cultural moment that has passed with the advent of spongees, detergents and Dyson vacuum cleaners. But if you are writing a regional novel set in 1960s Stoke, or one of your characters is a grandfather from Hanley with a typical working-class turn of phrase then this will influence how you write him into dialogue.

Try This: Dialogue and Conflict

Write a scene in which you have two contrasting characters. One is from a different social circle and class from the other. Invent a situation for their encounter and develop a scene through dialogue that expresses their different social and class cultures. Remember that some people regard regional language as an inferior mode of expression, while others consider it a sign of authenticity and grass root reality. How strongly do your characters feel about language and how regionalism defines identity?

Dialogue Is 'Voices'

All this means that not only do you have to have fine-tuned antennae for the sounds and rhythms of language – what I have called the music of speech – but also an inner ear, an awareness of the social and psychological resonances of speech. What I mean by this is that each person has an individual 'voice', or particular vocabulary and verbal mannerisms that identify and distinguish them from other people. But this voice changes according to circumstance: the way a teenager talks to her mates is different from the way she does to the headteacher in her school, to her brother, or her grandmother. In one situation she may be boastful, gossipy and slangy, in another she may be respectful, subservient-seeming and more formal in her speech. If she has to talk on the phone to a counsellor, or respond in an interview, her 'voice' will change yet again. Writers need to note these differences and have that 'ear' not just for their character's voice but for all the nuances of that character's 'voices'.

Now if one of your characters uses the phrase 'the social and psychological resonances of speech', just what kind of person would you have in mind, and in what context have you placed that character? Is s/he trying to impress, even browbeat a listener with this sonorous phrase, with the academic voice? Imagine a tutor in college talking like this in a tutorial to a naïve young student. Could you convey the academic detachment – even the self-importance – of the tutor, while at the same time mocking/implying the gullibility of the student? The student could use a hybrid academic/colloquial vocabulary and hesitant expression to show they have not quite got the appropriate voice for academia, and the tutor could be shown 'performing' through the use of extended rounded 'speeches' with lots of subordination in the sentences, and some jargon.

This contrast of 'voices' could create real punch and point to your scene. So make it even more resonant and have your characters of different sexes. And what do you get? A young working-class woman, grappling with the intellectual challenges of H.E. wanting to impress, and an educated middle-class, middle-aged tutor grappling with a sense of his own dullness and aware he is just going through the motions. Willy Russell, of course, has written *Educating Rita* out of just such an encounter. But the tutor could be boundlessly enthusiastic and the student tired and cynical, in which case the dynamics of the scene would change and the dialogue with it.

Try This: Active Dialogue

Write a scene that takes in some of these elements. Decide whether to first 'place' your two characters, or launch straight into dialogue relying on the spoken word to communicate the situation and location to the reader. You could of course start with three or four lines of dialogue and then try some narrative in-filling and scene-setting before picking up the dialogue again.

Dialogue Belongs to Characters Not to Writers

Some writers treat characters as if they were alter egos, or use them as mouthpieces for their own views, or just as mouthpieces. This is not to say characters should not express views or opinions, political, religious or philosophical, but that these should be as much a *part of them* as temperament and disposition. It's worthwhile, then, creating characters who speak very differently from the author. If you're a male writer create dialogue for women characters. Ask a female friend to read your work for hints of gender bias and stereotyping. If all your female characters seem passive in their expression, liberate them from your own obsession and create something more feisty, or better still create a number of female characters expressing a range of characteristics and attitudes. Set one character or group of characters to challenge others and create diversity and drama in your fictional discourse.

Dialogue Is Multipurpose

To some extent what you as a writer want from a scene will dictate the kind of dialogue you write for it. Back to the tutorial. If you want to ridicule the jargonising that passes for understanding in education then this will show in the vocabulary you put in the mouths of tutor and student. The key to good dialogue and successful scenes is *that more than one thing should be going on at the same time*. So, for instance, in our tutorial scene, the satirising of modern education can be developed at the same time as the theme of innocence and seduction, sexual and institutional power and so on. And the two characters will be revealed, their contrary motives, their backgrounds, their temperaments, aspirations, anxieties.

Much of the composition of this fictional complexity, which only reflects life's own variety, depends on the writer's intention/purpose/position with regard to the characters. For instance, the writer may decide on a strategy that juxtaposes simpler student language and the magisterial tutor voice for the purpose of puncturing the latter's pretensions. But then you may not be on the side of your student character. As a writer you may want to be more balanced, and this will effect how you shape the exchange between your characters.

As well as revealing character, back-story and charting themes, dialogue impels the narrative. Out of one scene comes the impetus for the next. Suppose that, at the end of their tutorial, the tutor offers to give the young student extra help with assignments, and lightly touches her knee as he leans to pick up a fallen book: this then becomes a topic for a subsequent conversation between the student and her flatmate. Here the tutor's reputation may be an issue.

Whatever the upshot of their talk, the student now has a dilemma (Is the tutor making a pass at her? What should she do about it?), which will, in turn, influence her behaviour in the next meeting.

Dialogue Is Contextual

Dialogue isn't an isolated feature of fiction. It exists in context, the context of the whole story and the context of the scene. Many fictional scenes mix dialogue with narration of action, with description of location, with interior reflection, with authorial commentary, with reported speech, and the art is to keep all or some of these elements in the air and balanced at the same time.

By now our tutor character is getting tired. He's been running end-to-end tutorials for two hours and is dying for a coffee. How do you communicate bored? Do you have the author simply state the fact to the reader? That's the most precise method. But you may feel it is better to show not tell and thus you interleave between passages of speech little gestures like pencil tapping and window gazing. And you write a final summing up by the tutor which sounds like a well-worn script, mechanical and mainly cliché and jargon.

One of the dialogue arts then is that of complementing and juxtaposing contrasting physical images with spoken words. After all, many of us use language not to reveal but to conceal things, to say one thing but feel/think another. Words often counter and contradict body language. It isn't true to say 'watch my lips' and all else follows. So remember your characters are communicating not just through speech, but through gesture and pose and mannerism, and dialogue is only one element in a rich communicative context: the automatic nervous system, for example, gives an observant person plenty of information by manifesting itself through sweating, trembling, palpitation and other involuntary signals. Dialogue is more than the words that characters say.

And there's yet another crucial element supplementing, modifying and often contradicting the oral and the autonomous, and that's the cerebral – the mental and perceptual world. The thoughts of your characters represent another 'voice' in the conversation of any scene. Indeed, they may represent more than one 'voice' because so often our interior world is riven by opposing feelings, ideas, sentiments, opinions, realisations. And so often it is though conversations with our inner selves, that dilemmas are resolved or debated or highlighted or exacerbated or whatever. Good page dialogue gives some hint of this busy clamorous interior life.

Try This: Dialogue Gives Information

Write the opening of a story with a passage of dialogue in which you aim to give as much information as possible about two characters without making it obvious and sounding like a synopsis.

Dialogue Is the Kiss of Life

Speech is a sign of intelligent life, and though dialogue is not an inevitable constituent of fiction, it is if you want to create convincing characters and dramatic situations. Up to 18,000,000 people watch weekly soaps on UK television. Visuals may dominate the medium, but dialogue is more than just an add-on. Try watching serial drama with the sound off. You'll be lip reading like mad. In fact, the best soaps are those that rely primarily on neither dialogue nor visuals, but balance the two modes of communication. In this, they bridge the gap between film and theatre.

Nevertheless, good dialogue does give *immediacy* to fiction. It shows things as they happen. A scene of convincing dialogue in a novel or short story is like the curtain going up to reveal a well-lit stage; it creates anticipation and excitement; it animates characters. Till they speak they are stiff, hardly more than cardboard cut-outs. Put words on their lips and they come to life. Listening to dialogue puts us readers on more intimate terms with characters, draws us in by invitation as it seems, to share dilemmas and predicaments, heartache and triumph.

Now, take a look at the following extract from Dave Eggers's bestselling novel, *A Heartbreaking Work of Staggering Genius.*

Beth and her brother are talking to their dying mother, trying to persuade her to go into hospital and have her nosebleed treated before she starts choking.

'They're waiting for us.'
'Call another nurse.'
'Mom, please.'
'This is stupid.'
'Don't call me stupid.'
'I didn't call you stupid.'
'Who were you calling stupid?'
'No one. I said it was stupid.'
'What's stupid?'
'Dying of a bloody nose.'
'I'm not going to die of a bloody nose.'
'The nurse said you could.'
'The doctor said you could.'
'If we go in, I'll never leave.'
'Yes you will.'
'I won't.'
'Oh, Jesus.'
'I don't want to go back in there.'
'Don't cry, Mom, Jesus.'
'Don't say that.'
    . . .
'Fine, bleed. Sit there and bleed to death.'
'Mom, please?'
'Just bleed. But we don't have enough towels for all the blood. I'll have to get more towels.'
'Mom?'
'And you'll ruin the couch.'
'Where's Toph?' she asks.
'Downstairs.'
'What's he doing?'
'Playing his game.'
'What will he do?'
'He'll have to come with us.'

The characters are by turns exasperated and distressed by having to play out of character and adopt uncomfortable parental roles. Uncertain, they become wound up and overheated. Though the mother uses her illness as a bargaining tool, her attempts at resistance only serve to highlight her vulnerability. The short tight phrases and sentences underscore the tensions in the encounter and give it that jerky apprehensive feel. And then the scene collapses, as does the mother's resistance, into the prosaic ending, and her sudden acquiescence confirms the air of inevitability that hangs over the whole episode.

Throughout, dialogue captures emotional intensity, delineates character, hints at the complex dynamics of family life, and insinuates some strong visual moments. These are inferred, for instance, from the exclamation: 'Don't cry, Mom.' and from the comment about needing 'towels for all the blood'. This latter image shakes the reader and at this point the tension collapses into ironic banality as one of the children points out that the couch will be ruined. The domestic rises above blood and death, and normality makes a show of reasserting itself. In the same way the mother's innocent question, 'Where's Toph?' is her way of seeking solace in the ordinary and mundane, a return to the comfort of her caring maternal role. The scene finally ends in quiet acquiescence.

Dialogue in Practice

Attribution – he says, she says – can be a problem. Some hesitant writers try and avoid repetition of the common verb 'to say' by using alternatives such as 'reply', 'respond', 'answer'. As these options run out, more and more exotic alternatives are tried such as 'aver/concur' for 'agree', or 'ejaculate/expostulate' for 'exclaim', or 'pronounce' and 'articulate' for 'say', or even 'adumbrate' for 'explain', or 'interject' for 'interrupt'.

The art is to keep it simple: don't be frightened of repetition; make your voices so distinct you don't need constant attribution.

But you could use more descriptive/image-based attributions such as 'murmured', 'whispered', 'sighed', 'wept', 'hissed', 'smiled'. There's a whole auditory and visual vocabulary out there. Poor dialogue resorts to the needless adverb and the adverbial phrase to gloss speech. An example:

'Get out of my sight,' he shouted angrily.

The spoken words suggest anger, which makes both the attribution 'he shouted' and the adverb 'angrily', redundant. The art of good dialogue is to make the spoken words carry tone, emotional force and even gesture if possible. The general rule is: reduce attribution to a minimum.

Another way to handle attribution is to place it in the middle of a sentence or passage of speech and not at the end. This way dramatic pause can be created. Compare:

'No,' he hissed. 'I will not have it.'
with
'No, I will not have it,' he hissed.

Isn't one more dramatic and forceful than the other? Consider the pacing of the two sentences and the stressing of syllables. Do you notice anything significant?

Or, put the attribution at the beginning of a line of speech like this:

He stood up, and looking in her eyes said, very slowly, very quietly, 'I'm going to kill him.'

Now that's how to delay crucial information till the last syllable and thereby create suspense. No sentence you ever write should be complete till the last syllable sings.

Dialogue and Exposition

Try and avoid using dialogue to 'set the scene' or explain action. Dialogue should not be the equivalent of stage directions in a play. Certainly it is important to contextualise action and say where characters are coming from, account for their present situation, appearance and so on, but if you have to do it through dialogue, make it so 'natural', so seamless the reader doesn't realise s/he is being fed vital preliminary information.

Pacing

As with all writing, pace and rhythm are critical. Consider how you can alternate passages of emotional intensity with those where you relax the reader. If you're writing a scene between two old friends reminiscing, it has to be gentle and slow-paced, probably with interludes of interior reflection, and gestural and descriptive moments. Pace may be expressed in terms of long sentences with plenty of qualification. On the other hand, if you're writing an action-packed thriller, pace and sentence shape in dialogue are altogether different. Scenes of high tension feature sentence fragments, short phrases, plenty of monosyllables, exclamations! And no dialogue lasts more than half a page before we are off on another high-speed scene.

Banality is Avoidable

Some writers mistake realism for naturalism, thinking that the nearer you can get to normal daily speech in fictional dialogue the better and more convincing, that is, real, it will sound. No way. The dullness of transcribed speech is a glory to behold. Some writers also believe, with justification, that the ordinary and everyday should be as much a preoccupation for artists as the unusual, the hidden and the extraordinary. Indeed, the one does not preclude the other. Thus a scene where two soccer fans discuss team selections over a pint may be a common experience in fact, but in fiction it is fraught with cliché and platitude.

Of course a good writer creating a pub scene will turn cliché to advantage as Graham Swift does in his Booker prize-winning novel, Last Orders.[1] Read the second chapter. Ray, a bookie, Jack, a butcher, and Vince, a garage owner, are drinking late in The Coach and Horses. Ray keeps repeating his dull joke about the Horses never going anywhere. However, though the repetition may bore his listeners, it works a strange magic on the reader, and by the end of the chapter the images of Coach and Horse take on an ominous and prophetic power. The writer has turned brash bar-room cliché into gold. Read how he does it.

Dialogue Begins Anywhere

New writers are often hesitant about writing dialogue. I think the best way to write good dialogue is to read good dialogue, and then have a go yourself. So, study Graham Swift, Dave Eggers, David Mamet. Now set yourself a limited number of characters in a recognisable location and write their talk. Go for it.

Further Reading

Jean Saunders (1994) *How to Write Realistic Dialogue* (London: Allison & Busby).
    A basic but very useful guide.
Lewis Turco (1991) *Dialogue* (London: Robinson).
    A useful general introduction to a range of dialogue-writing techniques.

Basics: Paragraphing

In written expression, you could be said to be working at four levels: word, sentence, paragraph, chapter. The last three are ways of organising information that a reader may access. As you will see in chapter 14, 'White Space: Page Design', the intelligent use of white space makes your writing inviting to the reader. So too will skilful use of the paragraph. When a paragraph ends, you are giving readers a break. You are saying that a chunk of information they were being asked to digest is now over, and so they have a small break – the white space created through taking a new line and indenting – before a new batch of information comes at them.

In the nineteenth century, long paragraphs were the norm. It was a textual era. During the twentieth century, our civilisation became a visual one, and as a result, vast monoliths of black text are no longer appealing to readers.

So in general, go easy on paragraph length. Here are some further suggestions:

- The beginning of your story, section or chapter is more likely to engage your reader if you use short paragraphs and short sentences.

- A new speaker needs a new paragraph.

- If the focus in fiction shifts from one person to another, take a new paragraph.

18 It's Showtime: Immediacy

Robert Graham

I once heard a BBC radio documentary on which a researcher for Ace Records was talking about being in the vaults of the major label that owns Otis Redding's recordings. He was ploughing through tape-box after tape-box, sifting for recordings to lease for reissue, when he came across a box labelled 'Otis Redding – Dock of The Bay – Take 1'. He described playing the tape for the first time. He explained that the sound effects – the waves washing the shore, seagulls – had not yet been added and the whistling solo was fluffed: 'Otis wasn't actually a very good whistler.' What the researcher said of the experience was, 'It put you right there on the studio floor.'

The point of writing immediate fiction is putting the reader 'right there on the studio floor' – right there in the action. Rather than recounting the narrative, you want the reader virtually to experience it. This, I would argue, is the reason that, in Percy Lubbock's words,

the art of fiction does not begin until the novelist thinks of his story as a matter to be shown, to be so exhibited that it will tell itself.[1]

Showing not Telling

I've touched on showing and telling in chapter 12, on characters, but in my experience, students find the difference between the two confusing, so I'm going to say more on the subject now.

Telling, Wayne C. Booth contends, amounts to 'summary' and is 'inartistic'; showing involves the use of 'scenes' and is 'artistic'.[2] Like most writers, I have often found it difficult to spot when I am slipping into telling. The difference between telling and showing, according to Monica Wood, can be expressed thus: showing involves 'using vivid details and engaging the senses ... painting a bright descriptive picture for the reader' while telling is 'uninspired narrative that only serves to explain what is going on in the story'.[3]

But what's the point in me telling you about it when I could show you?

Telling

ALL THIS HAPPENED, more or less. The war parts, anyway, are pretty much true. One guy I knew really *was* shot in Dresden for taking a teapot that wasn't his. Another guy I knew really *did* threaten to have his personal enemies killed by hired gunmen after the war. And so on. I've changed all the names.[4]

This isn't immediate. It's somewhat an author's note, really, but Kurt Vonnegut (whose work I really like) has put it in as his first paragraph – possibly the one paragraph in a novel that has to work harder than any other. No doubt Vonnegut did so deliberately. Maybe he was challenging the boundaries of truth and fiction, I don't know. Whatever the author's intention, the register of this passage is narration, or explanation, or monologue. It's the author addressing the reader directly and when that happens, you can be sure that, rather than being shown, you are being told something. You will find passages of telling in any great novel you care to name. Henry James does it. Richard Ford does it. And Carol Shields. And on and on. Is it a bad thing? Well, perhaps it's a case of horses for courses. All I know for sure is that showing is more dramatic and dramatised fiction is more engaging. And I also know that nobody will read your novel if it is entirely told. Not even your doting mother.

Showing

That evening, Cody went out to the porch and looked northward some more in the twilight. Ezra came too and sat in the glider, pushing back and forth with the heel of one sneaker. 'Want to walk toward Sloop Street?' Cody asked him.

'What's on Sloop Street?'

'Nothing much. This girl I know, Edith Taber.'

'Oh, yes. Edith,' Ezra said.

'You know who she is?'

'She's got this whistle,' Ezra said, 'that plays sharps and flats with hardly any extra trouble.'

'Edith *Taber*?'

'A recorder.'

'You're thinking of someone else,' Cody told him.

'Well, maybe so.'[5]

This is immediate fiction. There are only two registers present here: what the characters do and what they say. Note also that there is conflict. Cody and Ezra, who are brothers, are also rivals. Finally, how is the conflict communicated to the reader? Indirectly. Look at the line where Cody, clearly rattled, says, 'You know who she is?' It shows us that Cody did not expect Ezra to know Edith, and that it bothers him to discover it.

There are two other things to note about Tyler's scene. First of all, it takes place somewhere, and this is a useful indicator of whether a piece of writing is showing or telling. Authorial summary and exposition come to you out of the ether. They don't take place anywhere. But a scene always has a setting. More importantly – and this is so obvious, it wouldn't be hard to miss it – a scene always has characters. (Of course, authorial summary has characters, too, but I would argue that they aren't actually present: they're just being talked about.)

You now know enough to write fiction that shows the reader something.

1. Use characters.

2. Record what the characters do.

3. Record what the characters say.

4. Record where it all takes place.

5. Have your dialogue demonstrate conflict *indirectly*.

Try This: Staying on the Surface

Write a one-page scene, in which the setting is a dentist's waiting room. John walks in, sits down and spots a woman he knows on the other side of the room. They say hello. He can't remember her name. Follow the advice in the box above.

Offstage, Paring your Fingernails

Suspending the narrative to address the reader is a surefire way of destroying immediacy. Apart from the collapse of the sense of immediacy for the reader, the other problem with this device is that the story has temporarily stopped. You do a lot of work to get your reader interested in your story; why would you want to have to begin that work all over again? (You could argue the opposite of course: addressing the reader directly offers a break from the use of scenes and change is always good. But this chapter is about immediacy.) The author and the narrator are not usually the same person – but keeping the author or the narrator offstage 'paring his fingernails' as James Joyce put it, promotes immediacy. This is a matter of showing the reader how a character feels by the way he behaves and, often less directly, by what he says. That, for impact, is repeated information: showing will begin with what the characters say and what they do. Immediacy is promoted by avoiding the use of exposition, explanation, lecturing – anything which would bring the author on-stage.

Showing? Or Telling?

Still, most learning writers find it difficult to tell showing and telling apart. Renni Browne and Dave King's definition of a scene is helpful: 'In scenes, events are seen as they happen rather than described after the fact.'[6] Another way in is the illustration I often use in workshops: which would be more engaging, watching *One Flew Over the Cuckoo's Nest* or listening to me recount the film blow by blow? You might almost say that it's the difference between experiencing something vicariously and being told about it.

Perhaps Bernard MacLaverty's litmus test may help. MacLaverty is an Irish writer who has proven himself a master of the art of showing. His novel *Grace Notes* was shortlisted for the 1996 Booker Prize. His short stories have been compared to Chekhov's. In the field of short fiction, compliments don't come any better than that.

MacLaverty's Showing/Telling Litmus Test

Imagine you are pitching what you write to the film producer David Puttnam. If he thinks your material can be filmed, he will be offering you a £1 million contract. If he thinks your material is unfilmable, he will boot you out of his office.

You have two versions of the material. One goes like this:

> Jimmy was in love with Jane.

Short and sweet. The other goes like this:

> Every morning, Jimmy waited at his bedroom window for the moment when Jane would emerge from the house opposite. And each day as she walked out to the bus-stop, he would stare as she walked by and sigh when she disappeared from view.

Which version of the material should you pitch?

Try This: Showing? Telling?

Read the first chapter of any novel you can pluck from your bookshelves. Using MacLaverty's litmus test, go through the chapter, highlighting the places where the author has told rather than shown. (As you are about to find out, it isn't always wrong to tell – it's just normally a good idea to keep it to a minimum.)

When to Tell

It's tempting to think that there's a quick-fix rule that will make your life as a writer straightforward, but fortunately that isn't the case. Sometimes telling will be desirable. Renni Browne and Dave King[7] have come up with three separate reasons a writer might have for using authorial summary:

1. When you want to vary the rhythm of your writing.

2. When you need to include a good deal of repetitive action.

3. When you want to include plot developments that are trivial enough not to need showing.

Let me fill in the detail of that.

On the first point, it's simply a case of variety being the spice of life. Showing is the optimum mode for writing fiction, but you can get too much of a good thing.

On the second point, it's to do with making the material you show have the maximum impact. At the moment, I'm writing something about a comedy double-act. Obviously, the story will often feature them on-stage or on television. If many of these are summarised, it means that the ones that are presented as scenes will have a greater impact on the reader.

Finally, if something involves only minor characters or amounts only to a minor event, it may be better to summarise it.

The Scene

One way to maximise your chances of producing immediate fiction is to think in scenes. This is fundamental. If a piece of fiction doesn't have scenes, it isn't immediate. It may be exposition, or a lecture, or a monologue, interior or otherwise, it may be recounting or summarising – but it won't be immediate fiction.

The word 'scene' makes you think of films or plays, which is only right, as a scene should be *dramatic*. Something is dramatic when it has been dramatised. You dramatise when you use conflict to reveal character. If the author tells the reader about it, it has not been dramatised. It won't have much impact, either. Remember the often-quoted wise words of the American short-story writer, Flannery O'Connor: 'Readers aren't going to believe something just because you tell them.'

Dramatising is showing. If you show them something, readers will believe you. If you dramatise your material, it will have impact. You've already learned enough to make the basic elements of a scene. (Record what the characters do. Record what the characters say. Have the dialogue demonstrate conflict indirectly.) Let's develop that.

The Function of a Scene

A scene moves the action forward. At the end of a scene, things are no longer as they were at the beginning. The way a scene moves the action forward is by having characters *act* and *speak*, and demonstrate conflict indirectly.

A scene also explores and reveals character and motivation. By the end of each scene the reader should know more about the characters. The way we learn more about them is by seeing what they say and do in response to the conflicts they face. A scene must happen somewhere. When writing a scene, you have to make clear where and when the action is taking place, the setting of the action. A scene will have an emotional mood or atmosphere: funny or tragic, hopeful or desperate. For more on this, see chapter 13, 'Setting'.

Advice on Making a Scene

■ The scene begins when the blue touch-paper has already been lit – not on the trip down to the firework shop.

■ A scene, especially if it is an opening scene, may well have a hook to snare the reader.

■ A scene will often have a reversal. If it starts with a plus, it will often end with a minus. (Jill asks Jack out at the start of the scene; Jack falls down the hill and fractures his skull at the end of the scene.)

■ Narrative tension in a scene will rise steadily. (It will not be static. It will not suddenly leap from low-level tension to nuclear alert tension.)

■ As a scene develops it will often start to read faster – achieved through shorter sentences, dialogue and paragraphs.

■ The scene will have some kind of climax – a revelation perhaps, a cliffhanger situation or a hook that pulls the reader on to the next scene.

■ As soon as possible after the climactic moment, the scene will be over.

Try This: A Scene

Using the list above, have a go at writing a scene. Here's your starting point:
    'I was aiming for the neo-punk look.'
    'You missed.'

Exposition

If you are using the pluperfect tense you are failing to create a sense of immediacy. Exposition (background information) often comes in the pluperfect, by far the weakest tense – since it is most removed from the immediate – for the fiction writer. The pluperfect is the 'had been' tense:

> For as long as she could remember, Louise had hated bus-stops. She had once been mugged at a bus-stop, and it had been at a bus-stop that Dan, the great love of her life, had told her it was over between them. Bus-stops had always been bad news.

And if you want to know what's wrong with exposition, think of it this way: a reader wanting answers to questions creates narrative tension, in seeking answers, the reader is working. Exposition provides the reader with answers to questions they haven't even asked and requires them to do no work. The skills you use in fiction create narrative tension, which might be represented as a taut, ascending wire. Introducing exposition is akin to dropping a heavy weight on your carefully constructed taut wire. All you're left with is a flaccid wire.

Narrative Distance

A further factor in the creation of immediacy is the distance between events and the way in which they are brought to the reader. It's the distance between the narrative and the story – or, more helpfully, between the narrator and the story. The narrower that distance, the more real, the more convincing the fiction will be.

To look at some of the ways in which this distance may vary, it will be helpful to choose a novel where the narrator participates in the action – J.D. Salinger's *The Catcher in the Rye*, for instance. Some of the time Holden Caulfield, the narrator-protagonist, will address the reader directly:

> If you really want to hear about it, the first thing you'll probably want to know is where I was born, and what my lousy childhood was like, and how my parents were occupied and all before they had me, and all that David Copperfield kind of crap, but I don't feel like going into it, if you want to know the truth.[8]

In this celebrated opening, Holden, the narrator, is talking about the story at some distance. Here, before the narrative gets going, Holden isn't anywhere. Readers have begun the novel, but there isn't any action or setting, just a narrator addressing them. Thus, to put it in terms that you already understand, the reader will not feel very close to the story, because the author, in the guise of his creation, Holden Caulfield, is telling rather than showing. (Of course, the reason readers stick with Holden in their millions is because of his idiosyncratic voice, and voice is a way in which you may compensate for shortcomings in your narrative – but that's a whole other point, and one for a another book.)

I first described Holden as a narrator-protagonist, a narrator who participates in the action. As such, in addition to suspending the action to address the reader directly – in the example given, the action hasn't even begun, but it amounts to the same thing – Holden will sometimes comment on the action as it is taking place, as we see here in a scene where he meets up with Sally Hayes, an old girlfriend, to go to a matinee:

> 'We better hurry,' I said. 'The show starts at two-forty.'
> We started going down the stairs to where the taxis are.
> 'What are we going to see?' she said.
> 'I don't know. The Lunts. It's all I could get tickets for.'
> 'The Lunts! Oh, marvellous!'
> I told you she'd go mad when she heard it was for the Lunts.
> We horsed around a little bit in the cab on the way over to the theater. At first she didn't want to, because she had her lipstick on and all, but I was being seductive as hell and she didn't have any alternative. Twice, when the goddam cab stopped short in traffic, I damn near fell off the seat. Those drivers never even look where they're going, I swear they don't. Then, just to show you how crazy I am, when we were coming out of this big clinch, I told her I loved her and all. It was a lie, of course, but the things is, I *meant* it when I said it. I'm crazy. I swear to god I am.

Twice here, Holden breaks off from the scene to address the reader: firstly, when he says, 'I told you she'd go mad when she heard it was for the Lunts.' Secondly, when he tells us that he's crazy. The rest of the time, he's sticking to his day job and conveying a scene through action and dialogue. (There might be a couple of points here where the register is between the two, but it's easier to compare the more black and white examples.) If suspending the narration to address the readers directly – as in the first excerpt from *Catcher* – is the equivalent of the theatrical soliloquy, then commenting from within the scene would be an aside.

You can see that there is a difference between the forms of narration just cited, where the narrator addresses the reader some or all of the time, and that which is going on during the rest of the novel, when Salinger writes immediate fiction from the viewpoint of Holden Caulfield:

> Finally I got out of bed with just my pajamas on, and opened the door. I didn't even have to turn the light on in my room, because it was already daylight. Old Sunny and Maurice, the pimply elevator guy, were standing there.
>
> 'What's the matter? Wuddaya want?' I said. Boy, my voice was shaking like hell.
>
> 'Nothin' much,' old Maurice said. 'Just five bucks.' He did all the talking with the two of them. Old Sunny just stood there next to him, with her mouth open and all.
>
> 'I paid her already. I gave her five bucks. Ask her,' I said. Boy, was my voice shaking.

In a strictly show don't tell world, this third passage is what you would be aiming for. However, there are advantages to having the narrator address the reader directly. For one, as a narrative stance it amounts to an invitation to the reader to enter into a relationship with the narrator. The narrator is implicitly appealing for sympathy. The reader cannot help but feel more intimate with the narrator. In *Catcher*, whether Holden is addressing the reader out of the ether, commenting on a scene while it's happening, or simply sticking with his day job and presenting the narrative with immediacy, the aims are surely the same: to make him engage the reader. At the same time, using these three forms of discourse offers variety, or possibly complexity, one of the attributes of real life.

Try This: Varying The Immediacy

Write a page or so in which you include the narrative modes just listed (addressing the reader out of the ether, commenting on a scene while it's happening and writing a proper, immediate scene). Your stimulus: three people who have been in a car too long.

Further Reading

Anne Tyler (1992) *Dinner at the Homesick Restaurant* (London: Vintage).
Nick Hornby has called Tyler the best novelist at work today, but of
course, there is no best. (And there are plenty of American women writers
ploughing similar furrows just about as well; to name three: Anita
Shreve, Sue Miller and Alice Hoffman.) But Anne Tyler on form is
a guaranteed page-turning read, and if you want to learn how to write
immediate fiction (and how to avoid exposition) you won't go wrong
studying the work of the bard of Baltimore. She is also a mistress of
characterisation. She has been turning out skilful novels since the early
60s, so if you become a convert, there's plenty of good reading ahead of
you. For my money, *Homesick* is her finest achievement, but *Ladder of
Years* and *The Clock Winder* are very good reads, too.
Patrick Gale (2002). *Rough Music* (London: Vintage).
Gale has published a string of novels and *Rough Music* comes decorated
with critical acclaim. His use of exposition is instructive: take a look at
the first 50 pages of this novel and weigh up for yourself the respective
merits of immediacy and exposition.

Basics: Apostrophes

Plenty of learning writers fail to understand how apostrophes work. This may well have been the case in years gone by. I know Scott Fitzgerald couldn't spell, and I presume the editors at Scribners, his publishers, sorted that out for him. He would probably get short shrift in present-day publishing houses. Editors now expect manuscripts to arrive perfect, not only in terms of narrative, but also with every 'i' dotted and every 't' crossed.

So. The apostrophe has two functions:

1. To indicate possession.

2. To indicate abbreviation: that a letter or letters have been omitted.

Possession

The DVD's case = The case of one DVD
   's = singular possessive

The DVDs' cases = The cases of more than one DVD
   s' = plural possessive

The dog has lost its collar.
   its = singular possessive.

There's no apostrophe on the *its*, because that would confuse the issue: *it's* is always the abbreviated form of *it is* or *it has*. Which brings us on to the second function of the apostrophe.

Abbreviation

Straightforward: the apostrophe here indicates that one or more letters have been omitted.

It is > It's
He cannot > He can't
She will not > She won't
It is not > It isn't
They would not > They wouldn't

If you've gone through the British education system's recently rejigged National Curriculum, the theory is that you already know all of that. If you haven't, or if you don't, as far as the apostrophe goes, the above should be enough to get you by.

Size Matters...

Dear Auntie,
My story just keeps getting bigger
and bigger! Every time I work on
it, I get another brilliant idea
that must go in and I think it's
turning into a novel, and the limit
is 3000 words. Please help!

When writing a first work, whether it be a short story, a play or even a novel, writers often find themselves fighting a strong impulse to stick everything in: it's very tempting in the first rush of ideas to want to include them all. Besides that there is the vanity of creativity. Many a writer has set out believing that their work will be the final say on a particular theme, and they'll set out to research everything and anything to put in it: they want their first novel, short story, play, poem to be tremendous: not only will it present a new angle, it will present every angle. It will be everything. It will be all-encompassing. It will be universal. But if anyone ever did manage to pull this trick off and put the entire world into a piece of writing, there'd be nothing left to say in the next one. It can become a bit of a displacement activity to keep searching out more great ideas rather than working with the ones you've already got. So, be content to leave out some of your ideas; you can always use them in another piece. If you're writing to a tight deadline, then have a cut-off point at which you stop working in new ideas, and work solely with the ones you've already got.

The other thing to consider is that in the big bad professional world of writing, word limits must be adhered to. If an editor needs 3000 words, then only 3000 words will do, the issue being print space. You cannot think that another 500 won't hurt. So be professional. If you're over the limit, stop driving! Be savage and edit.

In all probability the work will be more powerful if it is uncluttered, and in the end, too many ideas can be as bad as too few.

19 Cut it Out, Put it In: Revision

Robert Graham

The wastepaper basket is the writer's best friend. (Isaac Bashevis Singer)[1]

Raymond Carver claimed to do up to thirty drafts of a story, and never less than ten. Tolstoy was always revising – right through to the galley stage. And Jann Martel, author of the 2002 Booker Prize winner, *Life of Pi*, is so bent on getting the words right that he is happy to finish a day's work having written a page.

Fiction is made through a mixture of drafting and redrafting, and obviously there can be no redrafting without the first drafting that precedes it. However, for me, redrafting is where the real business of shaping fiction is done. (And don't forget, this is where you are free to unleash your internal critic, your conscious mind – a fatal inhibition when you're writing a first draft, but you won't be able to redraft without using it.)

The poet John Ashbery claims that

> because of my strong desire to avoid all unnecessary work, I have somehow trained myself not to write something that I will either have to discard or be forced to work a great deal over.[2]

I wish I knew how he has achieved this happy knack! Like Bernard Malamud, who says, 'Revision is one of the true pleasures of writing',[3] I love revision, and I particularly like cutting. Last week I heard a radio programme about James Joyce's *Ulysses*. At one point, the presenter alluded to the fact that Joyce, while revising the galleys – in other words, while making a final check before the book was printed – expanded the whole by one third. *One third*. I don't think I have always done it, but in recent years, by the time I have finished with the first draft of a novel in manuscript, I have *reduced* it by at least a third. Maybe I'm a sloppy writer of first drafts. Whatever, I love redrafting. One aspect of what you're doing is polishing, finishing off. When you've worked on something for a year or two, what's not to like about polishing and finishing off?

At one stage, the word count of my last but one novel was 115,000. Later, it had shrunk to 93,000, and the final draft was less than 73,000. In Ashbery's terms, this is wasteful. However, even if I could do anything about the waste, I suspect I would not. I like the story of the sculptor who was asked how he made such lifelike sculptures of his subjects: 'I start with a block of stone and then I remove everything that doesn't look like the subject.' The real shaping of a piece of writing is in the revision process. Furthermore, I would argue that fiction isn't created simply through invention followed by revision: as we see in chapter 25, 'Narrative Design', invention leads to revision, but revision leads to more invention.

So. That sounds pretty straightforward: take out the stuff that doesn't belong and leave everything else.

Try This: The Things You Make Them Carry

'At the beginning of the story, the writer is giving the reader things. Think of them as things they will need – sleeping bags, a knife, a snack, a compass – as they climb the hill you are sending them up. You don't want the reader getting to the top and being pissed off about the things you made them carry up the hill for no reason.' (Frank Conroy)[4]

Using a draft of one of your stories, go to what amounts to the top of the hill in the narrative and see what readers actually need when they get there. Now begin at the beginning and search for and remove all the extraneous information you have burdened them with in the early stages of the narrative.

A Few Words about Revision

I'll get into some detail about revision in a moment, but first a few pieces of general advice. I don't honestly think there is much point in trying to revise until you have a complete first draft. You risk never finishing a first draft if you keep stopping to rework. Revising is a matter of looking at your work and seeing what it says to you – as Jane Smiley puts it here:

> Your only task is to let what you have talk back to you and teach you what is missing or superfluous or not quite right, and then to suggest what would be better than what you have.[5]

A further consideration is that you won't get anywhere trying to revise immediately after you've completed a first draft. You need distance from the story; you need perspective. Revising is seeing the story afresh. Janet Burroway has this advice:

> *Put it away.* Don't look at it for a matter of days or weeks – until you feel fresh on the project. In addition to getting some distance on your story, you're nailing it to your unconscious.[6]

The main thrust of this quotation is important, and obvious enough. It's probably just worth emphasising the value of the closing point. Revising is perhaps a combination of wrestling with things in your conscious mind and giving up and leaving them to your unconscious mind. It's what people do when they say they are going to sleep on an impending decision.

It's also helpful to remember that you don't have to approach the task of revision all by yourself. When it comes to freshness you will be hard pressed to beat that which readers bring to your work. They might only confirm things that you knew yourself, but often they will see things that you can't – because they're not you. I think I developed the habit early on of farming my work out to friends who would generously look at it and offer their responses. However, I don't believe I would ever have thought to join a writer's group had I not been thrust into one by the experience of doing an MA in Creative Writing. That was more than ten years ago, and I benefited so much from the feedback on my work offered by the workshop members that I have made sure to be in a workshop (see chapter 10, 'Writing Together: Groups and Workshops') or group ever since. The advantages are great. It offers you an audience, which every writer needs, and in doing so, I think it gives you more confidence and helps you to think of yourself as a writer. For what it's worth, I approach processing this form of feedback in the following way. I jot down everything that everyone says unless it is plain stupid – very rare. Then I live with the advice for a while and eventually use the suggestions that still appeal a few weeks later.

A lot of writers swear by reading the work aloud – even better if it's to somebody else, because as you read it out you will see it through their eyes. In the absence of an audience, you will still find reading aloud to yourself an effective way of finding flaws in your writing. Read it to the wall.

One other thing before we move on: don't think revising is just about eliminating the bad stuff; sometimes you will have to eliminate good material, too. 'Murder your darlings,' G.K. Chesterton famously wrote. In revising you will almost always have to remove phrases, sentences, paragraphs or whole chapters not because they don't work in themselves – but because they *don't work there*.

The rest of this chapter consists of two lengthy writing exercises, for each of which you will need a first draft. Use the same first draft for both exercises. As you work at these exercises, bear in mind that good fiction is not written, it is *rewritten*. I have yet to meet the Writing student who redrafts too much. In writing fiction, you should do as many drafts of a story as you have time to.

Technical Redrafting

> INTERVIEWER: How much rewriting do you do?
>
> HEMINGWAY: It depends. I rewrote the ending to *Farewell to Arms*, the last page of it, thirty-nine times before I was satisfied.
>
> INTERVIEWER: Was there some technical problem there? What was it that had stumped you?
>
> HEMINGWAY: Getting the words right.[7]

In *The Fiction Editor, the Novel, and the Novelist*, Thomas McCormack talks firstly about 'the *dermal*' flaw.[8] The dermal consists of blemishes on the surface of the novel and McCormack lists a good many examples of them:

> Failures of diction, grace, freshness, materiality, credibility, pace, vividness, understand-ability, interest…clichés, repetitions, stale modifiers, abstract generalities where concrete specificities are needed; phrases, images, and metaphors that simply misfire.[9]

These are all failings that are worthy of your attention when you come to revise. As Jonathan Swift put it, 'Proper words in proper places make the true definition of style.' For my money, however, the most common form of dermal flaw has less to do with style than what McCormack is talking about. The most common form of dermal flaw, and the one that needs your attention first, is when your writing is simply technically wrong.

What to Look For, Technically Speaking...

Here is a range of common technical errors that turn up in early drafts. Use it as a checklist, until you've acquired the checklist habit. Begin by using your word-processing programme's spellchecker. Remember, however, that it won't find every mistake – and it will sometimes tell you to do the wrong thing, so read each suggestion carefully before hitting the change button.

Having tested your spelling and grammar against the software, track the work for the things given in the checklist below.

Layout

- Make sure the first line is not indented.
- Thereafter, every first line of each paragraph should be indented – except the first line of a new scene or section.
- When you go to a new scene, leave one line's worth of space.
- Do not leave one line's worth of space after paragraphs – only to indicate a break between scenes.
- Each new speaker requires a new paragraph (new speaker, new paragraph).
- Each suggested shift of viewpoint needs a new paragraph (new person, new paragraph).
- Titles of books, films and albums need to be in italics.
- Titles of short stories and songs just need speech marks.

Punctuation

- Check that each sentence really is a sentence (and not two).

- A colon (:) goes before a list or an example.

- A semi-colon (;) breaks a sentence in two, usually into a main clause followed by a modifier. Think of it as stronger than a comma, but not as strong as a full stop.

- Punctuation of direct speech always goes inside the speech marks. (*'That hurts,' he said*. <u>Not</u> 'That hurts', he said.)

- Speech tags after dialogue don't begin with a capital letter. RIGHT: *'Yes,' she said.* WRONG: *'Yes.' She said.*

- If you have a whole sentence in brackets, the punctuation goes inside the brackets. *(Gualchos is in Spain.)* But otherwise not. *We had a great holiday in Gualchos (which is in Spain).*

- Mum and Dad – better with a capital initial letter.

- Questions always need a question mark, don't they?

- Don't overuse exclamation marks. One will do! But not at the end of *every* sentence!

- Don't forget the apostrophe – where a letter has been omitted (don't, can't, wasn't, hadn't) or to indicate possession (the car's wheel, John's shirt, the house's size) – except for possession where it is concerned, where you don't use an apostrophe (the horse had hurt its leg). The reason is that it would be confused with *it's* as an abbreviation of *it is*.

Grammar

- If the subject is plural then so is the verb. (*The school children were very well behaved.* <u>Not</u> *The school children was very well behaved.*)

- Watch out for subject and object. When the first person is the subject, it's *I: I kicked the ball.* When the first person is the object, it's *me: The ball thumped me in the face.* Same with *who* and *whom. This is the woman who loves me.* And *This is the woman whom I love.*

Try This: Technical Redrafting in Action

Take a draft of something you've been working on, or something from your journal. If it's on a word-processor, print it out: reading for drafting is often easier when the work is on paper rather than the screen. Read it. Apply the checklist to it. Now you'll see why double-spacing is so useful: it enables you to scribble between the lines, noting the changes you want to make.

Creative Redrafting

The second kind of flaw that McCormack recognises, the internal flaw, is more serious and more difficult to diagnose. McCormack lists among its symptoms the following:

> A disappointed sense of its not meeting us at the station, of its having missed some unnameable opportunity, of its lacking a life-supporting temperature, of inertness, of inconsequence, of meaninglessness to events, of something, somewhere in the book, gone profoundly awry.[10]

Internal flaws are not only difficult to diagnose, they're troublesome and time-consuming to fix: you may find yourself having to unravel and remove a whole subplot. Speaking of which, it's probably worth saying that many internal flaws concern the plot. So, before you have a go at the next writing exercise, here are a few well-chosen questions that Jane Smiley poses on the matter of revising plot:

> Is it clear who the characters are? Is it clear what the conflict is, and whom it is between? Does the reader have a concrete sense of where the characters are in space and time? Is there a climax or is the climax implied rather than depicted? Is the climax dramatic enough, long enough, weighty enough to balance the length of the rising action? Does the denouement get the reader gracefully and meaningfully out of the climax? Does the denouement bring the story to a state of equilibrium?[11]

A Checklist for Creative Redrafting

This might take some time: redrafting is not something you start an hour before a submission deadline.

Narrative Tension

- Does your story intrigue the reader at once? What is the first reader question? How soon does it come?

- Does the story begin at the beginning (or towards the bottom of the first page)?

- Is the dialogue dull, or does real conflict get expressed?

- Does the dialogue move the plot along?

- Drama is life with the dull parts left out. Have you left the dull parts in?

- Have you told the reader what you should have shown?

- Is there always something at stake? Or are you chewing with no gum?

- By the end of a scene, things will no longer be as they were at the beginning. This is even more the case when thinking of the whole story.

- Have scenes been fully developed? Look for implicit drama in what's written and think of ways to milk it more than has happened in the first draft.

- If you have used flashback or exposition on the first page, get rid of it.

- Is the story too internal? (Have you spent too much time inside the character's head?)

- Is the conflict static? Jumping? It ought to rise steadily.

- Does the story end when it should? (Or does it run on after the end has been reached?)

- Does the ending satisfy?

Common Flaws

- Are you in viewpoint? (Your reader can only *know, hear, see* what the viewpoint character can. Make sure you haven't slipped into another character's viewpoint by mistake.)

- Have you shifted out of one tense and into another?

Characters

- Have you used more characters than you really need?

- Do your characters always speak and act characteristically?

- Avoid giving characters names with the same first name initial letter.

- Remember that things happen off the page. It's appealing when the reader learns that a character has a life of his or her own, away from the plot of this story.

- Have you told the reader how your characters feel? Don't. Let the reader discover how a character feels through action and dialogue – what the character says and does.

Style

- Are action and dialogue balanced? (Watch out for too much of either.)

- Is there too much description?

- Is your description static? (The ideal is that description is incorporated into action and dialogue.)

- Is your description specific enough? (A *Ford* rather than *a car*.)

- Is there too much action?

- Are you writing with verbs and nouns?

- Have you avoided clichés?

- Have you removed all superfluous speech tags?

- Are your speech tags plain and without the encumbrance of an adverb?

- Have you written directly? Make cumbersome sentences straightforward.

- Remove anything that delays the information going straight from your head to the reader's.

- Weed out vocabulary repeats – the same word used twice in quick succession.

- Watch out for redundancies. (They met at 8 am in the morning.)

- Is there an interpretation of any sentence that is not the one you intend?

- Have you avoided qualifying what you say? (Get it right in one.)

- Have you used active and not passive language? (*He took her to the shops.* Not *She was taken to the shops.*)

- Any weak intensifiers? (*The dog was totally dead.*)

- Do a word search for 'seemed'. If you find it used often, replace it with alternatives.

Try This: Into Action on the Creative Battlefield

Use the same piece of work as before. Or select another. Apply the checklist to it. Some points may be more pertinent than others, or you may wish to track merely for characters, or theme, or description. You can redraft by scribbling over the printout, or cutting up paragraphs with scissors to reorder them. Use nice pens. Enjoy the process!

Further Reading

Raymond Carver (1993) *Where I'm Calling From* (London: Harvill Press).
   Carver is the king of economy. If you want to see how bare a sentence can be, read any of his collections of short stories. (This one collects nearly all his stories.) The language isn't just missing the flab, it has been cut to the bone. Carver's style isn't for everyone, but study him and you will conclude that your prose needs to go on a diet.
James Friel (2001) 'Redrafting Your Novel' in Julia Bell and Paul Magrs (eds), *The Creative Writing Coursebook* (London: Macmillan – now Palgrave Macmillan) pp. 261–270.
   This consists of a list of the things you should be (*Be Kind, Be Curious, Be Stealthy*) when revising. The structure may be playful, but the advice is good, and – as befits the subject matter – succinct. And I don't know anyone who doesn't think this is the best British book on writing craft published so far.

20 Poetry for People Who Don't Like Poetry

Heather Leach

Walk into a seminar room and ask a normal-looking bunch of students whether they like poetry. Watch their reactions. Most people will screw up their faces as if they'd smelt something disgusting; a few will grimace awkwardly and waggle their hands in an awkward *maybe, maybe not* gesture. After a few moments one or two brave individuals – three at the most – will raise a finger, looking round the room to make sure they're not alone.

These days poetry is apparently not very popular. I say apparently because if you were to continue the experiment and take each one of the members of the seminar out of the group and ask them about their experiences of *writing* poetry, you'd find that quite a lot of them would confess (and confess is the appropriate word here) that they'd actually jotted down the odd poem or two: an interesting contradiction, my dear Watson.

One of the problems is that Poetry is a word burdened with a big P: a word that needs to be pronounced in a special, rather reverent, voice. Poetry, as it has been handed down to many of us, through school English literature – or litterachooer as Tony Harrison called it[1] – is often experienced as serious and difficult to understand, needing translation and explanation by an expert, usually a teacher. This is a bit like having a joke explained: by the time you've got the point you've lost the point, if you see what I mean. I am not going to argue that all poetry should be easy to understand but I do think that for many of us, this high literature approach to poetry is not the place to begin. However, before I talk about alternatives, I have a confession to make.

A Confession

I am not a poet or at least only a poet with a small p. This might seem like a bit of a cheek given that here I am writing a chapter on poetry, but I have two excuses. The first is that there is another chapter in this book written by real poets. My second is that there is a lot of small-p poetry in the world and a lot of small-p poets who need encouragement. Here are my poetic credentials. I began writing rhyming verse when I was 12 or 13 and filled a few notebooks, going on to read some of my efforts to friends and family. There are two memories associated with this period: one good, one excruciatingly bad.

The good one was being asked by a girl in my class to write a poem for her father's birthday card (fame at last!). The bad one was reading a poem aloud to my mother and grandma. I can't remember all of this poem but, for reasons, which will become clear, the last two lines are burned into my memory. Here they are:

And dances like the daffodil
While silver fishes leap at will.

After I'd finished reading there was a long silence. Then Grandma said: Who's Will? before going back to her newspaper. My mother said, 'Haven't I heard the bit about the daffodil before?'

I was mortified: a laughable double meaning and a crude copy in only 11 words.

Sometime later, during my cooler teenage years, I stopped writing poetry. It was obvious that I could never be a real poet and anyway, who cared about poetry when there was rock and roll? I threw away the notebooks, embarrassed by the evidence.

You're Already a Poet, But You Don't Know It!

As adults we may be cynical about our childish and adolescent poetic efforts when comparing it with the 'real stuff', but that would be to miss some key points. In my daffodil line I was certainly plagiarising Wordsworth, but this was because I had learned some of the pleasures of pattern and alliteration and wanted to use them for myself.

We all learn by copying to begin with, and we all write emotional stuff which sometimes goes over the top: the only difference between adolescent poets and real ones is that the real ones don't give up. You may have written poems when you were younger. You may still be writing them but keeping them secret. Some of these poems may be song lyrics and many may explore deep emotions: love, anger, frustration, despair. A large number probably also draw on existing poems and songs as models. By the time we are adults most of us have heard and unconsciously learned poetic styles, methods and patterns from hundreds, if not thousands of poetry-with-a-small-p examples. We all know a lot more about poetry than we think we do.

Happy Valentine, Deepest Sorrow

A popular outlet for poetry is the greetings card. You know the kind:

> Here's a card just made for you
> With lots of love so rich and true
> Dum de Dum de Dum de Da
> Dum de Dum de Dum de Da.

Quite a few people would deny that this stuff is real poetry at all, and I have to admit it isn't my cup of tea. But it does have pattern and rhythm and it can provide a template for beginners to build on. I suggest you read as many as you can and then try to write your own with care and feeling. Or you could write a subversive version.

The other place for popular rhyme is the newspaper obituary. These also often follow a well-worn format, but some people rewrite and adapt the verses to fit their own circumstances, which makes them more moving and original. It is striking that many people feel that the deepest emotions are best expressed in poetic forms.

Try This: Obituaries

Have a look at the obituary columns. You can also find some great poems on gravestones. Now write one or two of your own. You could write about someone you were close to who has died, or an imaginary one about yourself. Use the existing templates only as a jumping off point. You can vary and subvert the forms and patterns. And remember that

obituaries don't always have to be sad or serious. They can also be cele-
bratory, funny or gothically macabre.

Song Lyrics

If you love contemporary popular music, you probably know the
words of many songs. Song lyrics are not exactly the same as poems
meant to be read or spoken, as they also rely on the music, but
many poems have been made into songs, and many songs are
powerful poems. There are huge variations. Some lyrics are recognisable and simple, greetings card style: The Beatles' *Love Me Do*[2] is
a good example. Others are wilder and more complex. Look at and
listen to some of Bob Dylan's 1960s lyrics. I suggest 'A Hard Rain's
Gonna Fall' from *The Freewheelin' Bob Dylan*.[3] Both of these rely
on recognisable poetic forms: repetition; sound patterns: alliteration
and assonance,[4] line scanning and rhythm. The Beatles song uses a
familiar and conventional end rhyme pattern and the Bob Dylan
song does use half-rhymes or almost-rhymes and much repetition.
You do know this stuff!

Try This: Song Lyrics

Choose a song lyric you particularly like. First play it, sing it or read it and
listen to the patterns and rhythms. Then write it down and examine the
ways it produces its effects. Next write your own, using some of the same
techniques. You could also use the examples above as models. Try to
avoid cliché by choosing an unusual subject to write about, e.g.: Sport;
Food; Clothes; Dogs; Money; Computers; Television; Spoons. If you write
about a 'poetic' subject (e.g. Love; Nature; Strong Emotions) try to find
fresh words or patterns.

Rhymes and Riddles

All children, if they get the chance, love wordplay. Many of the
first poems we learn are nursery rhymes: Jack and Jill; Baa Baa
Black Sheep, although these days we're more likely to get them

from television: Postman Pat, Bob the Builder and so on. See how many you can remember and, if you can cope with the embarrassment, recite or sing them aloud, preferably in a group, in order to recapture the sheer pleasure of playing with word and sound. You could have a go at writing an alternative grown-up version of one of your favourite nursery rhymes or jingles, using the same patterns and musicality. Although you may need to pick your audience carefully, as many of my students have produced rhymes that are far too rude to reprint.

There are also many riddle poems, and children and poets invent new ones all the time. A riddle poem is a puzzle. Here are a couple of examples:

> It's the beginning of eternity
> The end of time and space
>
> It's the start of every end,
> And the end of every place.
>   (*Author Unknown*)

Read the poems *Metaphors* and *You're* by Sylvia Plath,[5] and see how long it takes you to work out their subjects.

Try This: Riddle Poem

Write a riddle poem for a common object

- First decide on the object.

- Then list as many descriptions of the object as you can. Try to think metaphorically, the way Plath does, e.g. if your object was a spoon you could describe it as: -lip-sipper/ sip-lipper/ soup-slurper/ the way lovers sleep/ silver bowl on silver arm/ fork's mate, etc. Keep going, the best ones often come when you have reached the limits of rational thought.

- Then choose 5 or 6 of the best and shape into lines.

- Next try to make these lines work together as patterns and sound. If rhymes develop, use them, but don't force the material into awkward shapes to make a rhyme.

- Try it out on other people. If they guess it too easily, make it harder. If nobody gets it, make it slightly easier.

Making Poetry Belong to You

Up to now I've been emphasising the playful and musical aspects of poetry, and as I said earlier, this is partly to de-couple the idea of poetry from literary pretentiousness. However, it's important not to throw the baby out with the bathwater and to remember that poetry can be emotional, serious and committed: it's an ideal form to express strongly felt personal and political meanings.

Try This: Step By Step Poem

This exercise below is a way of developing a poem through a series of stages and is adapted from one set out by Sandy Brownjohn in her useful book *Does It Have to Rhyme?* aimed at schoolteachers. This is a way of developing a poem through a series of stages.

- Chose an incident, or a moment that involves people who are in a close relationship with each other: parent/grandparent/child; brothers and sisters; close friends; lovers/partners; husband/wife. You should be one of the people. Write a description of the incident in prose. Write out the story of the incident in prose.

- Make a list of words or phrases which describe aspects of the place/people; sounds sights, smells, touch.

- Make the first draft of the poem by putting it into lines.

- Read aloud to yourself and pay attention to the patterns, rhythms and music.

- Find ways of making the poem stronger and more truthful to the experience by redrafting until it feels just right.

Further Reading

Sandy Brownjohn (1980) *Does it Have to Rhyme?* (London: Hodder and Stoughton).

M. Hulse, D. Kennedy and D. Morley (eds) (1992) *The New Poetry*. (Bloodaxe: Newcastle upon Tyne).

Paul Hyland (1993) *Getting into Poetry* (Bloodaxe: Newcastle upon Tyne).

Peter Sansom (1994) *Writing Poetry* (Bloodaxe: Newcastle upon Tyne).

21 Words and Images
John Singleton

Words Change the World

At one level, a word is a substitute for the real thing: it is a label or sign, not the object itself. As signs, words can be either visual (like these in front of your eyes now), or aural (which they will be if you read this aloud), and may be visual/tactile (if they are carved on stone or punched into Braille). They could even be gustatory if swallowed as alphabetti spaghetti. And from the first moment cave dwellers daubed on the walls of their Neolithic open-plan bed-sits, writers have exploited this physicality.

When we use (speak/write) these signs, images of the objects to which they refer are conjured up in the mind's eye, drawn mysteriously from that vast in-built database we call memory. These images come not as photographic records, but weighted with feelings and emotions mellowed by remembrance, and combine their charge with the sensory power of words. By 'sensory' I mean the capacity of verbal images to evoke textural, auditory and visual sensations. It is this alliance of the sensory and the affective that gives force to writing, and, employed well, compels and engages readers. Indeed, some people argue that word-derived images of things can have a more pronounced effect on the mind and the imagination than the thing itself. Though William Wordsworth doesn't actually say this when he famously describes poetry as 'emotion recollected in tranquillity', his phrase does indicate what powerful surrogates word-images can be.

The thing is, words do reach beyond themselves, or rather beyond the thing/idea they represent. They move from being images to motifs or symbols. In chapter 23 of Charlotte Brontë's *Jane Eyre*[1] Jane walks into a garden redolent with the last scents of the day. She observes 'a great moth' go humming by, which moments later

Mr Rochester says reminds him of a 'West Indian insect...a night rover'.

Take this image and all the images of flowers and heavy dropping fruit and you get a paradisal impression of the place; it is alluring and sensuous. But Rochester then cruelly teases Jane until his heartlessness is interrupted by a violent storm coinciding with Jane's extreme distress. After the rain and wind and lightning fade, the great chestnut tree at the bottom of the plantation is discovered split in two.

In the narrative, globed gooseberries big as plums, heavy exotic moths, lightning flashes, split trees work at the sensory descriptive level, but they also hint at other realities: the exotic 'rover' may be a figure for the quixotic Rochester, unnaturally present in an English garden. The paradisal garden itself may represent the richness and prodigality of creation and Jane's potential for love and life; the storm, a parallel for Jane's emotional turmoil and Rochester's disruptive power; the split tree, a symbol of the divided sides of his nature, and a prophecy of disaster.

Try This: Follow The Line

Consider Billy Collins's poem 'Velocity' from his collection, *Nine Horses*, published by Picador. It's about the poet sitting on a train hoping to use journey time creatively by writing.

You don't have to take a train to do this, but try scribbling, doodling, scrawling, graffiti-ing to see if, out of the patterns, any surprising trails open up. They may be poetry or prose doodlings. Follow them wherever they take you. After a bit you may have to take bearings and seek some direction so that your wanderings are not just aimless. Behind 'Velocity' is a strong controlling – even manipulative – influence, despite the poet's pretence that he is not into writing a poem at all.

Word Encounters

Some people argue that words *are* images, one and the same, not just signs *of* them or *for* them. You can't think images without the words used to say them, and when the writer of Genesis said, 'In the beginning was the Word,' he meant it literally, so they say. Of course 'Word' in this context means the creative agency of God the maker. So in this sense words are creators, the beginners of things, bringing them into being, at least in our mind's eye.

But *do* I need words to trigger images? I can conjure up the picture of blue, for instance, in my head, with all the feeling of blue-ness, all the tinges, tones and tints of blue without uttering a single word. But it's read-only stuff. If I want to communicate with others I have to use words – of blue. So I talk blue: blue this, blue that. And you talk blue and before long our blues merge, and the palette of our personal meanings, our databank of images, has subtly changed in the encounter. In other words, language doesn't merely reflect or record the external world, it changes perceptions of it.

But after reading Thomas Hardy's poem, 'Beeny Cliff'[2] I've new images of blue to contend with: they're laid down in the memory now, quietly composting, ready to surface anytime and enrich my writing as well as my perceptions of things. It's as if I've laid down new images in the memory: and these will be among the ones that respond to the word in future.

So, if language does indeed refine our perceptions, changes the way we see things, I'll have to modify what I said at the beginning of this chapter where I stated words are substitutes, or labels and tags for objects. It is obvious they are more active than that. They enable us to see and hear and describe the world, but they also change us as we experience and use them. It's a two-way thing.

Juxtaposition

There are other aspects to the word/image/object relationship that complicate the picture. The word 'chair' for instance can refer to all kinds of seating shapes, seating materials, seating construction tech-niques. There is no precise one-for-one relationship between word and image. There are hundreds of differing chairs in the mind's eye all stacked inside that 'chair' image, and what's more, if you weren't made, as I was, to bend over a chair at school to be caned, then the word 'chair' (and 'cane' too) may have a very different impact on you than it does on me. Your 'chair' is different from mine! Mine shares in the pain: words aren't inert labels for things; they hurt too! They hurt me.

And they aren't loners. They are sociable. They work with other words to produce elaborate strings of images or rather composite images. As in the phrase: 'Madame's red velvet chair'. When you read this phrase I suggest you have whole scripts of words and images starting up in your head, including an idea of who Madame is, her appearance, a sense of the room in which the chair is set, even of the city where she lives and works. One image chases the next onto the mind's stage.

And one word changes the word it sits next to: 'velvet' becomes deeper, richer, more textured for being next to 'red'. If it turns out that 'Madame' is a high-class courtesan living in late nineteenth-century Paris then the colour and the material take on added significance as images of sensuality if not sexuality. And if 'velvet' was regarded as a brash inferior material in the 1870s then the word in this context takes a moral, even judgemental, significance as well. Context shapes us like it shapes meaning.

Setting one image off against another is one of the ways writers capture the rich contrariness of life and experience. It is one of the required writing skills to develop an eye for telling juxtaposition of images. The 'red velvet chair' succession of images above is a complementary juxtaposition to create a sensory experience for the reader and to illuminate the character of the woman. Equally a writer might want to create dissonance or ambiguity or surprise or shock by setting opposing images against each other or pairing images, which are normally strangers. In a sense, this is what happens in figurative language where metaphor and simile are used. If you say a toad looks like an old woman's purse one is startled into recognition by the oddness and aptness of the comparison, the yoking together of the unexpected.

Red Shift

OK. But some words, probably most, are composite images themselves. They have a whole family of related images attached by association. It is the associations of words that give them their richness. Take the word 'red' again. It runs deep. It associates with blood, rawness, wound, life, roses, sex, books, communists (now a fading image), passion, Manchester United, anger and so on. Skilled writers will play on such associations and resonances to give texture and depth to their work.

We are conversing all the time with the material world, with the language of others, and the two – world and language – shift and change meanings restlessly. Nothing stays still despite dictionaries giving us authoritative definitions of words as if they are set in concrete. They are not. Words wear out, die, reinvent themselves just like every other bit of creation. Writers can save them. Kill them. Hijack them. Anyone can.

Does the dictionary tell us how the word 'asylum' has fallen on hard times? Instead of being a positive term it now conjures up images of shifty-looking young men, and is associated with crime, dirt and disease, with shadowy figures jumping over security fences or gathering in threatening gangs on street corners. The word itself isn't responsible for these images. We are. The users. Trouble is, now we've lost a word that enshrines the values of fairness and hospitality that have, up until now, been an integral part of our national culture and psyche. When comes such another? Our public life is the weaker for the loss. Words and images matter. A lot.

And it's interesting to consider how TV images of asylum seekers running to hitch lifts on chunnel trains have altered the word 'asylum' and brought it into disrepute: a case of the image shafting the word.

Words Are Things Too

Now the word 'asylum' is different from, say, the word 'pebble'. 'Asylum' is what we call an abstract word as opposed to a concrete word such as 'pebble'. A concrete word is linked very strongly to an object and the image it evokes. As suggested above, that image will be sensory, intimating the visual, tactile, aural qualities of the object. But abstract words are different in the sense that they don't have an immediate image equivalent. They are ideas not objects. But that is not to say they aren't objectified in some way. Indeed, giving ideas a tangible presence/existence is a crucial function of language. If, for instance, we could associate 'asylum' with images of smiling kids and men building walls we'd rescue the word from the hands of bigots, eliminate our sense of anxiety about strangers in our midst, and re-establish decency and justice as watchwords in our national consciousness.

Wow!

Just think of how we imagise 'war', 'peace', 'love', 'God', some of the great abstractions in our lives. We do it, not through words that facsimilise, but through associated concrete, particularised images. We give them, as Skakespeare says, 'a local habitation and a name.' And one of the strongest effects achieved in poetry for example, is where ideas are rendered concrete say by personification, or metaphor or symbolism. When Gerard Manley Hopkins writes in his poem 'The Wreck of the Deutschland':[3]

Hope had grown grey hairs
Hope had mourning on...

he is giving a cold concept real substance by dressing it in powerful sensory and emotive images.

Onomatopoeia

My assertion that words are no more than labels for objects is wrong in another sense too. Words are much closer to the object they describe than that. They are intimate with the thing in their lives to such a degree that words and even bits of them can sound just like the object they stand for. Hasn't the word 'grind' something of the real live action about it? Doesn't 'whisper' mimic its own meaning? Doesn't 'slap' mime itself? The truth is words are mimetic, a fact that all good writers exploit. Sure, a word is more than the image it conjures up; it shares in the presence of the thing itself almost as if it were the thing.

Concrete Poetry

Verse that exploits the visual qualities of words and print has earned the name 'concrete poetry'. Its foremost practitioners were members of the avant-garde in the early twentieth century – the Futurists, the Dadaists and later, the Surrealists. They introduced a new visual poetic, which more recent experimenters including poets such as Edwin Morgan and Ian Hamilton Finlay have been intent to exploit. They have broken conventions and pushed the boundaries till they give way altogether, yielding a hybrid form of art based on visual patterning, unusual spatial alignments, repetitions, chance effects where words and visuals enjoy shifting relationships and meaning is a flux not a fix.

Try This: Concrete Poetry

Find an example of a concrete poem.
Try one yourself.
Does it work for prose?

Words as Real Things

Finally, the word as object in its own right exploring the interface between verbal symbol and concrete reality, visual, aural or tactile, has been a preoccupation of a number of writer/artists over the last 50 years. There has been a long tradition of the illustrated book (the *livre d'artiste*) for instance, ranging from early Celtic manuscript illumination through works like William Blake's *Songs of Innocence and Experience* to contemporary pieces like Tom Phillips's *A Humument*.[4]

A Humument[5] is a celebrated example of a different visual image/word relationship. In this case, the artist has taken an obscure Victorian novel and brought out the visual possibilities of the printed text by masking and blanking whole blocks of type with coloured inks. This way each page becomes a picture frame, and each chapter is akin to a film-maker's storyboard. These strongly patterned and pictorial panel-pages complement the verbal narrative that Phillips creates by isolating phrases, sentences, paragraphs to create a wholly new 'narrative' from the novel's existing stock of words.

The implication is that within this novel there are thousands of other 'hidden' narratives that the artist can expose if he chooses. What makes this book different from, say, a traditionally illustrated book, is its typographic inventiveness, its fusion of the visual and verbal elements and its break with the conventions of page layout; not to say its willingness to repudiate the primacy of the word itself in the thing we call a 'book'. It's an iconoclastic work, and an ironic one because, among other things, Phillips is obliterating the text with ink, the very medium that embodied the original words!

I wrote above about the possibility of there being an infinite number of narratives embedded in Phillips's 'treated' novel. The possibility of perming words into seeming endless combinations has been a game other writers have consciously played. Raymond Queneau, the French writer and literary experimenter, for instance, devised a work called *Cent Mille Milliards des Poêmes*[6] where he wrote 14 sonnets and made it possible to combine any line (from a total of 140) with any 13 from any of the other sonnets. Others have turned this experiment into paper sculptures, and Nottingham University's website[7] includes an interactive page where a machine allows the user to create some of the millions of poems into which Queneau's 14 can combine and multiply.

Other experimenters too have played fast and loose with the constituent elements of the book. In the early twentieth century,

Marinetti, the Italian writer, literary impresario and central figure in the Futurist Movement, along with others, experimented with a highly inventive typography that exploded the conventions of page layout. It was he who paved the way for the more adventurous and complex artistic phenomenon known as the Artist's Book.

In the 60s, across Europe and North America, artists and writers began pushing the boundary definitions of what a word is and what a book is. Words began to be realised as sculpture in their own right, books were seen as a space for a new kind of artistic practice and product. Again Tom Phillips offers an intriguing example. On his website (see note 5) you can see one of his word sculptures. It's entitled *Miami Beach* and shows a pile of wooden book-shaped blocks piled up into a tower each with a one-word 'title' on the 'spine'. In the light of the artist's own interpretation of this piece quoted on the web page it's worth considering how the sculpture interrogates the relationship between image, word and object.

All writing concerns itself with the arrangement of words, but thinking about words and images might lead you to the following chapters: 13, 'Setting'; 20, 'Poetry for People Who Don't Like Poetry'; 23, 'Writing Play'; and 22, 'Trying Something Else: Poetry Writing'.

Further Reading

Ken Cockburn and Alec Finlay (eds) (2001) *The Order of Things* (London: Polygon).
> Features the work of Scottish concrete poets within an international context and includes contributions from such major figures as Edwin Morgan, Tom Leonard and Ian Hamilton Finlay.

Tom Phillips (1998) *A Humument. A Treated Victorian Novel* (London: Thames and Hudson).
> A rich and endlessly inventive narrative reworking and recycling. It raises all kinds of questions about the nature of reading and the dynamics of the word/image relationship. A good starting point for those interested in visual poetry writing.

M.E. Solt (1970) *Concrete Poetry: A World View* (Indiana: Indiana University Press).
> An enthusing anthology showing the range and scope of concrete poetry. This book is out of print at the moment but every good library should have a copy.

22 Trying Something Else: Poetry Writing

Robert Sheppard and Scott Thurston

Moon in June

Writing poetry, or beginning to write poetry seriously, seems to throw up unique problems. We're often faced with students who are either filled with dread at the prospect of writing a poem, or ones who feel quite confident about what is required, but know very little about it. It's sometimes easier to encourage the first group, than it is to redirect the second. In fact, both groups are often labouring under the same illusions. Perhaps you, too, are prevented from achieving a breakthrough because of your notions about what poetry is.

One of the biggest blocks is the notion that poetry has to be full of sententious thoughts, mediated through a voluminous and unusual vocabulary, that there is a necessary special language, even code, in which poetry is written, a poetic diction that it falls to the clever reader to locate. I'm not saying that some poetry isn't difficult (or that difficulty isn't part of the fun), but that similes, metaphors, imagery, or symbolism need not be necessary complications.

Secondly, it is often assumed that poetry can only be poetry if it rhymes and if it is in metre. Plenty of poetry doesn't rhyme. It's actually a very simple device. Metre, however, is complicated. This is the pattern of the syllables in the line. There are hundreds of such patterns, but the most common is the iambic beat, which alternates weak stresses with strong ones. Metrical theory is a fascinating subject, but it can operate as a block to new writers. The dedication to rhyme and metre often produces weak writing, where the rhymes carry the poem along, the limited available words distorting the meaning of the poem: if there's a moon in it, it'll have to be in June! All too often the result is a piece of verse that swings between rhymes like telegraph wires between poles. The name of this is doggerel.

The third misapprehension is that poetry must always be personal, the exposure of some traumatic emotional wound or of the ecstasies of love, for example. Doubtless, these have been subjects for poetry, but they needn't be yours! If you're a student writer, or belong to a writing group, you'll have two responses to this. Either you will be horrified at the thought of having to commit continual acts of literary self-revelation, or you will revel in it, seeking to shock or impress your audience. Neither is fair; neither is productive.

Let's try something else.

Poetic Hygiene

Firstly, think small. Many poems are short anyway, but this is not the result of exhaustion, but of condensation *in* the act of writing, and in editing after. One of the shortest types of poem is the Japanese haiku. Probably the most famous haiku is the near untranslatable one by the seventeenth-century Zen Buddhist monk, Basho. Our version goes like this:

> An ancient pond, yes –
> The frog there, leaping into
> Its own rippled splash.

Formally, the poem consists of three lines, with the simple syllable count of 5 – 7 – 5. Try writing in this form. Don't think poetry. Think description: describe the moment of arriving in the space you are now in. It'll get you used to the form.

There are a couple of other 'rules' to help you. At the end of the first, or at the end of the second line, there is a slight pause, a change of theme, an articulation, a hinge. It might be marked by a punctuation mark: a full stop, a semi-colon or a comma. Or you might like to omit formal punctuation altogether and use a dash or a space. We call this the 'turn'.

In the traditional haiku there is always a recognisable word (called a *dai*) which tells you what season the poem was written in. (For example, the frog in Basho's haiku suggests it was written in spring.) Our next two haiku demonstrate variations of 'turn' and '*dai*'. What is the effect of the different position of the turn?

> September morning –
> a blackbird runs along the
> edge of a shadow

> The daffodils dance
> and frost is hard this morning:
> but doesn't break them.

Basho believed that a poet learns about 'a pine tree from a pine tree, about a bamboo stalk from a bamboo stalk', and contemporary Japanese haiku writers have followed this by adopting the technique of 'on the spot composition'.[1] The writer, preferably standing before the object, enters 'into the object, sharing its delicate life and feeling'.[2] Haiku should try to 'contain feelings that have come from the object', in the words of one of Basho's disciples.[3] In other words haiku are all about what's out there, immediately in front of you, not about what's inside you. Slip a small note pad into your pocket and step outside into the world whose moments will offer you numerous potential haiku. The trick is to keep on writing them. Perhaps haiku writing, with its immediacy, will become an habitual part of using your writer's journal, even if you don't focus on poetry. As an exercise, try writing them in your head.

Try This: Haiku

1. Write a list of 10 *dai* for the season. You are not in Japan watching frogs and bamboo. What do you associate with the season?
2. Paying attention to the form write up to 10 haiku, using one *dai* per poem.
3. Think about each word and describe some aspect of the season.
4. Remember to use the articulation of the 'turn'. If it's just one long sentence, it lacks tension.
5. Pick out the most successful, the most surprising. Why does it work?

The haiku was a great influence on a group of poets called The Imagists in the early twentieth century, and some of the things their leader, Ezra Pound, said about this 'school' of poetry are relevant today. He proposed a haiku-like 'Direct treatment of the "thing", whether subjective or objective.'[4] This involves the use of the 'Image', which Pound defined as 'that which presents an intellectual and emotional complex in an instant of time'.[5] It gives 'that sense of sudden liberation', the instantaneous sense of surprise, feelings evoked by objects, that you get with the very best haiku, where the focus is objective (that is, in the object seen not in the self observing).[6] Pound added, 'Use absolutely no word that does not contribute to the presentation.'[7] This is good advice for any kind of writing, of course, but Pound's lessons in poetic hygiene had in mind the kind of wordy pseudo-poetry we dismissed in our opening. But he is also agreeing with another useful saying (although it was an architect who first said it): 'Less is More'. Pound's demands were specific: 'Use no superfluous word, no adjective, which does not reveal something.'[8] The poet Basil Bunting went further: 'Fear adjectives; they bleed nouns.'[9] That is, in poetry adjectives seldom act as 'intensifiers' as linguists call them; they actually 'dull the image' as Pound said of a cliché like 'dim lands of peace'.[10] According to Pound, this 'mixes an abstraction with the concrete'. As William Carlos Williams puts it: 'No ideas but in things'.[11] This is a particular way of expressing a more general creative writing maxim: 'Show, don't tell'.

Pound's most famous Imagist poem is called 'In a Station of the Metro', which is a kind of haiku, though it is only two lines long (but originally was over fifty lines long, and itself a miniature testimony to his monumental editing skills). Have a look at this poem and many other Imagist poems in Peter Jones's *Imagist Poetry*, and see how they did (and didn't) stick to Pound's 'rules' (which are also reprinted there in full).[12] Our poem is modelled upon Pound's:

> A PAVEMENT CAFÉ IN WARSAW
> The pushing of this person through the crowd;
> A figure-head on a sharp, high, prow.

The word 'image' is often used loosely in discussions of poetry, almost to the point of meaninglessness, but I want you to think about it quite literally as things we can see (at least in these exercises). I want you to forget everything about figurative language you've been taught, and to think for a moment only of similes: those markers of similarity marked by the word 'like' (or 'as'), and only of ones you can see. 'His teeth were stained like a Victorian urinal,' may not be very nice, but you can see it! 'His teeth were as loose as a call girl's morals!' is very funny, but you can't see it! This is the sort of simile I want you to avoid; it is one of Pound's abstractions. Notice how in our poem the word 'like' could have been added. We have used the line-break as a sort of hinge, a kind of 'turn'.

Try This: From Simile To Image

1. Decide on a visual image for exploration.
   We suggest: images of teeth, good, bad or decaying; an image of a crowd: at a railway station like Pound, or at a café table in our version, or a concert or football match; an image of a single person in movement: a dancer in full flight, or an athlete in action, or somebody moving inelegantly.
2. Write a short first line that states the subject, as in 'A Pavement Café in Warsaw'.
3. List as many possible second lines you can. If it helps, use the word 'like' or 'as'.
4. Select the most effective, the one with the greatest surprise.
5. Delete the word 'like' or 'as'. Place at the end of line 1 the most appropriate punctuation mark. We've followed Pound in using a semi-colon, but we could have used a colon for a more direct sense of equation between the object and the image.

We have yet to pay attention to another of Pound's injunctions, which was: 'As regarding rhythm: compose in sequence of the musical phrase, not in sequence of a metronome.'[13] A metronome is a device for measuring equally spaced beats, very useful for learning to play a musical instrument, but too regular to use in a real performance. Pound explained: 'Don't chop your stuff into separate iambs', by which he meant a strict, repetitive metre.[14] He was advocating what is sometimes called 'free verse', although this has never been a satisfactory term. A common misconception is that free verse has no rhythm. All language has rhythm, but not all language is in a regular metre. 'Free is properly a synonym for "nonmetrical" and it follows that the prosody of free verse is rhythmic organisation by other than numerical modes,' or by counting syllables, writes Charles O. Hartman.[15]

The chief problem for any writer in this form is how and where to break the line (and stanza). Pound has some solid advice about what is often called enjambment, that is, the act of breaking a line while continuing the sense: 'Don't make each line stop dead at the end, and then begin every next line with a heave.'[16] Look again at lines 2 and 3 of our 'September' haiku. The demon of beginners in non-metrical verse is that they (unconsciously) arrange their lines as phrases because that is where a 'break' appears to be (a worse habit is to put a comma at the end of each line). 'Let the beginning of the next line catch the rise of the rhythm wave, unless you want a definite longish pause.'[17] This question of line is strictly a question of judgement. Pound's Metro poem, and our Café poem, both have a deliberately irregular pattern of heavy syllables in line 2, which slows the poems down. As Bunting said: 'Vary rhythm enough to stir the emotion you want but not so as to lose impetus.'[18] One sound guideline from Pound is to remind the poet that 'your rhythmic structure should not destroy the shape of your words, or their natural sound, or their meaning'.[19] You need not distort your ordinary voice. The best way is to try this out for yourself before we suggest some more technical ways of doing this. We often tell students to 'get a feel for the line'. Different people perhaps have personal rhythms.

Pound is clear about rhyme in these freer structures, where it is not necessary: 'A rhyme must have in it some slight element of surprise if it is to give pleasure.'[20] Notice how in our example (like Pound's) there is a half-rhyme at the end of both lines, but it is neither intrusive nor mandatory.

Try This: Imagist Poem

1. Study this section so far and go outside or sit at a window with a view and write freely.
2. Try putting feeling into a description of a landscape.
3. Try to evoke an emotion in the piece without naming it. Your ideas must be completed articulated by *things*.
4. See if you can develop several images in one poem.
5. Let the poem flow. Try to think in lines as you go. Avoid end-stopped lines except where necessary. Experiment with verse breaks.

In revision:

1. Check the poem for abstractions and consider replacements.
2. Check that you haven't written the piece in lines that are phrases, and relineate until you are happy with the 'flow'.
3. Change any clangy rhymes or remove altogether. (If you are an habitual 'rhymester' practise doing without this prop.)

Small Machines of Words

William Carlos Williams famously defined a poem as 'a small (or large) machine made of words.'[21] A poem is not often thought of as a machine, with parts that can be built up to make a whole. While any poem should work *as a whole*, it may be useful in the writing of poems to think about how its mechanisms may be isolated, and even pulled to bits and reassembled. When a group of poets around Williams developed Imagism further, they called it Objectivism, not because they were being objective towards the world, or writing about objects, like the haiku writers, but because they thought of writing poetry as the making of these machine-like objects. We are going to pretend that there are only three parts to the poetry-machine: line, line break and enjambment. The line break will be thought of as a hinge.

We don't often think enough about line. But it is the basic component of a poem. Think what a line break does to the flow of language that would otherwise be 'prose'. Derek Attridge writes:

> Free verse is the introduction into the continuous flow of prose language, which has breaks determined entirely by syntax and sense, of another kind of break, shown on the page by the start of a new line, and often indicated in a reading of the poem by a slight pause.[22]

This means that where the line breaks, the point of enjambment, becomes crucial. Take a piece of prose – your own from your journal, perhaps – and put it into different arrangements of lines: experiment with the 'break' described above. 'Enjambment', Giorgio Agamben writes, 'reveals a mismatch, a disconnection between the metrical and syntactic elements, between sounding rhythm and meaning, such that...poetry lives...only in their inner disagreement.'[23] We prefer to speak of tension between the parts of the poem, instead of disagreement. It is clear that there is a tension between the sentence and the line-lengths it trails along and breaks. In writing your small machine, you will be able to play off line-length against sentence (or syntax), and punctuation against enjambment.

THE SNIPER, WASHINGTON
The observer –
spotted with crooked
elbow

the sights parallel
with a loaded
rifle image –

camouflaged. The
cuff exposed, the
mobile hovers

above the head
a dis-
connected thought

Williams was a master of this kind of enjambment:

in all its kinds and degrees: phrases and clauses splay, leap or crawl across line and
stanza breaks, in deliberate violation of natural pauses and syntactic boundaries.
Some poems play frequently enjambed lines against end-stopped stanzas; others
build up successively stronger enjambments in order to emphasize one big stop.[24]

Try experimenting in the light of this inspired description. A good
way to help you practise these skills is by using photographs, as we
have in 'The Sniper, Washington'. Daily papers often have excellent
quality images to work from; unlike the world itself they are often
dramatic, but they are also static, Imagist and Objectivist in their
own way. Also try paintings as in our next poem, in homage to
Williams' late poem *Pictures from Brueghel*.

LADY WRITING A LETTER, WITH HER MAID (Vermeer)
A thought
Approaches her cap:
A slender leg.
The discarded implements
Compliment the marbled floor;
Implicate a visitor

Just departed.
The maid watches
Him go.

Her lady
Addresses
The page.

However visual and imagistic the contents of these poems are, there
is a different kind of visualising required: to read the text with the
eye. The line and stanza breaks are visual shapes as well as (possibly)

representing a pause in sound. Williams may have invented new forms of typography and lineation inspired by his use of the typewriter, the word processor of his time. Text is a visual entity (a process accelerated with our use of white space and computer screens, hypertext and cyberpoetics) and there is hardly a language to talk of this, but it is our hunch that writers have always been aware of it, and that, if a poem is a machine, then the three gears of listening, looking and meaning, must work together (and in tension). An easy way of remembering this is to think: sound, shape and sense.

Try This: Objectivist Poems

1. Obtain some newspaper photographs.
2. Select one that impresses you.
3. Write a poem, thinking hard about line, syntax and enjambment.
4. Never use words like 'in the photograph'. Just be there, capturing what you see.
5. Revise in the light of this. Check the flow of the lines. Is it smooth or jagged? Which is appropriate to the object or image captured?
6. Reading for the Ear. Read your poem out loud. How does it sound? Experiment with ways of reading it. Test out Attridge's remark about a slight pause between lines and stanzas.
7. Reading for the Eye. Look at the poem as a shape upon the page. Does it look right? Does it feel right, for you?
8. How do sound, shape and sense work together (or in tension with one another) in your poem? Does this suggest how you might redraft it?

Then Try This: Writing An Objectivist Sequence

Late in life Williams was incapacitated by a stroke. During this time he wrote his book *Pictures from Brueghel*, relying on a book of the artist's pictures. He was writing on an early electric typewriter and this encouraged him to experiment with dropping punctuation completely (as we nearly have in our 'The Sniper, Washington').

1. Select a book of paintings by any representational painter (other than Brueghel: go and read Williams' sequence instead). We picked Vermeer, who often painted scenes of ordinary life that would have appealed to Williams.
2. Repeat the objectivist method in terms of form and focus
3. Optionally, experiment with removing punctuation.

All these things will sensitise you to line and will enable you to experiment with appropriate ways of maintaining the tension between line and sentence, form and content, as well as between sound, shape and sense. All of these exercises may be adapted (just think of all the images you might use, from your own snapshots through to the dozen images on a calendar). Part of the reason to concentrate on short poems is the lesson of concision in writing and editing. Basil Bunting's advice to young poets was 'Cut out every word you dare,' which represents editing and redrafting as a daring enterprise.[25] But he adds: 'Do it again, a week later, and again.'[26] Go on. It's a good preparation, whether you end up exploring the texts we recommend below, or whether your taste leads you back to traditional poetic forms.

Further Reading

J. Rothenberg and P. Joris (eds) (1995, 1998) *Poems for the Millennium*, in two volumes (Berkeley, CA: University of California Press).
  We teach from the second volume, *From Post-War to Millennium*, but the first contains the works of Pound, Williams and Bunting. Each poet's work is accompanied by excerpts from his or her poetics, or philosophy of composition, which gives an insight into both general attitudes and questions of technique. A generous international cross-section of work, and a useful source book for poets.
H. Smith (forthcoming) *The Writing Experiment: Strategies for Innovative Creative Writing* (Sydney: Allen Unwin).
  This book, published in Australia, is a different kind of creative writing book, in keeping with the focus of our exercises here. It covers prose and narrative as well as poetry, but is focused upon a language-centred approach rather than expressing yourself or using traditional forms, although it suggests new ways of writing about life-experience.

23 Writing Play: On and Off the Page

Heather Leach

After a century of film and fifty years of television, the use of short fragmented images is now so familiar that most of us have become skilled at processing them. This jump-cut style, which was once experimental and is now commonplace, fits well with the pacy, complicated lives that many of us lead. It's a filmic narrative art that helps us make sense of our real lives. Yet give the average reader a copy of James Joyce's *Ulysses* or Virginia Woolf's *Mrs Dalloway*, both novels which use fragmented voices, thoughts, feelings, shifts of viewpoint and location, and they're likely to give it you back after a few minutes, asking where's the story. Many of us find these textual narrative forms hard to read, unfamiliar and therefore uncomfortable.

Jeff Noon, an experimental fiction writer himself, a few years ago had a justifiable pop at stick-in-the-mud readers, and also at publishers unwilling to take a risk with something that doesn't follow the conventional linear narrative structure, arguing that in the internet age, we need a different kind of narrative art.[1] He makes a strong point but there's a lot more to this story-business than meets the eye. It isn't only the reader's conservatism or crude capitalist greed that keeps much of today's fiction in the safe middle ground, but our addiction to linearity: to beginnings, middles and ends. Perhaps this love of linear narrative is built into the human mind/culture in some way and has useful survival value: once you are able to imagine a bear in a forest and can speak, then, if you're particularly smart, you can begin to tell the others a story of how we could all get sharp sticks and then we could go quietly under the trees and then we could surround it all together and...well you know how it goes. These days many of our stories are more complex and rationalised.

But we still turn even the smallest event into dramatised stories: *this happened, then this happened and then*...In an unpredictable universe, the predictable linearity of story helps to order experience and keep chaos at bay. However, as Noon points out, we live in an increasingly fast-paced world and are becoming skilled at handling complexity. So why should most of our stories continue to be such simple and singular lines?

Another way of thinking about this is to remember that as well as order and safety, most of us (if we haven't had it schooled out of us) also like play, ridiculousness and nonsense. Children are the experts here: babies begin to play with words from the moment they can speak; toddlers babble and sing nonsense; juniors laugh their socks off at silly puns, rude jokes, any kind of daft word play. All of them break the rules for fun, treating language as malleable *stuff*.

Blue-Sky Writing

Scientists, academics and entrepreneurs have something called *blue-sky research*. This is the kind of rare research that people invest a lot of time, effort and money into without any guarantee of a payoff. Creative experimentation with language is blue-sky research into the way the mind works; into the emotions; into different ways of being in the world and into language itself.

But Is There a Point to It?

Does everything have to have a point? What's the point of a baby; a Harley-Davidson bike; a rock anthem; the colour purple? Play doesn't necessarily get you anywhere: *that's* the point of it. Ask a group of eight-year olds to describe the useful educational qualities of hide and seek and you'll end up with a bunch of gloomy-looking kids. Loosen up. Use language like toddlers use paint: mess with it! Here are some familiar word games to get you in the mood:

Anagrams

Rearrange letters to make new words. One of the keys to good anagram solving is to keep an eye out for words that will work together, making a link between the original word and the new one. Here are a couple of good ones:

dormitory = dirty room
desperation = a rope ends it.

Sadly, these two are not mine but are collected by Jim Kalb and listed along with thousands of other anagrams and palindromes on his website.[2]

Palindromes

Words, lines and sentences that spell and read the same forwards as backwards: Madam, I'm Adam is the most famous. There are some fiendishly clever ones on Jim Kalb's site: one of my favourites is:

A man, a plan, a canal: Panama!

As I said above, play is play and doesn't have to justify itself with a purpose but, inevitably as a side effect, these games will enable you to notice words more, will extend your vocabulary and help you learn from their interactions, their odd possibilities and rich potential. A word of warning – this wordplay is serious fun but also a desperate time waster. Do not start unless you've got a few hours (or years?) to spare. Some people, who probably have started off as simple word lovers and would-be writers, have ended up word-game crazy: Lawrence Levine, for example, produced a palindromic novel 31, 957 words long, which is seriously sad. Palindromes are the heroin of the word game world. Keep well away. You have been warned.

Codes

There are an enormous number of codes and ciphers, many in daily and essential use: Morse code; Braille; sign language, for example. Think of the 26 letters of the alphabet as a computer programme, a pack of cards, a codebook. Use them to randomise, to make new combinations. Languages are codes: as translations of each other and as signs for thoughts, emotions, objects, people; anything that we can perceive, imagine, name. Writing itself is a form of code.

Try This: Code Writing

Write a story in which someone is using code to communicate with another person. Why? What kind of code are they using? Can the person receiving the letters work out the code? Is the code key lost? How will the reader work it out?

Words and Pictures

It isn't only writers who miss out on fun but also adult *readers*. Go to the children's fiction section of a library or bookshop, have a good browse and then come sadly back into the adult fiction section. What's missing? Pictures, of course. Not only pictures, but colour, variation, interactivity. Children's books, particularly for under 7s, come in all sizes and shapes; they incorporate things you can press and stroke; pages with holes that you can put your fingers through; there are letters in envelopes; tags to pull; doors to open; whole double page spreads which unfold into butterflies, castles, space ships. Many children's books also allow text to stray out of its usual rigid linearity: instead of large plain black chunks; words come in small blocks of colour; they curve into spirals, and scatter across the page as freely as paint.

Give me one good reason why, when we become adults, most of this should have to stop. There *are* plenty of reasons, and no doubt you've heard some of them:

> Adult readers use their imaginations to visualise places, characters, events, etc.; pictures and fiddly bits would detract from that inner world.

True, but children use their imaginations too: their inner visions are fed by the richness that, if they're lucky, they get from picture books. You might use a similar argument against film or television drama. Read my lips: we do not have to choose. The imagination can be fed and stimulated in many different ways; through inner and outer visions: word and image. This is a both/and world, remember, not an either/or.

> But some people will never read proper books if you give them pictures: the inner life of literature could die out, swamped by the visual.

Well, *hello*. Many people, far too many people, *already* stop reading fiction when they reach adolescence. Perhaps they are daunted by pages of colourless print. Perhaps they get sick of being told how very good *'proper'* reading is for them and swamped by piousness, they miss out on the real fun. Children who love reading read both Philip Pullman and *The Beano* without pride or shame. Adults have a lot to learn from them.

Some Grown-up Examples

Fortunately there are an increasing number of books and writings, aimed at an adult audience, which use pictures and image, textual innovation, cut-outs and pop-ups and so forth, alongside language. We need a lot more. The following descriptions cover just a few. I have focused on those where the language arts: narrative; drama; character; poetry; dialogue and so on, are at least equal in importance to the visual arts:

Book Arts: Pop-ups and Textual Play

Remember pop-ups? If you live with small children, then you're probably still lucky enough to get your hands on some. I recently brought a couple of books into a class I teach, passing them round while we talked about the potential of book art for the writer. I had thought that this might take a few minutes, giving me time to move on to other examples. Wrong. The whole class plan fell apart as every person insisted on going through each book pulling and pushing every single tab and fold. People were actually wrestling the books away from each other, and those farthest away were hopping up and down with impatience. These were BIG people. This just goes to show how much fun most adults miss out on. Where are the adult pop-ups? Where are the books that have pockets, foldings, secret compartments, cut-out revelations? Where are the stories and poems which use papery-ness, its origami potential to interact with text?

Most of the time, the conventional book (bound pages inside covers) is simply a medium for writing: a container for the stories, poems, ideas, inside it. The form stays static, largely unnoticed, allowing the message to do its work. If writers want to display their work to the best advantage, it will be worth their while to think about fonts, layout on the page, white space and so on. For most of us that's usually as far as it goes. Fine. Most people most of the time regard a book as a plain collection of bound sheets of paper between card covers, but sometimes we might want to play with alternatives. Let's face it: why should children have all the fun books?

Try This: Make Your Own Pop-Up Book

…but without using pictures or illustrations. Make the text itself move, hide, appear, enfold itself or whatever.

Graphic Novels

Put your hands up those of you who still read comics. The bad news is that after a certain age, stories about men with sticky feet who can walk up walls lose their charm for most of us: simplistic good and evil narratives; bug-eyed monster worlds and macho scenarios begin to seem shallow and repetitive in a more complex and adult culture. The good news is that there are grown-up alternatives.[3] I've commented on just two here to give you a taste.

Nausicaa, by Hiyao Miyazaki,[4] is described by many as a work of genius. Begun and continued through volumes as a Japanese Manga (comic) and made into a film, this saga tells the story of a girl journeying through a strange country searching for meaning and a pure land. See the fan website for a full synopsis, history, plus details of production.

Raymond Briggs, the well-known children's writer and illustrator, famous for *Fungus the Bogeyman* and *Father Christmas*, has also produced a number of graphic novels for adults. Take a look at *When the Wind Blows* and *Ethel and Ernest*: both are funny, sad and intimately personal, as well as subtly political. Story, text and image work together beautifully and convincingly.

Things to Think About if You'd Like to Become a Writer for Comics or Graphic Novels

- Many writers in this field operate as part of a team, rather than as lone workers – this is similar to the way television scriptwriters work.

- Do you have a strong visual sense?
- Do you have illustrative talent as well as writing? If not, can you find a collaborator?

Writing and Computers: Web and Interactive Writing

It can't have escaped your notice that the web is now a repository of writing. The world has been transformed by computer programmers during the past twenty years: new ways of reading texts through hyper-textual links, new ways of integrating image, word, sound and so on. Millions of people are playing online games, many of them with dramatic storylines. Many of the comics and graphic novels discussed above have been or are being developed for online and interactive computer environments. There is a lot of experimental writing out there.

On the other hand don't let's get too carried away. A lot of these games might be fun to play with but very limited in terms of character, narrative complexity, ideas: many of the more serious experiments are difficult to read on a screen. You can't read a laptop in bed or in the bath, and the promised hand-helds haven't reached us yet. But, hey, these are early days. It took film many years for its full potential to be realised. The web is a writer's experimental playground, full of collaborations, advice, information, and other writers. It can be overwhelming, and there is also a great deal of dross out there, but if you're not technophobic and you have access to a networked computer, particularly if it's free, then I suggest you at least *look* at some of the wonders out there. You may even want to have a go at interactive writing or multimedia play for yourself.

Illustrious Examples

Geoff Ryman: 253 – A Novel for the Internet: www.ryman.com

This is an award-winning site. *253* is structured in blocks based on the coaches of a London Tube train. Its characters are the passengers scattered through these coaches. You can click on each person, identified by seat number, in any order you choose, but there is an underlying story and plenty of small stories to keep you clicking, and there are also witty and thoughtful side-shoots to the structure. There are no bells and whistles, no pictures or multimedia, just text organised to work online and interactively. This writer has something to say and stories to tell and the tube train structure helps the reader to understand where they are and how to read. There is a printed version and you might want to compare the two. Any writer with reasonable computer competence could produce something like this. You don't need specialist skills.

Poems that Go: www.poemsthatgo.com

This site shows and discusses poetry that interacts with sound, image and computer code. The web authors describe it as:

> Space on the Web as a creative field for this generation's artists and writers. One which challenges you, the new viewers, readers, writers and artists, to discover extraordinary ways to make sense of language, art, and narrative in a way that is both critical and entertaining.[5]

Try This: Writing Hypertext

Think about a story that can be told in a non-linear way. For a first attempt use a form you already know: e.g. letters or postcards; people waiting in a bus queue.

- Write the story in short sections, trying to let the events and actions reveal an underlying dramatic structure.
- Type up each block on a separate page.
- Use the web-authoring tools within your computer software to make it interactive.
- Decide how you want the reader to read it: in any order? in an order you choose?
- Think about how it looks, what the reader sees on the screen.
- Test it out on readers. Then revise.

Crossing Boundaries

The history of writing is also the history of experimentation: plays; novels; modern poetry; feature film scripts; television drama; all were at one time new and unusual writing forms. There have also been plenty of experiments which failed to make it into mainstream culture – that's the nature of experiment, of course: something that begins as a tentative adventure may turn out to be a whole new journey or an embarrassing dead end. I want to finish this chapter by pointing you towards some examples of innovative writing that remain inside the covers of the conventional book in order to emphasise that you can experiment with words and narrative form being a computer expert, a musician or a stand-up performer. What you *do* need is an interest in the way language works, and in the way that forms of writing interact with forms of thinking and being.

The Golden Gate: A Novel in Verse by Vikram Seth[6]

A novel written in sonnets: all 307 pages of it. You wouldn't think this could possibly work but it really does, mainly because Seth builds the story through the tried and tested novelistic techniques: character, setting (San Francisco in the 1980s), drama plus a lot of wit. This isn't for everyone, but lots of people love this book and I can vouch for it being readable to the end: if you get beyond the first 20 pages and give it a fair bash, you really do begin to care what will happen to John, the sad and lonely computer programmer.

The House of Leaves by Mark Danielewski

This is a horror story, a thesis, a film script, an autobiography. The horror is based on a strange house that has a mysterious and threatening labyrinth somewhere inside it, and the story is told through voices and documentary archives, some of which contradict each other. The whole book is a series of layers and interconnections: narratives that may be truth, fiction or lies – without a key as to which is which. There are many typographical tricks and twists: there are blank pages, upside down text, footnotes and footnotes of footnotes. This book may drive you mad but the story is genuinely scary and the narrative voices are a convincing mix of realistic and weird. It's a book that shouldn't be missed if you are interested in contemporary writing.

Have fun!

Further Reading

Nick Bantock (1994) *The Griffin and Sabine Trilogy* (London: Chronicle Books).

Now also a wonderful interactive CD-Rom: Bantock, N. (1997) *Ceremony of Innocence*. Real World Multi Media.

L. Haines (1998) *The Writer's Guide to the Business of Comics* (New York: Watson-Guptil).

Does what it says on the tin.

Style: Subject, Verb, Object

If the subject is plural then so is the verb.

WRONG: *The school children was very well behaved.*
RIGHT: *The school children were very well behaved.*

On a slightly different point, watch out for subject and object confusion.
When the first person is the subject, it's *I*:

I kicked the ball.

When the first person is the object, it's *me*:

The ball thumped me in the face.

Same with *who* and *whom*:

This is the woman who loves me.

And:

This is the woman whom I love.

24 The Polyphonic Spree: Other Narrative Strategies

Robert Graham

Aristotle believed a plot required a beginning, a middle and an end. Wayne C. Booth argues that this notion fell out of fashion during the twentieth century. It is unrealistic, he says, to 'begin at the beginning and plod methodically through to the end.'[1] In support of this, Booth points to Ford Madox Ford who promoted a model which involved moving backwards and forwards over the protagonist's past – the non-chronological approach that is a hallmark of modernist fiction. Just such a narrative strategy can be seen in postmodern fiction, too: Peter Barry contends that for the postmodern writer, fragmented narratives are:

> an exhilarating, liberating phenomenon, symptomatic of our escape from the claustrophobic embrace of fixed systems of belief.[2]

'Polyphonic' is one way of describing the approaches to narrative that I'm going to touch on in this chapter. One definition of 'polyphonic' is *many-voiced*, which nearly gets it, but there's more to what I'm talking about here than that. Part of the approach to constructing fiction that I prefer has to do with what I call 'breaking up the monolith'. (The term probably derives from Henry James's observation that first-person narrative tends towards the monolithic.)

Breaking Up the Monolith

One of the ways in which I interpret this term is in the use of breathing space. Even in eras where readers may have had longer attention spans, there has always been a need for breathing space in fiction. At a fundamental level this begins with allowing the reader to participate in the text by letting them do some of the work – in what, for instance, remains unexplained or not fully described. (Perhaps Dickens described London in more detail than Martin Amis because his provincial or international readers did not have access to cinema and television and would not have much idea of how the metropolis looked.)

It also involves, as Laurence Block explains in *The Writer's Digest Handbook of Short Story Writing*[3] making use of the passing of time, geographical movement, leaving one set of characters and focusing on another, pulling back the focus, plus the use of what he calls collage – which I call quilting – rather than linear plot to tell the story.

In the use of breathing space, as in the more general aim to avoid the monolithic, my ambition is simply to keep the contemporary reader – and myself – stimulated. This may be achieved by breaking chapters into brief sections, making chapters and paragraphs and sentences shorter or using a range of narrative techniques. More variety, more complexity.

Another way of breaking up the monolith is using multiple viewpoints – of which, more in a moment – and flashbacks, which I have to say I've gone off. I like a narrative to keep moving forward, and the risk with a flashback is that readers may forget where they were before it began. Having a non-chronological narrative, where different time-periods occupy the space of a whole chapter, seems to me a less risky approach. It's less disruptive to move around in time by the chapter rather than *within* a chapter. Speaking of time, leaving gaps in the chronology of days, months or years is another way of creating breathing space. Alternating between main and subplot also contributes to creating a various text.

Masculine Narrative Strategies

What I'm calling masculine approaches – and obviously I'm simplifying here: all writers use both masculine and feminine narrative strategies – tend to be task-oriented and target-related. (For example, the simple linear plot, the reversal plot – anything, in fact, that could be defined by a plot structure, which consists of hook, steadily rising conflict, climax and denouement.[4]) Most Hollywood films use the kind of narrative structure I'm talking about here. (If you want a quick understanding of the difference between masculine and feminine narrative strategies, watch the Spike Jonze/Charlie Kaufman film *Adaptation*, the first two-thirds of which are feminine in approach with the final third conforming to the regular Hollywood, and more masculine, structure. It's very illuminating.) If you want to know how to vary your simple linear plot, Ronald B. Tobias's *20 Master Plots*[5] is a useful guide.

One thing that's helpful to bear in mind about plotting of this kind is that you can usually benefit from slowing down the changes that take place. In Alison Lurie's *The Truth About Lorin Jones*, narrative tension is sustained throughout the concluding sections by negotiating change more sparingly than it might have been: the suspense is kept tight; the resolution comes an inch at a time, while the level of drama is maintained and often increased. For example, Lurie is able to keep us guessing about whether or not the protagonist will get her man. (For more how pace is related to description, read chapter 13, 'Setting'.)

Try This: Dual-Viewpoint Story-Building

Find an object, think about the following questions and make notes. It may be helpful at times to close your eyes and ponder the situation.

Where are you?
What you can see?
What can you smell?
What can you touch?
Is anyone else there?
What is the weather / atmosphere / mood like?
How do you feel?
What do you wish?
What does the object mean to you?
What is the problem at the moment?
What has led up to this moment?
What do you think will happen next?

Your notes should create a character in a situation. You'll need at least two characters, so repeat the exercise to create your second character, making the responses very different to make the second character distinct from the first.

Use the notes to write the first draft of a short story in which you write scenes, alternating the viewpoint, so that the story is seen through both your characters.

Don't try to write it all in one sitting: let the ideas gestate. Though it may not amount to a spree, a dual-viewpoint story is a first step on the road to being polyphonic.

Feminine Narrative Strategies

Feminine approaches tend towards plurality: of viewpoint and of narrative strategy. These approaches offer an alternative way to achieve what every narrative must do: maximise reader involvement with the text. In any number of contemporary novels distinctively feminine narrative techniques are deployed. They are deployed with exemplary skill in Morrison's *Beloved*, Erdrich's *Love Medicine*, Tan's *The Joy Luck Club*, Tyler's *Dinner at the Homesick Restaurant*, Walker's *The Color Purple*, Shields' *Larry's Party* and Garcia's *Dreaming In Cuban*.

Anne Tyler's family saga, *Dinner At the Homesick Restaurant*, is a *tour de force* in the use of multiple viewpoints. Each member of the Beck family has at least one chapter written from his or her point of view. An earlier model for this multiple-viewpoint approach is William Faulkner's *As I Lay Dying*. Multiple-viewpoint fiction offers more variety: the author is entirely removed from the text and no one point of view is given credence above any of the others, thus suggesting that no one character's reality is objectively true. For the writer, it's very stimulating, if only because, like an actor in a one-man show, you have to adopt a series of personas.

The use of multiple viewpoints is a prominent feature of the work of Amy Tan. In her novel *The Joy Luck Club*, for instance, the author has no overriding or unifying plot in the traditional sense. Instead, the novel is divided into four thematically linked sections, in each of which, four viewpoint characters have one chapter apiece. Jing-Mei, the central character who links the other characters, has the most chapters. She is the unifying thread linking other viewpoint characters.

The Joy Luck Club, and other similar texts (those cited above, for example), may occupy the middle territory between a novel and a collection of short stories, but their appeal is that they offer an alternative to the traditional narrative. It's something like the pleasures of a compilation tape over those of a whole album by one artist.

Another interesting feminine narrative strategy is quilting, which is used in all of the novels mentioned so far. It amounts to fashioning a textual patchwork, whether through altering viewpoint, moving through time and space in a non-linear fashion, or, like Lucy Ellmann's *Sweet Desserts* (see chapter 25, 'Narrative Design') using a collage of writing modes (in this example, jokes, recipes, letters, personal ads, and other found texts).

Elaine Showalter has written about narrative quilting in some depth. She notes Judith Fetterley's argument that nineteenth-century American women writers were freed from the pressures of the novel form[6] – the one 'most highly programmed and most heavily burdened by thematic and formal conventions'[7] by, as Showalter puts it, 'working with the piece or the story'.

Let me try to summarise (very briefly) her account of the history of this development. Women found that the short story form – 'the short narrative piece' allowed them more freedom. The growing importance of the book and novel form in America at the time led them to collect their stories together. In some cases, the collections later evolved into novels 'with narrative structures developed out of the piecing technique'.[8] She goes on to examine a short fiction by Kate Chopin, 'Elizabeth Stock's Story'.

Stock wants to write, but is daunted by the masculine, linear narrative form which she describes as 'original, entertaining, full of action, and goodness knows what all'. The feminine narrative form, which she attempts, is made up of patches in the manner of literal quilt-making, and according to Showalter, 'seems to offer a more authentic, but less orderly plot'. Chopin's story ends with Elizabeth Stock dying and her work being edited, condensed, and preserved according to the consecutive and linear models of the male tradition, with all her craziness and originality lost.[9] The male editor in question prefaces Stock's patchwork narrative with an explanation of his task:

> I was permitted to examine her desk, which was quite filled with scraps and bits of writing in bad prose and impossible verse. In the whole conglomerate mass, I discovered but the following pages which bore any semblance to a connected or consecutive narration.[10]

In many respects this is how I think the quilted narrative works: the author acts as masculine editor of his or her own feminine text. On the one hand the narrative may be various, making use of multiple viewpoint, collage, the epistolary; on the other, the author needs to give it some structure that causes the whole to cohere and compel.

Why not have a stab at polyphonic fiction? One voice good: many voices better. One narrative mode, fine: many narrative modes, finer.

Basics: Colons and Semi-colons

This is a colon:
  It goes before an example of something:

Martha was especially passionate about Australian films: anything by Peter Weir or Gillian Armstrong was her idea of bliss.

Sometimes a colon may precede a list:

The bowl was overflowing fresh fruit: apples, bananas, mangoes, mandarins and cherries.

And sometimes a colon may introduce an idea:

John and Yoko say: war is over (if you want it).

This is a semi-colon:
  A semi-colon is more emphatic than a comma, but less emphatic than a full-stop or period. A semi-colon may separate the main part of a sentence for a clause, which qualifies it in some way. For example:

2004 Belfast has a thriving restaurant scene, with a range of international cuisines; you're almost spoilt for choice.

It may also be used to separate out items in a list that consist of phrases:

Driving involves many skills: changing gear; steering the car round corners and pedestrians; and not crashing.

The one lesson to take away from it is this:

Don't use a semi-colon before you present an example of something; doing so will upset me. A lot.

25 Narrative Design: Pattern, Plant and Pay-off

Robert Graham

Form was another matter. It grew out of the materials of the tale and the teller's reaction to them.[1] (Sherwood Anderson)

Almost any writer you talk to will admit that the execution of a piece of work never lives up to the original conception, the vision of what the piece will be. So, while we're talking about the way work is composed, it might be comforting to look at part of an essay on the subject by Annie Dillard:

You are wrong if you think that in the actual writing, or in the actual painting, you are filling in the vision. You cannot fill in the vision. You cannot even bring the vision to light. You are wrong if you think that you can in any way take the vision and tame it to the page...Words lead to other words and down the garden path. You adjust the paints' values and hues not to the world, not to the vision, but to the rest of the paint...And so you continue to work, and finish it. Probably by now you have been forced to toss the most essential part of the vision...The work is not the vision itself, certainly. It is not the vision filled in, as if it had been a coloring book. It is not the vision reproduced in time; that were impossible. It is rather a simulacrum and a replacement.[2]

This, to my mind, is a helpful articulation of the processes we all go through when we are producing a piece of writing. The end product, Dillard is saying, may always be a pale shadow of the original idea. But, in Sherwood Anderson's view of the writing process, that in itself is an advantage: the final form of a piece of writing will be shaped by the writer's relationship with the elements involved. This should feel both liberating and exciting: you may never write what you thought you were setting out to, but the organic nature of literary production allows the possibility of ending up with something stronger than your original conception.

Sharples includes a diagram[3] which 'shows composing as a cycle of contemplating ideas, specifying plans and intentions, composing text and interpreting the text, leading to further ideas and continued composition'. What may be most interesting to you here is the idea that the three stages of writing – planning, composing and revising – are spiral, not linear. Any one stage is as important as the others are: more than this, each stage is entirely dependent on the others.

Sharples' cycle may be helpful for you to bear in mind as we approach an aspect of narrative design which I regard as important to the overall effect on the reader: pattern. The creation of pattern may take place during planning or composition or at the revising phase, or during all three. Sharples says of revising that looking at the first draft 'prompts the writer to interpret it and contemplate ways in which the plan could be extended, leading to a new round of planning'. Or as Rob Watson puts it in his *Extracts from a Work in Progress: Writing Life*:

> thoughts only exist with time. They need time to find their shape and size, and time to establish contacts and continuities.[4]

Pattern

Pattern seems to me a useful word for one of the results of this process. The kind of pattern I am thinking of involves creating repetition in much the same way as rolls of wallpaper make use of a repeated image. Let's look at one particularly developed example of pattern.

In her novel *Sweet Deserts*, Lucy Ellmann creates a structure where the narrative is frequently interrupted by a number of different kinds of asides. Some of these have no relation to what goes on before (or after) them, while some in a strange way do comment on, or add emotional colour to, the narrative in which they are embedded. One of these strands consists of recipes, or sometimes only fragments of recipes:

> Bone two large eels, fill them with diced truffles. Wrap in a piece of muslin and tie with string. Cook in wine and well-flavoured fish stock. Drain, unwrap, and cool under a press.

Another strand is letters sent or received by the narrator, Suzy Schwarz:

> *Dear Suzy, I don't want to hear any more talk about killing yourself. It would be a terrible loss to the world, and to your family. Cheer up! Make friends! Don't be sad.*

Sometimes Ellmann incorporates found texts:

> THE MUSK-DEER inhabits the steep slopes of the Himalaya. He lives an active but lonely life and feeds on grass and lichen.

(At one stage, she even uses a found text to theorise this approach:

> Many artists have used Chance and ready-mades in order to obscure their exact involvement with the work of art.

Other patterns in *Sweet Desserts* include tick-box questionnaires, snippets from language textbooks, snatches of song lyrics and jokes:

> Goldberg's a private in the army. His mother dies, and his superior officers don't know how to break the news to him. His sergeant volunteers to do it. He calls the whole platoon out, makes them all stand to attention, and then says:
>   'All those with mothers still living, step forward!'
>   They all step forward.
>   'Not so fast, Goldberg!'[5]

What Lucy Ellmann is up to is a form of collage. Unconnected images create an effect when they are placed next to one another in a visual collage, and so too do unconnected pieces of text. Often one piece of text can be used to comment on another: the joke just quoted is a way for Suzy Schwarz to deal with the fact that her father is dying. Taken all in all, Ellmann's use of pattern helps her construct a novel that is the very opposite of monolithic.

  Pattern has a positive effect on the reader because it is a means of making sense. When the reader comes across the second example of something in a novel, he or she can think, 'Ah-ha – I've seen one of these before. I know what they are.' (The process may not be conscious. I don't think it matters to the writer, though, whether the reader registers the pattern consciously or unconsciously.) For the writer, being aware that the reader will know what is going on is not something to be underestimated. I think there is more to the effect of pattern than this, though. Certainly it may give the reader the impression that he or she is making sense of the text. I believe it may also give the reader an indication that *the writer* knows what is going on. The pattern shows that the text has been designed. It shows that there is a design and, therefore, a designer. Furthermore, it shows, I think, that the designer is conscious of what he or she is doing. The text is not just something that tumbled unformed from the writer's mind. On the contrary, it has been shaped with a purpose. My own view is that these are positive responses to elicit from a reader, that reader reactions along these lines are the kind the writer wants – perhaps because they involve the reader wanting, and receiving, reassurance.

Try This: Narrative design

You'll need a first draft for this.

- Look for guns that don't go off. I once tried to be clever at the outset of a novel in manuscript. I thought I'd let the reader discover the name of the first-person narrator by having him read his name on an envelope. However, instead of revealing the character's name without actually telling the readers, I made them wonder what was in the letter – and the answer was, of course, nothing important to the plot! So the letter was a gun inadvertently planted, which would never go off.

- Look out for flourishes that you could turn into recurrent motifs or running jokes. In her novel *Things To Do Indoors*, Sheena Joughin makes frequent use of the small, but appealing, device of rendering song lyrics as reported speech: 'Dylan [was] singing that someone must say hello to his girlfriend, who might be in Tangiers.'

She uses the same device a handful of times throughout her novel. Each one raises a smile, and the effect is cumulatively amusing.

Plant and Pay-off

Perhaps the most efficient illustration of plant and pay-off is Chekhov's much quoted observation that the gun in the first act must go off in the third. The plant is the first (or second, third and so on) mention of whatever it is. The pay-off is when whatever it is is used at a key moment in the narrative.

In my teaching, I use a clip from *Toy Story* to illustrate the – I think really effective – skill of plant and pay-off. Halfway through the film, Sid, the nasty kid from next door, sets Andy's cowboy doll Woody on a barbecue and jams a match in Woody's empty holster. It is clear he means to torch the doll. However, Woody escapes. Then, at the climax of the film, Woody and his friend Buzz Light-year have the chance to catch up with their family, the Davises, if they can light a rocket attached to a roller-skate. Woody remembers the match – textbook plant and pay-off. (Except, in this case the screenwriter chooses to play with the convention: once ignited, the match blows out and the dolls have to find another way of lighting the rocket.)

A Symbolic Home

In the examples described so far, pattern has been achieved by using a fairly straightforward and brief plant and pay-off. A novel that uses plant and pay-off very effectively is Rose Tremain's *The Way I Found Her*. Three major elements of plot are sustained through the use of this device: the ability of Lewis, the narrator, to play chess; his growing skill at negotiating the rooftop of the Paris apartment building where he is staying; and the construction, by his father back in England, of a garden hut, and this last is the most impressive use of extended planting and paying-off in a novel bursting with it.

Lewis and his mother Alice are staying with Valentina in Paris for a summer while Alice works on the English translation of the novel Valentina is writing. Lewis' father, Hugh, is left at home, where he is planning a surprise for his wife when she returns from Paris:

> Hugh said: 'Lewis, I'm going to build a hut in the garden...It's a secret between you and me, OK? I'm building it for Mum. We'll put a desk and a chair in it. It'll be a place where she can sit and read or work in the summer.'[6]

The garden hut is mentioned a handful of times and it seems as though Tremain's intention is comic relief: in these references to the building of the hut, Hugh appears ridiculous

> Because I knew exactly what was going to happen to the hut: it would remain empty for ever. A desk would be put in it for Alice and a gas heater, even. But Alice would never spend any time there, not even in summer.[7]

All the garden hut planting is paid off with considerable resonance when we learn, in the book's penultimate page, what happened to the hut:

> So I tell Hugh, I don't want to sleep in [my bedroom] any more; I want to sleep in the hut...So that's more or less where I live now, separate from the house, separate from Alice and Hugh.[8]

In effect, the hut has become a kind of symbolic home for Lewis, and with a fetching poetic justice: it was intended to be a place of solitude for Alice, but by the end of the narrative, Lewis is the one who really needs to be solitary.

Further Reading

Mike Sharples (1999) *How We Write* (London: Routledge).
   This is an academic text, but written in an accessible style. If you're interested in thinking about how we write, it's well worth a look.
Rose Tremain (1998) *The Way I Found Her* (London: Vintage).
   Tremain is one of the finest contemporary British novelists. Apart from what I've said about her use of plant and pay-off, much can be learned by studying her work. Hers is always a beautifully realised fictional world, finely textured without ever being dense.

IV
Going Where?

It's Finished. What Now?

Dear Auntie,
I have a story finished, what do I
do with it now?

The Writers' and Artists' Handbook, and *The Writers' Handbook* both have lists of small presses and magazines accepting unsolicited material. *Writer's News*, a subscription magazine for writers, regularly gives details of annual competitions and small press magazines seeking new work. There is a growing community of web-based magazines seeking new work.

If you want to send work out to magazines then have the courtesy to read them first. This will help in three ways: you will get a sharper idea of what their editors are looking for; you will understand better what kind of a writer you are by finding work you either like or dislike; and finally, small press magazines need new writers and new *readers* to survive.

There may be little or no financial reward for publication, and entering competitions will almost certainly involve entrance fees, and there can never be any guarantees that you will get into print or eventually win a competition: writing doesn't operate on a merit system; 'I've entered one hundred competitions, it's definitely my turn to win'... But those writers who do succeed are usually those who didn't give up at the first, second or forty-third hurdle, and these hurdles may be the size of several novels and a hundred or so short stories sent fruitlessly out.

If this sounds bleak, then take heart. You should write for the love of it; after all, writing purely to get rich and famous is a precarious journey, beginning in blood and sweat and often ending in tears.

Admittedly, some writers do strike it lucky with their first attempt, and some writers are people who make their own luck. Be one of those latter people; get yourself into the right place at the right time by sending out your work! Make sure it's good. Make sure it's properly presented. Make sure it's what the editor is looking for. But most of all: make sure you send it out!

26 Getting Published
John Singleton

First: Write The Book

The hard yards: write a *good* book; one that excites you, not your Mum, not your kids, not the vicar, not your imagined reader. *You* are the first, last, and most important reader of your work. Nothing else matters.

You, however, are not the only reader of your work. There are people out there who will have a say in what and how you write – if you want to get published and read. They form the market – agents and readers and distributors and editors and publishers and reviewers and librarians and booksellers and teachers. And though all these interested parties will impinge on your choice of material and approach, they shouldn't control what you write or how you write.

Taking too much notice of the market by trying to write what you think the market wants is a recipe for failure. Another novel about the serial dating of three or four 25-year-old typical city-somethings will probably produce a dull, typical, and unsurprising, write-by-numbers book. Find what works for you and stick with it. If it's familiar fictional territory you must enter give it your own spin. Do something different. Surprise the reader. It's *your* voice we want to hear, not an imitation; a real voice, not an echo. If you want to write popular family drama go for it. If you want to write gritty fiction about the chemical generation do so. But do it your way, not the Irvine Welsh way.

On the other hand, taking too little notice of the market may leave you isolated and unpublished. What it comes down to is this: everyone has to work out for themself how to balance market demand and personal aspirations as a writer. My view is this: yes, keep a weather eye on the market, but first get that book done. It's a good book that will impress an agent or a publisher, not some clever pitch and market savvy narrative. Leave it up to the professionals for guidance on adjusting to market conditions.

And here is another crucial point. Having a book accepted for publication is only the beginning of a long evolutionary process. You will inevitably be asked to revise it, maybe a number of times. Revisions may well be driven by market considerations, but editors and agents have made these decisions for you, and you will follow their advice to the letter because you're not going to pass up a chance to be published, are you?

Six months after acceptance, many letters and phone calls later, the text is finally agreed and the book goes into production. You've kept your artistic integrity; others have adjusted and helped you fine-tune the product for an eager readership out there.

As with all advice this lot comes with conditions and small print. Here's some of it: your book may be great but, the market still has to want it. Like all markets, publishing is subject to the whims of change. Take the non-fiction sector. At the time of writing social history is the going thing. Hocus-pocus is out. This includes all those books with titles like *The Mysteries of the Pyramids* and *Blood Guilt: Human Sacrifice and the Ancient Aztecs*. Books with single titles like *Cod, Salt, Spice, Diamond* are also out. But in the mid-lit field of quality readable historical fiction things are on the up. Books like *The Girl with The Pearl Earring* and *Tulip* have been big hits, and anything set in eighteenth-century Japan will be snapped up.

In Popular Fiction, chic-lit is out; the old hands like Freya North and Jill Mansell and Marian Keyes have carved up the territory anyway. Because the Bridget Jones experience is currently out of literary favour, so too, for the time being, is the diary as a popular narrative form. And don't try to be a second Joanna Trollope. First, remember your writing isn't homage to other writers; it's about your voice sounding loud and thrilled. Second, you won't succeed as a Trollope clone because no publisher wants Aga-sagas anymore. But, if you are sensitive to the market and consider trends in demographics, you will notice that more and more readers are active into their eighties. So, you might want to consider Saga-sex as your subject!

But sex is one subject where you do need a bit of protection. Write about underage sex and no one will publish your work. And don't make your protagonist a sexually predatory librarian. Librarians sit on book selection panels and award committees: it doesn't pay to upset them. Publishers tend not to be keen on religious themes either. They don't like vicars in children's stories. God and Satan are out everywhere: mention the devil, and editors will exorcise your manuscript. Teenage necrophilia is definitely off limits. Restriction, if not censorship, is alive and well in every fiction executive's office.

Research Your Market

Research is commonsense, but worth spelling out. And you must be dedicated. If you're not prepared to research, don't expect to be published. You do research because it's the first step to maximising your chance of getting published.

The first thing you might find out is that recent changes in the market are not helping writers. Large companies are buying up small independents and forming huge conglomerates. When profit is the bottom line, risk, innovation and adventure disappear out of the market. In other words conglomerates could be less likely to risk money on an unknown writer especially as most of the market (editors and agents) are desperately looking for the next mega-seller.

In the big organisation it is harder to create that crucial personal touch and the nurturing environment that good editors in attentive publishing houses manage. The upside, however, is that the profits from highly successful enterprises such as the *Harry Potter* series mean that the publisher can afford to develop new products, new imprints, and even put money aside to invest in new writers.

Before...

First, there is what I call before-writing research, the useful enquiry you can do *before* you write. I'm assuming you are writing fiction. You're doing the first bit of research by reading this chapter. Next, check on the bookshop shelves. See what's happening in crime fiction – women and forensics and pathology are the in thing – but for how long?

Maybe you want to consider another angle. Thinking of writing a children's novel? How long will it be? At 100,000 words your story may prove too expensive. A publisher may be reluctant to put up the money for a first-time writer and a 300-page teenage novel, unless your name's Philip Pullman. What age ranges do publishers divide the kid-lit market into? Are you aiming for the 7–9 year olds? Or the 11–13s? What's the average length for each category? What sort of book is getting published here? Do kids' books divide along genre lines like adult ones do? Are there crime novels for children? Sci-fi? Horror? If so, do they interest you? Read a few. See what the standards are like. Are you after character development and psychological reality, or a fast-paced narrative where plot is king? Is it social realism you want, or a good escapist read? All this is before-writing research and will help clarify your fictional aims and add a touch of market realism to your grand ideas.

Select your readership. Browse in Waterstone's and sample read over cups of cappuccino. You'll be surprised how bad some published work is, and how much better you could do. Read magazines like *The Bookseller, Publishing News, The Rights Report* for trends and insider knowledge. These trade publications offer you an inside glimpse of market workings. For instance, you might see what a particular agent is interested in from reports of their recent acquisitions and deals. If it looks from these accounts that they could be interested in your kind of work, give them a ring. In this game you've got to push yourself and sell yourself. Shrinking violets needn't apply!

But, remember it's different if you're just browsing the market for ideas on *what* to write. I'm talking about a situation in which you already have an idea for a book and I'm suggesting how you can save yourself a lot of time and heartache by using research to make sure your work fits into the requirements of the market.

...And After

The other kind of research is the after-writing kind. By this I mean sussing out, not the products out there, but the main players – primarily agents and publishers. Here you are an outsider and dependent on a few expert guides on how the market drivers work. Apart from the trade journals mentioned above, the two best guides and essential reading for new writers are *The Writers' and Artists' Year Book* and *The Writer's Handbook*. Both list all UK and some overseas book and magazine publishers, all literary agents, and both offer sound advice on presentation of manuscripts and proposals.[1]

Agents...

These days more and more publishers are refusing unsolicited manuscripts, so start with agents not publishers. Today, publishing houses are relying on agents to do their initial sifting out of the good from the bad, the unpublishable from the publishable. Even publishers who do read new material often employ freelance readers to go through their 'slush' pile (unsolicited manuscripts) and depend on them for recommendations.

So, a good agent is the key to getting published. It follows therefore that nowadays, it's harder to get an agent than it is to get a publisher, and you want a *good* agent, one who will know your work, and know which publisher is best for you. What an agent does is promote you, enthuse others – editors, publicity and marketing people – about your work, advise what will and won't sell, keep your publisher in line and, if you're really lucky, do some sharp editing of your manuscript and advise on changes.

Not-so-good agents will not set up an initial meeting, will not offer market or editorial advice, will hand over everything to publishers (if they get one for your work), will not keep an eye on progress, will not talk and report back often over the phone enthused and optimistic, will never take you out to lunch, will not discuss future projects. Remember a good agent wants you for life, wants to build up a good working and personal relationship with you, wants to map out your future writing with you. A good agent is a networker who keeps their finger on the market pulse, who has contacts not just in the UK, but in Europe and USA through their associated agents and subagents, and who knows everyone in the trade. And more importantly knows what's happening inside publishing houses. She might find out on the grapevine that one publisher is looking to develop a new list in children's books and wants writers who can turn in socially real, hard-edged material.

Now how could any writer know about this critical info? It takes a good agent, ear to the ground, to know this and seize the opportunity on your behalf. Thus, what you are getting for your money (you pay an agent 10 per cent of royalties as a fee) is an unrivalled knowledge of the market and a powerful advocate for your work.

A good agent knows how to wheel and deal; she is someone with commercial savvy; she can talk to BBC film producers or French subagents on your behalf at the Frankfurt Book Fair or the Bologna International Children's Book Fair; she is someone who is familiar with contractual arrangements and she can check through the 20-page contract a publisher is offering you and advise on its appropriateness, and she controls the translation rights, subsidiary rights, and manages film options, and how advance royalties are paid and so on. This sort of advice is critical nowadays. Contracts are getting more and more restrictive. Good advice about the legal aspects of publishing also comes from *The Society of Authors*, the writers' union. Other brilliant sources of information are listed below.

...And How To Get One

Convinced you need an agent? Here's how to get one.

First, I repeat, *Write a Good Book*. If it's good, it will get taken up by an agent and it will get published.

Next, go through the agents given in one of the guides mentioned above. The entries will tell you what kinds of genre they deal in; make a list of the ones most suited to your work. Obviously, if you've written a historical novel, don't send it to an agent specialising in biographies and technical subjects. Be realistic. And eliminate from your shopping list agents who state, 'no unsolicited manuscripts'. This means they have a full client list and are not taking on new ones.

Having made your list, ring each one up to ask whether they are still taking on new clients. Check their submission requirements. This is usually: 2/3 chapters (typed, double-spaced, A4 one sided), synopsis, and a covering letter explaining who you are, a bit of background, target readership for your work especially if non-fiction, and where you think your work fits into the market. Enclose an SAE and address it to a named person. If the guide doesn't give the name of the editor you want, phone and find out, especially if you have an old guide. In this business, people change jobs often. Getting the right person gives a good first impression.

The submission letter should convince the agent they are dealing with someone who knows what they're about, has done their research and has a commercial proposition. For non-fiction works you really need a proposal: this includes an extended summary of the book, with main argument, chapter headings if possible, a statement of market appeal, a rationale for the book in commercial terms, and three sample chapters. Keep a copy of your submission. Agents and publishers always run a disclaimer that they are not responsible for loss or damage to the work.

If you've not heard from an agent within three weeks, call and make polite enquiries. Polite, because that's the way you are: why antagonise people who may be able to help you? A middle-sized agency may get up to 100–200 manuscripts a week, and it's tough turning that amount of reading round quickly.

The Marketing Buzz

So, you've got an agent and the agent has come up trumps: the book is with the publishing house. Home and dry? Not quite.

An unhelpful trend is the increasing power of marketing and publicity teams within big publishing houses. This is two-edged again. If your work is taken up by a big house, they will have the resources to push your work with wholesalers, reviewers and booksellers prior to launch, and to market you strongly after launch. What publicity departments aim to do is create a 'buzz' about a book, talk it up within the company so everyone inside is gunning for the book. They want everyone onside to push it with distributors, librarians and award committees so that a wave of expectancy rises with publication date and the book becomes a bestseller. A good agent will also try and create a buzz when selling a book to publishers, talking it up over the phone, over lunch and so on. And once a book is sold, agent and publisher work together to promote it.

On the other hand, if a book is slow to sell, it is Marketing who decide to remainder it, just as it is Marketing and Publicity who decide whether to promote a book strongly or ignore it in the first place. Your publishing editor has no say in these critical decisions, however much he or she believes in the book.

Perhaps most telling is the growing management habit of appointing marketing people as editors in their publishing houses. What happens to literary quality then, and to real editorial guidance and advice so essential to new writers on the brink of being published?

But you can help the marketing department. Make suggestions. Listen to theirs. And keep smiling. Do the readings. Sign the copies. And smile.

Alternative Forms of Publication

Community publishing

Co-operatives set up within a community centre, Adult Ed. class or arts centre offer opportunities for group publishing, especially collections of shorter works such as poetry and short stories. Research is the answer here. Check in local libraries for information.

Small Presses

They publish poetry and short story collections/anthologies as well as works of fiction. See the Independent Publishers' Guild (ipg) website listed below for details.

Arts Projects

Regional Arts Boards through their literary officers *promote* writing through a wide variety of schemes which include publishing ventures. Contact the local Board for details or website.

Self-publishing

Not to be confused with vanity publishing where a company offers you a flattering assessment of your work and thereby persuades you to part with a lot of money in exchange for publishing your book. Self-publishing is about taking advantage of desktop publishing technology and producing your own book with the help of a local printer. See *Self-Publishing: Not So Difficult After All*. Contact: 25 St Benedict's Close, Church Lane, London, SW17 9NX.

Electronic publishing

The Internet offers a different kind of outlet. Just set up a web page and fill it with a few biographical notes and the text of your book?

Easy! And there are off-the-shelf electronic publishers. They have different levels of product. And pricing structures. You can get a book in plain format (title and text only), or with illustrated cover and text or with state of the art design and formatting. It works like this. You select what quality of product you want, pay by credit card and one master copy is stored and catalogued on the publisher's web site. When a reader comes along who wants to buy they pay by credit card and are then able to download your book. Easy again. See Barnes and Noble's web pages.

Facts and Reassuring Figures

The good news is this: 120,000 books were published in 2002, and the numbers are not going down. Surely one of those could be yours. And my tip for the top? Children's books. There's a big surge of interest amongst publishers and readers, especially for cross-readership works, ones that are read by kids and grown-ups. Books by Philip Pullman, J. K. Rowling and Mark Haddon fit into this category. At the time of writing 70 per cent of the Harry Potter readership is adult!

And Finally...

Now write the book.

Further Reading

Chris McCallum (2003) *The Writers' Guide to Getting Published* (London: How To Books).
    Covers all aspects of writing – fiction, non-fiction, poetry and script-writing. And all markets from small presses to the Internet.
The Writers' and Artists' Yearbook (London: A & C Black).
    The essential market tool. Many useful articles on aspects of writing and publishing as well as exhaustive lists of agents and publishers, national and international.
Michelle Howry (ed.) (2002) *Agents, Editors and You: The Insider's Guide to Getting Your Book Published* (New York: Writer's Digest Books).
    An American publication but contains good general advice and opens up a larger world of opportunity to the writer.

Rhonda Whitton and Sheila Hollingworth (2001) *A Decent Proposal: How to sell your book to an Autralian publisher* (Melbourne: Common Ground Publishing).
Excellent step-by-step instructions for Australian writers seeking markets.

Almost Famous

Dear Auntie,
I'm a brilliant writer, but no one's discovered me yet. Why is it that only my mother thinks I'm any good?

And have you sent off any work yet?

Er...not exactly...

Bad news for writers: no one's going to come knocking on your door, and discover you for a grateful world, and publish all the novels gathering dust under your bed. Think about it: if you don't send out your stuff, how will they know which door to knock on?

Is it because you fear failure?

Maybe

I've seen this happen so many times. Does this sound familiar? You've taken the advice in the books, started early; you've not waited for inspiration, but written yourself into being inspired; you've paddled valiantly against the rip tide of the bad days; you've surfed the magnificent rolling waves of the good days, and now – oh, momentous day – the thing is finished. What a feeling. You have conquered. You are a Champion. And then, through the rose-tinted binoculars of desperate hopefulness, you see the distant shoreline of publication and instant success, and the leaves on the trees are fluttering like cheques.

And then the ominous music starts. Fins slice the water. The sharks of doubt begin to circle you! So you spellcheck everything again. You read the manuscript through again, and realise that everything is terrible; you'll have to rewrite it; you'll just change that word; you'll check over that part again; and change that word back again. And when you read it all through again you find that it's not terrible anymore: it's worse than terrible! It needs totally rewriting. It needs screwing up. It needs burning. You can't possibly send it off to anyone in this state...

And so, dear Writer, yet again, you don't actually finish writing, let alone getting to the point of sending it out anywhere. The fear that it might fail prevents you from letting go, because – take a deep breath – if you don't send it out it can't fail.

But it can't succeed either.

27 Writing As Self-Invention

Julie Armstrong

Why do people want to write? It can, after all, be a frustrating activity, and a very lonely job, as Stephen King notes in *On Writing*. However, whether one is a published writer or not, writing is rewarding, if not a compulsion, a way of life.

The Autobiography in Writing

Writing is self-expression. When we write, we preserve emotions, thoughts, experiences, relationships and memories: writing captures the importance they had, just as photographs can capture *defining* moments. Writing enables us to mourn our losses and celebrate our joys. All writing is autobiographical in that the fictional worlds you create come from you: undoubtedly, the trace elements of your unique experiences are in your narratives, waiting to be found by someone who knows what they're looking for. And what autobiography is ever totally and utterly as it happened? Writing gives you a second chance: you can take revenge; you can refashion the dialogue as you wish you'd said it. Rebuilding and rewriting events from our lives, however much they are framed as things that happen to our characters, helps us make sense of them. Writing is thus a way of discovering who you are, and working through the parts of your life that trouble you. Alice Sebold has done both in her memoir, *Lucky*, and the companion novel *The Lovely Bones*.[1] In other words, if you want it to be, it can be a form of therapy, psychoanalysis even.

Writing is often seen as a search for some kind of truth. Maybe life doesn't seem 'true' until it is written down and encapsulated

257

in a form. Whatever your views, if you want to write, writing has to be essential to your well-being as an individual. If not, why do it?

So what *exactly* is it that makes us want to write?

As well as being a craft and an art form, writing is an intellectual and philosophical pursuit. As a student of writing you will be a thinker: you'll observe life, reflect upon it, then explore your findings and experiences through creative writing. Why? What is it that makes YOU want to write? Why do you choose to express yourself in this way? Why words and not paint, your body, a musical instrument? It's an interesting and endlessly fascinating question, to which you may never find the answer.

Why Express Yourself Through Language?

Jot down some thoughts and ideas in response to the following questions:

■ Why do *you* express yourself through language?

■ How do you see the world?

■ What is the use of reading? And writing?

Writing can offer a different way of looking at things and the world: it is often about asking and answering questions; you should take some time to ponder the reasons for your wanting to engage in the process of writing.

What follows is a list of questions for you, the answers to which will give you insight into your motivation for writing. Don't worry if you can't answer some of them straight away: mull them over. The answers fill form over time.

■ *When did you first start writing?*
Some writers have written for as long as they can remember. During childhood, they may have simply scribbled in notebooks or kept a diary. A diary can be a place where we take refuge, as Anne Frank did. Other writers take it up out of the blue. There's no advantage in either position (readers can't tell that you've always wanted to be a writer!).

■ *What was your first piece of writing about? What inspired you to write it?*

Your first piece of writing – and by this I mean a longer work, something you've spent time crafting – may well have been autobiographical or it may have been an escape world you created, in the same way that a child has an imaginary friend.

■ *What is your favoured form? Why?*

There are no rules: you don't have to stick at writing just poetry, or fiction, or scripts. And you can write in any genre you choose, be it science fiction, magic realism, romance or thriller, whatever. However, the chances are you'll find yourself gravitating towards a particular form and genre. Experiment and discover what is best for you.

■ *What themes recur in your work?*

There are often repetitive themes across the body of a writer's work: these will reflect the ideas and subjects that fascinate the writer. They will also reflect a world-view, of which the writer herself may be unaware. When you've finished a piece of work, sit down and ask yourself: what's it all about? How does this compare with other pieces I've written?

■ *Do you have to write?*

If the answer is no, forget it. Writing has to have relevance in your life. Writing *is* a life. Yes, it's a slog, fraught with disappointments, but it's also fulfilling and fun. It can also be a means of escape: while he was writing during his lunch hour, Stephen King was transcending the workplace and his boss!

■ *Do you look at the world differently when you write?*

Of course, it's personal, but I suggest it's like putting on a pair of glasses: some things are blurred; others are in sharp focus. The world takes on a new perspective.

Answering such questions helps you become a more self-aware writer. Having read this chapter you might want to read chapter 9 'Looking Your Words in the Face: Reflection'.

A Journey of Self-discovery

It is worth contemplating the notion that writing is a journey of self-discovery, one in which we construct through language a sense of self. Writing is empowering, it can enable us to *save* our lives. Through writing we explore our identities, confirm and affirm them, and find a sense of control over our lives (however illusory that sense might be). It enables us to make sense of the world, and our role in it. Through the act of writing we solve problems, record, order, process and express our experiences and communicate these to others, the reader being the 'other'. We learn what it means to be human.

Other Worlds, Other Selves

As we've mentioned elsewhere in this book, if you don't read you'll find it very hard to be a good writer: reading is an excellent focus for a writer's craft. Ask yourself this: do you read to be entertained, or to be given something to think about? Perhaps both? And what do you like to read? Fantasy, horror, crime? Of course the list of genres is endless, but in each case, when you read, you enter other worlds, and so it is when you write: the virtual reality of the imagination, of writing, is one where writers and readers step out of real time and space into other dimensions, other worlds. Adam Thorpe speaks of taking the reader into his own universe, a universe that he likens to a wild garden or the forest.[2] When we make up other worlds, we can briefly forget this one. How liberating!

In postmodern times there isn't a single 'truth' or viewpoint: we are free to discover other selves and to create other realities. As writers, we have ultimate freedom to construct worlds outside and beyond our environment, beyond our experiences and cultural history. The only limitation is our imagination.

Try This: Fictional Worlds

Think of a world you experienced vividly when reading a book: you may have read the book years ago, and intricate plot details may have faded, but your memory of the world might still be as fresh as the day it was imprinted into your imagination. Describe it.

The Best Time to Be a Writer

Take time now to reflect upon your writing process. The process of writing is a *personal* journey, a different journey for every writer, but one of the most fascinating journeys you can make. We all have a time when our imagination is most fertile, a time when our creative juices flow unhindered. For some writers this may be at night, for others very early in the morning. These are quiet times, when we're more in touch with our unconscious, when we can inhabit the 'secret' place of our imagination and explore our secret lives, our lives beyond our 'real' lives. It's just a question of dipping into our creative drive. Chapter 6, 'Dreams and Visions' might help you now.

Try This: Self-Invention

In an ideal world what kind of person would you like to be? What attributes would you like to have? For example: I'd like to be able to fly. Now write for 10 minutes without stopping. Now put this character into a predicament and write them trying to work themselves free. You have the rough beginnings of a piece of writing. Take it further. Take it any direction you choose. Write with it for half an hour.

Further Reading

Natalie Goldberg (1986) *Writing Down the Bones* (New York: Shambhala).
   A marvellous book that should be on every writer's bookshelf.
Michèle Roberts (1998) *Food, Sex and God: Inspiration and Writing* (London: Virago).
   Roberts articulates wonderfully the private process of constructing identity and reinvention of the self through language.

28 How Not Being Published Can Change Your Life

Heather Leach

Not Thinking About Elephants

Here's a story. You wake up one morning and make your way slowly and carefully down to the place where they give you some coffee. You're nursing a headache: let's not go into the reasons why. You look out of the window and see whatever's out there: grass, street, traffic; the usual. Somebody, a friend, sits down opposite you and tells you to cheer up. You don't cheer up. They say, this so-called friend, 'OK. Well, just don't think about elephants', and then they get up and go away, whistling. Loudly. You stare at the tabletop and try to forget what they just said. You look out of the window and see, mixed in with the grass, street, traffic, the faint but unmistakable outline of an elephant. You shut your eyes. No, you think to yourself, I don't want to think of an ... But the word insinuates itself into your mind: the more you tell yourself not to think of an elephant, the stronger the thought-elephant becomes. Test this for yourself – with a little variation. Today, as you go about your normal business, try not to think about a giraffe. Try hard.

Writers are often told not to think about publication: just to get on and write their book, story, poem, script: to do their very best to forget about money, fame, the admiration of friends and foes, critical and commercial success. Love of words, language, story: that's the real point, we are told, it's what we tell ourselves. Art, inventiveness, creativity is what it's all about, not all that crass and greedy ambition. There's truth and value in this, of course there is, but, in my

262

experience, for most writers, not thinking about publication just isn't possible, and the more you try not to think about it, the bigger the thought grows.

Look Away Now

John Singleton's wise and witty chapter 26: 'Getting Published', gives a sound practical guide to the publishing world. As he rightly asserts, if you have writing talent, if you try hard and keep at it, then you have a fair chance of publication in some form or other. But in *this* chapter, I want to explore some of the more edgy and ambiguous sides of the drive to be published. There's a lot of good news to come but I'll begin with the bad news, so if you don't want to hear it, look away now:

- Most writers don't make much money.

- Most writers don't make any money.

- Most writers don't gain commercial success.

- Most writers don't gain critical success.

- Most writers don't get published at all.

There are lots of different reasons for this: the writing isn't good enough; the writer gives up too soon; they're not writing for the right markets; the writing is really good but nobody wants to pay for it; the writer hasn't got a famous dad; they don't live next door to a publisher; they didn't go to the right school. These are just a few reasons, but there are plenty more. You can't do anything about a lot of them, so it's probably best not to waste energy worrying about them. (I say probably because I have to admit to not always taking my own advice. I do get hot under the collar about versions of *my dad/brother/mother's auntie just happens to be a big publisher but it's never made any difference to me* ... but I try to keep it under control.) But you can make a difference to one or two of them:

- Buy more books, including poetry, by unknown writers. This is another version of reading as a writer. If you don't want to read other people's new writing, first novels and so on, how can you expect other people to want to read yours?

- Write better.

- Keep on trucking. If you have any reason at all to believe that you have writing ability and that you have something to say, then keep going. Don't give up in face of rejection.

That word: *rejection*. It's painful, awkward, humiliating. It has echoes of being the only kid in the playground who doesn't get picked, of being dumped by a lover, of not getting the job. And yet, despite the unpleasantness of the word and the experience, the majority of writers who send their work off for publication have to get used to being rejected as a part of the job. All those jokes about rejection letters being used to paper the walls: such light-hearted courage, such pitiful denial. We hear famous stories about writers who didn't get recognised to begin with: Charlotte Brontë, Emily Dickinson, Franz Kafka. And then the stories of people who sent off their books to publisher after publisher, each one of whom foolishly rejected it until the final ... well, you know how it goes; we think: that could be me ... one day it will happen, preferably before I'm dead. And it's true, it might. But, then again, it might not.

Perhaps you don't want to think about this. Let's face it, *I* don't want to think about it and I'm writing it. After all, I'm a writer too. And not rich or famous either. Yet. But this is a book for writers who want to *think about* writing, as well as simply to *be* writers. We need to find a meaningful and realistic way to deal with ambition and rejection and that means, I believe, looking at them hard.

I sometimes think that the writer's ambition for publication is like doing the lottery. You know that the likelihood of getting your work accepted is low and that there are so many other punters that your little story may get lost in the machine. But the dream itself is so compelling that you forget all that cold and scary realism and take your chance. You need to have a bit of the gambler in you to have a chance of making it as a writer: after all, if you're not in it you can't win it. But if the gambling becomes compulsive, if you think about publication as your be-all and end-all then you're probably on a serious loser. You have to think about it but not too much. You have to think about it without thinking about it. Like the elephant. No one said being a writer would be easy.

OK. Let's wind this one up. So it's hard to get published and most writers don't make it. So publishing is a buyer's market. So not many people read books by unknown writers and even fewer buy them. So what? That's the bad news. End of. If you're keen I won't have put you off. You've looked the Gorgon in the face and she hasn't turned you to stone. There's plenty of good news.

There Are Readers All Around You

Writers need readers but you don't have to wait for the big publishing break to find them. There are lots of opportunities to communicate, to try out ideas, to get a response from others – but you may have to think local, not global – at least as a start.

Write for Yourself: You're Worth It!

You are your own first reader. This is the way many of us begin: writing a diary or poetry about our lives, thoughts, feelings and there is no reason why you can't continue. You don't need to show anybody else what you've written, and you can allow yourself to be honest and direct in a way you couldn't be if other people were to read it. There are plenty of people who will knock this kind of writing, complaining that it isn't real writing: just therapy; an overflow of emotion or ego; too individual and personal et cetera et cetera. Ignore them. Writing belongs to you: do what you like with it. Writing for yourself is a way of deepening and strengthening your own ideas and sense of self; it can help you to understand the way your mind works; the way you relate to others; the way you change through time.

Writing doesn't have to be a stepping stone on the way to somewhere else; it can be an end in itself: a way of making yourself up as you go along. Even with this kind of writing, I think you should set yourself some expectations and challenges, otherwise you will lose momentum and the writing self you make up won't be as interesting as it could be. My checklist would be:

- Be as honest with yourself as you dare.

- Use the writing to learn: ask questions; be curious.

- Describe and comment on what you observe and experience, including other people as well as your inner world.

- Keep trying to find the best words, the most accurate description.

- Read other people's diaries: Samuel Pepys's diary is probably the most celebrated; still a good read and a good example of honesty, observation and lively writing.

Write for Your Family and Friends

'Every family needs a writer.' I can't remember who said this but it makes a lot of sense. Writers observe. They witness events: births and deaths; divorces and love stories; funerals and holidays. They describe people, houses, animals; they notice the things other people miss; they analyse and interpret; they keep a record; they pass on stories from one generation to the next. The sad thing is that most of the stories passed on in this way are written by established and published writers. Most family history and experience soon gets lost: people die and the stories they told get forgotten. Photographs and films usually show a happy but superficial world, but they lack an individual viewpoint, interpretation, creative narrative. A lot of people who would not consider themselves writers already write a little: speeches at weddings; eulogies at funerals; letters and the like, but there is a lot of scope to extend this, to make writing a part of a family's record, its story of itself.

Make Up Stories for the Children You Know

Think about what different age groups like. Try them out and choose the most popular. Read, give or send them to the children: email could be a good method if you and the children have access. Ask the children to comment on them; what they like and dislike. Ask them to be really honest. Write them down and develop them further. You could collect these stories into books.

When you're away from people, instead of, or as well as, normal letters or emails, keep a continuous written record of your experience in episodes. Edit and rewrite as you would any other piece of writing and then send or give them in chapters to people.

Write Greeting Card Poems for People You Know

Write a more personal, witty poem than the commercial ones. The opportunities are endless: birthdays, weddings, Valentine's Day, new babies, moving house, the death of the goldfish. Every family needs a poet.

Be the Recorder for a Special Event

Pick out what goes on at the margins as well as the centre. Use your writerly abilities: storytelling; detailed observation and description; listening carefully to voices and getting them down accurately; scene-setting; truth-telling. You could interview people during or after the event, and use their perspective to add to your account. Add your own viewpoint and interpretation – this is real writing not tape-recording. Write it up afterwards and lay it out as a booklet. Include an introduction explaining the way it was done and why it's important to be accurate and honest. Send or give copies to key people and ask for feedback. Then think of ways to distribute it. And don't forget the ideas given in other chapters: have a look at chapter 23, 'Writing Play' and then make a pop-up book to celebrate baby Joe's christening; Sally's graduation day; Gill and Jack's Golden Wedding...

Write a Description of Family Members/of Friends

Describe them in detail: looks, character, strengths. Include stories about them; things that have happened to them; the way they've developed and changed. Don't be cruel or hurtful but try to be accurate and particular. Miss out people you don't like. Collaborate with the photographer in the group and produce an album or exhibition: words alongside pictures.

Write Your Autobiography

Writing can be more subtle and more powerful than the spoken word – use it to communicate, to tell your own story.

Write Other People's Biographies

There are lots of people out there with really good stories to tell but without the skill or confidence to write them. Ask questions, find out about people and offer to write their stories. Tell them it will be collaborative with both your names on the final product.

I can already hear some readers going *aaaargh*! at these suggestions. It's true there are problems with this kind of writing. One of the biggest is bad writing. If you are determined to upset nobody, to tell only sweet stories, to avoid controversy, and to present yourself and everybody else in a shining and golden light, you will almost certainly produce bland and boring stuff. Those embarrassing round robins which people send at Christmas are often written in this kind of style, which is why they come in for so much stick. Many family histories and autobiographies are not very exciting and dynamic because they are written in syrupy-hindsight language. And the sins are multifarious: piety, self-congratulation, humourlessness, perfect lives with no mistakes, sex or swearing. They all equal tedious reading. Don't go there. Write the best you can, even if the audience is only yourself or one or two others.

Another problem is that you might annoy people: you could hurt feelings; you could lose friends and relations, although in some cases, let's face it, that could be a good thing. You will need to be thoughtful about whom you show your writing to and how you present it. But this is true of commercially published work too. Many so-called *fictional* stories, scripts and novels are thinly disguised autobiographies: many an angst-ridden poem is based on the real-life marriage and break-up of actual people. Think Sylvia Plath and Ted Hughes for starters. It's in your control how much you tell and how much you keep quiet: writing is not a court of law; you may want to tell the truth but not the whole truth. If you really can't bear to let anyone see what you've written, then write for people not yet born: speak to them directly, imagine them finding your words, show them this world, this time.

Start Your Own Group

Other chapters in this book have suggested contacting local writers' groups, writing festivals and competitions, details of which you can find in libraries and local arts boards. There are, however, plenty of other ways of finding your own readers.

■ *Find some like-minded people*
If you're on a course identify a few people you think you might get on with and arrange to meet once a week to read each other's work.

■ *Read / perform your work at a poetry slam or pub writers' event*
Some venues have a slot for anyone willing to stand up and try out their work on the half-drunk audience. You probably need to be half-drunk yourself, but it can be a great thrill to be up there with your adrenaline buzzing and those beer glasses flying.

■ *Produce your own writer's magazine*
These days you don't need much equipment, just a computer and a printer. Advertise for writers to submit their work: produce as many as you can afford and distribute them as widely as possible.

But It May Happen ...

You may not want to try any of these. You may consider them small beer compared to the 'real' thing and want to wait until *it* happens for you. Fine. You may make it happen: you might just write that great book or script, and it's funny, clever, beautiful, popular – everything you wish it to be. Accepted by a publisher and actually paid for, your work is recognised by the public, admired by the critics. Of course, it could happen. There is absolutely no reason why not. It has already happened to thousands of writers. Believe it and work for it. But while you're waiting, I think it helps if you can reflect on and reframe the ways you think about being a writer.

Think Hard about Why You Were Attracted to Writing in the First Place

I've included a questionnaire at the end of this chapter that you can use to reflect on your beginnings as a writer. The point of this exercise is to help you revisit the freshness of your early ambitions. You may have wanted to emulate a writer you liked or to put down on paper something you couldn't put into speech. You may have written something for a school project, which turned out to be good. There are all kinds of reasons writers start, but only rarely are they based on the desire for fame or loadsamoney. Most of us begin because we like it, sometimes with the added perk that other people (teachers/parents/friends) also like it. All writers need readers, but you don't have to wait for the big publishing break to find them. Of course, most of us change as we grow older: we become a little more cynical, greedy and egotistic. The world's a tough place. But from time to time it helps to revisit those beginnings, to rediscover that original spark and to make it burn again.

Remembering Why You're a Writer

Remember the first piece of creative writing that no one made you do: the piece you wrote just for yourself.

- Did you show the first writing you ever did to anyone? If not, why not?

- Who did you write for: was there someone you wanted to show it to but didn't? Who were your first readers?

- Were you praised for your writing? Or did you get negative responses? Give details.

- Who are you writing for *now*?

Not Waiting but Writing

Remember the bad news at the beginning of this chapter and don't wait too long. Think about all the other things people do: cycling, playing football, making music, painting, pig breeding, dancing. The pig breeder may sometimes dream of one day being recognised as the best pig breeder in Britain, Europe, the world: there may be big prizes to be won, and there is almost certainly a pig breeder's Man Booker prize. But does the pig breeder stay sulkily and artistically at home waiting to be recognised before he or she lets anybody look at his or her half-grown piglets? You know the answer already. That pig breeder is out there with all the other hopeful pig-breeders, *living* pig-breeding because that's what you do with life, you live it now. If your work lies unread in a pile on your desk or locked in a cupboard then it still isn't quite real. All writers need readers, so get out there and find them. Think laterally and creatively about ways to get your own and other people's work out there into a public space. *Live* writing. Oink!

Further Reading

D. Morley and K. Worpole (eds) (1982) *The Republic of Letters: Working Class Writing and Local Publishing* (London: Comedia).
A hotchpotch of information, ideas, writing and resources for writers beyond the fringe. A bit outdated, but still useful.
T. Olson (1980) *Silences* (London: Virago).
Another lucky bag of gorgeous stuff. A creative work in itself, the book explores the reasons and history and politics of many writers' blocks and silences.
R. Lathem, (ed.) (2003) *The Diary of Samuel Pepys: A Selection* (London: Penguin).
Speaks for itself.

V
Going Further

Writers' Websites

Creative Writing in Education

NAWE
National Association of Writers in Education
http://www.nawe.co.uk/scripts/WebObjects.exe/naweSite/
Shedloads of resources relating to creative writing – and not just relevant to those working in an education context. They are, they say, 'the one organization supporting the development of creative writing of all genres and in all educational settings throughout the UK.'

AWP
The Association of Writers and Writing Programs
http://awpwriter.org/
Especially good for writers' conferences and finding postgraduate programmes in the US. The AWP supports 'over 24,000 writers at over 370 member colleges and universities and 125 writers' conferences and centres.'

Varuna
www.varuna.com.au/
A wealth of writing experience with an Australian focus.

Getting Published/Performed

www.bloomsburymagazine.com
Clear precise guidance for new writers and a firsthand account of one writer's attempts to get published.

www.publishing-services.co.uk
An annotated catalogue of excellent web sites and a brilliant resource. Pick and choose.

www.writers.net
Especially useful for research that may lead to you finding an agent.

Independent Publishers' Guild
http://www.ipg.uk.com
This is the Independent Publishers' Guild's site and has an excellent list of resources for all kinds of publishing.

writersroom
http://www.bbc.co.uk/writersroom/
Like pretty much the whole of the BBC's website, this is brilliant, packed with writers' resources and an essential destination for anyone wanting to learn about writing for television, radio and film and, importantly, layout.

www.irdp.co.uk
Everything you ever needed to know about radio drama. Now go and listen to some!

www.booktrust.org.uk
Full of info about the book world, including links to sites like book-trusted.com – a resource for those writing for children.

Writing on the Web

www.trace.ntu.ac.uk
Online writing community created by Sue Thomas and based in Nottingham Trent University. Gateway to many cutting edge hypertext and multimedia experiments, plus debate. Accessible. Rich in ideas and experiments.

www.nickbantock.com *and* **www.griffinandsabire.com**
This is beautiful to look at, the love story works quite well, and it even has W.B. Yeats reciting his own poem. There is some inter-activity and the animated visuals, while enjoyable, are often unconnected to the storyline. Bantock is a good writer but a better visual artist and animator: the visuals are stunning and inventive; the story is good but without much depth. However, everybody who has seen it loves it, and as an inspirational example of a creative word/image/interactive project – this is one of the best so far.

www.cobralingus.com
Jeff Noon's idea is to apply techniques from dance music to the production of words. He begins with his own fiction or pieces 'sampled' from elsewhere and then puts them through some 'remixing' process. There are examples and you can have a go yourself. The idea of transferring a method or technique from one art form to another has been tried often before with mixed results but this site is worth a visit and you might get inspired.

British Electronic Poetry Centre, www.soton.ac.uk/~bepc
Electronic Poetry Center, www.epc.buffalo.edu/

Graphic Novels

http://www.mit.edu/people/rei/Expl.html
A useful summary of Japanese Manga.

http://my.voyager.net/~sraiteri/graphicnovels.htm.
Steve Raiter's website

http://www.guardian.co.uk/online/story/0,3605,544266,00.html
Tim Guest's article on web-based graphic novels is at *Guardian Unlimited* – a portal to many intriguing websites.

Writing Play

http://pharmdec.wustl.edu/juju/surr/surrealism.html
(Surrealism.)

http://www.iwm.org.uk/online/enigma/eni-intro.htm
(Codes and cyphers at The Enigma Pages: The Imperial War Museum website.)

http://www.philobiblon.com/isitabook
(*Is It A Book* website, an exploration and appreciation of various arts, looking at how they may enhance the life of the mind.)

http://www.wordsmith.org/anagram/advanced.html
(Word-play.)

Web Links

http://www.writersdigest.com/101sites/2003_index.asp
writersdigest.com is the huge site of the venerable American writers' magazine, *Writers' Digest* – not in the least to be confused with *Readers' Digest*. The link here takes you to their annual *101 Best Web Sites for Writers* and if that doesn't satisfy your lust for more, go back to the parent site and explore a raft of material on writer's craft.

A Writer's Bookshelf

Writers' Companions

Becoming a Writer, Dorothea Brande (London: Pan; 1996)[1]
Writing Down the Bones: Freeing the Writer Within, Natalie Goldberg (Boston: Shambala Publications, 1986)
Bird By Bird – Some Instructions on Writing and Life, Anne Lamott (New York: Anchor Books, 1995)
On Writing, Stephen King, New English Library (London: Hodder & Stoughton, 2000)
The Creative Writing Coursebook. Forty Writers Share Advice and Exercises for Poetry and Prose, ed. Julia Bell and Paul Magrs (London: Palgrave Macmillan, 2001)
The Writer's Workbook, 2nd edn, ed. Jenny Newman Edmund Cusick and Aileen La Tourette (London: Arnold, 2004)

Writing Fiction

Writing Fiction: A Guide To Narrative Craft, Janet Burroway (New York: HarperCollins, 1992)
The Art of Fiction: Notes on Craft for Young Writers, John Gardner (New York: Vintage Books, 1991)
How To Write A Damn Good Novel, James N. Frey (London: Macmillan, 1988)
Plot, Ansen Dibell (London: Robinson Publishing, 1988)
Self-Editing for Fiction Writers: Show and Tell, Renni Browne and Dave King (New York: HarperCollins, 1991)

279

Scriptwriting

Story: Substance, Structure, Style, and the Principles of Screenwriting,
   Robert McKee (New York: HarperCollins, 1997)
The Definitive Guide to Screenwriting, Syd Field (London: Ebury
   Press, 2003)
The Sound of One Hand Clapping, Sheila Yeger (London: Amber
   Press, 1990)
Writing For Radio, Vincent McInerney (Manchester: Manchester
   University Press, 2001)
The Writer's Handbook Guide to Writing for Stage and Screen, ed.
   Barry Turner (London: Pan Macmillan, 2003)

Writing Poetry

Getting Into Poetry, Paul Hyland (Newcastle-upon-Tyne: Bloodaxe,
   1993)
The Practice of Poetry: Writing Exercises from Poets who Teach, ed.
   Robin and Twichell Behne (New York: Quill, 1992)
Binary Myths, Andy Brown (Exeter: Stride Books, 2004)
Poets on Writing: Britain 1970–1991, ed. Denise Riley (London:
   Macmillan – now Palgrave Macmillan, 1992)
Modern Poets on Modern Poetry, ed. James Scully (London: Fontana,
   1966)[2]

Anthologies

Fiction
The Story And Its Writer, Ann Charters (New York: Bedford Books
   of St. Martin's Press, 1995)[3]
Scriptwriting
The Radio Times (UK TV and Radio Listings Magazine). Your
   guide to a conceptual visual and aural anthology!
Poetry
Poems For The Millenium, Volume 2: From Postwar To Milennium,
   ed. Jerome Rothenburg (Berkeley, CA: University of California
   Press, 1998)[4]

Basics

The Ladybird Book of Spelling and Grammar, Audrey Daly, David Till
    (Illustrator) (London: Ladybird Books, 2000)[5]
Eats, Shoots and Leaves: The Zero Tolerance Approach to Punctuation,
    Lynne Truss (London: Profile Books, 2003)
*English Repair Kit: Spelling Repair Kit/Punctuation Repair Kit/
    Grammar Repair Kit*, Angela Burt, William Vandyck (London:
    Hodder, 2001)

Style

The Oxford Guide To Style, ed. Robert Ritter (Oxford: Oxford
    University Press, 2002)
The Elements of Style, ed. William I. Strunk and E.B. White, 4th
    edn (New Jersey: Longman, 2000)[6]

Appendix
Self-Assessment/
Annotated Bibliography
and Reflection

Lisa Ratcliffe[1]

(Edge Hill, BA Writing, 1999–2002)

Self-Assessment

The idea for this story was inspired by the work I have been doing for the Romantic and Gothic Popular Fiction Module, but for the writing of it, I am indebted to the visiting writer, Gareth Creer, and his wonderful lecture/workshop on Vogel's 'Hero's Journey'.

Using Vogel's 12-point plan I found it easy to map out the story of Marjory and her strange psychotic guest, Chloe, to create a moving narrative which I hope works well in engaging the reader. Whilst it was difficult to employ each of the 12 steps in such a short story, as opposed to a screenplay, or novel, I found I was able to adapt it to suit my needs. For example, I omitted the 'mentor' but employed Chloe as a 'shape shifter'.

I decided on telling the story using a third-person omniscient narrator, with sparse use of the passive voice, though the point of view rests heavily with Marjory, as it is her story.

Once I began to write the story, I found I had to make changes in order to tighten up the story, despite my concerns about losing tension. I had originally thought Marjory picked up the girl in her car, but then thought it more effective to have her come to the house instead, so that I could have a sinister figure passing the window, building reader tension. I am pleased with the final choice of opening and hope it works to pull the reader into the story quickly and effectively.

I worked hard on the dialogue, trying to get the balance just right, so that the reader can infer the undertones of the story without being too explicit, though I did feel the scene with the box in the bedroom necessary as it is not something Marjory would have discussed with anyone, let alone someone like Chloe. I had trouble trying to set out the dialogue correctly, interspersing it with the narrative voice, especially knowing where to begin on a new line. Eventually I opted for a new line each time I changed character, though I have probably made errors with indentation.

Writing this story was like a breath of fresh air, an opportunity to allow my imagination to run riot. It has been a long time since I have enjoyed my writing, something I have been quick to blame on deadlines and conflicting course work. I now feel, after attempting a gothic psychological thriller, that perhaps it was my choice of genre instead?

Writing the gory scenes was fun although I did have problems trying to choreograph the violent scene at the end. I reminded myself of the openings and closings of some of Stephen King's short stories which helped enormously. I intertextualised with the movie *The Crow* in order to create the character of Chloe, leaving the reader to decide whether or not she truly deserves vengeance, or just feels she should be judge and jury for Marjory's sins. There are also overtones of King's *Misery* but I have twisted it so that it is a mother/daughter relationship, and it is the 'guest' who has the upper hand, not the homeowner. I also looked at Angela Carter's *The Bloody Chamber* to see how she uses description to evoke a sense of the sublime. I drew on the features of Gothic, such as the isolated country house, the secret from the past returning to haunt the present, and the disgusting masses of blood at the end.

Throughout this story I have tried to follow the normal with the strange and then returning to normal again. It opens with Marjory in her ordinary world, slips into the sublime as the figure runs past the window, and then returns to normality when Marjory realises it is a young girl on the fells. Normality begins to slip away again with reference to the girl's jacket, which has, 'a painted face on the back, distorted and mocking' (p. 2). This tension builds (I hope), as Chloe makes herself far too comfortable in Marjory's house, and continues to the major turning point when Marjory discovers the cat. I hope I have managed to achieve a rising intensity from that point on, leading up to the final climax of the story and the pseudo-ending.

The ending was problematic as I did not feel the story had closure with Marjory bleeding to death on the fells alone and also, I wanted the body to disappear so that the reader never knows if she was real or supernatural, another gothic element. I employed the technique of a brief epilogue in order to tie up loose ends and allow the reader to see Marjory has reached the end of her journey, a changed woman who has learned to come to terms with her past.

As the final piece of work for the fiction-writing strand of my degree, I hope I have managed to employ the techniques I have acquired over the last three years. I have made a conscious effort to avoid repetition and other superfluous wording, to keep the pace moving briskly along, building tension through careful use of dialogue and narrative to create a story which leaves the reader feeling satisfied.

With so little time to write this story, I am indebted to my readers who brought my attention to inconsistencies. Through discussing their ideas of the characters I was able to hone the writing down so that their vision became closer to my own. They also helped me to see the good parts too, giving me the confidence to rework the piece until it was as finished as it could be before the deadline.

I hope the reader will enjoy reading this story as much as I have enjoyed writing it. Never has a first draft come with such delightful ease since I stopped writing fairy tales and turned to realist prose. My only wish is that Mr Creer could have come sooner, giving me much more time to work on this story, though perhaps it might even make a good novella. I think I may have just discovered a side to myself I never knew I had!

Annotated Bibliography

Carter, A. (1995) *The Bloody Chamber* (Vintage)
    Re-reading the openings to these stories gave me a strong sense of
    how which words to employ in creating a sense of the eerie and
    unnatural.
King, S. (1983) *Different Seasons* (Signet)
King, S. (1988) *Misery* (Hodder & Stoughton)
King, S. (1979) *Night Shift* (New English Library)

King's stories gave me a taste for the sublime many years ago, and I had forgotten how much I enjoyed his work. Whilst I do not wish to imitate his style, I do find him useful for technique and layout for dialogue, not to mention his way of building tension and suspense in his work.

Other

Lecture given by Gareth Creer, visiting writer.
Invaluable presentation of Vogel's 12-point 'Hero's Journey'. Using this 'master plan' I was able to come up with a first draft with relative ease and enjoyed doing it. Having such a structure is important because not only does it give something to follow, but it is only in knowing the 'rules' or 'forms' of writing, that one can move on to break them effectively.

Reflection

Work on good prose has three steps; a musical stage when it is composed, an architectonic one when it is built, and a textile one when it is woven. (Walter Benjamin, One Way Street: 'Caution: Steps')

Having purposely avoided 'writing' as a modular choice three years ago, it was with trepidation that I attended my first 'writing' seminar at Edge Hill. Due to a clerical error that reeked of Fate, I was now faced with what I knew to be a demanding course with an astronomical workload. I was also about to risk a quarter of my degree on 'talent', but worst of all, I would once again have to confront 'The Blank Page' and go to war with 'The Internal Censor'.

I should explain at this point, that I have been having a love hate affair with writing for as long as I can remember, a compulsion rather than a choice. I have filled countless diaries and journals with everything from biographical material to some very embarrassing poetry. I attended a writing course at Liverpool University after the birth of my first child and took out a subscription to *Writer's News* over ten years ago, but it has been these last three years writing at Edge Hill which have given me the direction and support necessary to improve my work and develop as a writer.

The writing modules at Edge Hill have forced me to complete work by a given deadline, essential for someone who had consistently abandoned all previous attempts of completing anything. Whilst I was happy with poetry and journalism, I battled through the script writing and found the fiction ridiculously difficult. My first attempts at the short story were abysmal. I could appreciate the qualities in the works of other writers and yet my own work still lacked. I read *Writer's News* avidly, studied Jean Saunders' *How To Write Realistic Dialogue* and everything I could find by Michael Legat and still, my prose, contrived and verbose, hung uneasily on non-existent plots. Deadlines loomed large in the distance and the blank page dared me to come up with something better. Luckily, help was at hand.

One of the methods we have used at Edge Hill, to overcome the blank page, is to start each session with a 10-minute writing 'burst'. This exercise of 'writing a stream of consciousness' on a given subject has been beneficial as it allows one to overcome the internal censor (which usually stops me dead with two sentences with one snide remark or another) leaving one with enough material to begin work on. If there is one thing I have learned, it has been that you cannot redraft and edit unless you have something to work with. I particularly liked Helen Newall's technique of playing a song repeatedly whilst writing a stream of consciousness to help bypass the internal censor, and it was during this exercise that the idea for *Bear Cubs* was born.

Practising these techniques at home has allowed me to reach a stage where I can produce a page of inane scrawl with relative ease. It was a joy to discover that even the best writers draft their work endlessly, that drafting is not meant to be a minimal process used by writers who cannot 'get it right' the first time (like myself), but one of the most fundamental stages of the creative process.

Producing something I like enough to work with is a struggle however, and to solve that problem, I have had to investigate my own reasons for writing.

Bear Cubs, written in my second year, was the first story to bring me closer to a sense of satisfaction. Realising that the writer must be fully engaged with the text if there is any hope for the reader to be so, I chose a subject I know and understand, taking the age old advice of 'writing what you know'. I experimented with the narrative structure in order to produce something more original than I had been doing up to that point. Inspired by the female writers I encountered throughout the literature modules at Edge Hill, and particularly American Women's Fiction I & II (ENG 262 & 263), I felt more comfortable using my own experience to write about relationships and 'otherness'. At last I was able to move away from the traditional, chronological, rising crescendo and attempt to employ techniques such as quilting and multiple narrative voices. I had composed a story to first draft, structured it architecturally and then redrafted intensively, interweaving themes and colours so that the narrative became a richer tapestry than anything I had produced previously.

Stephen King says, 'Reading is the creative centre of a writer's life.'[2] I have to agree. Reading has been a fundamental part of the 'writing' modules at Edge Hill also. I read, and have always read, voraciously. Perhaps the urge to write is a side effect of having a love affair with books. I read for information, for ideas and for the sheer pleasure of being taken on a journey to somewhere else. I had to ask myself where it was I wanted to take my readers and what ideas did I want to share with them.

Over the last three years we have spent a great deal of time on basic writer's craft skills. I have learned valuable lessons about drafting and editing, about cutting excess wordage, and have gained confidence in my work. I have found the comments made by tutors extremely helpful, even if it has taken me a while to get the point fully. For example with *A Piece of Paper* I learned about balance and consistency in a piece, so that I can see now that the scene with the birth mother in the hospital is at odds with the rest of the text which is in a diary format. It was a work that still contained too much fact however, and whilst writing to purge and analyse can produce good work, I had forgotten how much fun writing could be. *The Last Laugh* was a breakthrough, as for the first time I was able to draw on my own experiences to write a completely fictitious story.

All of the stories I have written in the last two years, excluding the final piece, *Marjory's Guest*, have been realist prose. I have been feeling uneasy about writing what is largely semi-autobiographical material. It is not that it is too personal, or even that I must take responsibility for the stories I tell, but that I wanted to write real fiction, fiction where the author is 'dead'.

I cannot stress just how much of a problem I have had trying to overcome the blank page and the internal censor.

'How does one find original ideas?' I asked myself. 'And what *is* this thing called plot?!' I have learned that there must be movement in a piece, that there must be tension and peaks and that the characters must develop, but if I have managed to do these things, I must admit it has been by accident.

It took until last Friday, the final lecture of the final year, for Mr Gareth Creer to waltz in and hand out plot on a plate. Okay, so it was Vogel's plot but who is complaining? I am certainly not! It was so beautifully simple yet had eluded us for all this time: A 12-point journey which enables one to sit down and immediately apply a structured outline of plot to any story in mind, complete with all the necessary steps to create movement, tension, peaks and character development. The plan destroys the internal censor and the fear of the blank page because it is fun to imagine different scenarios without actually writing the prose. I also found that the very idea of 'Ordinary World' and 'Special World' freed my imagination and enabled me to leave the realist prose behind and regain a sense of fun from writing.

My final story *Marjory's Guest* has been influenced by the literature module, Romantic and Gothic Popular Fiction. Using the advice from Mr Creer I was able to outline the story very quickly. I wanted to write a gothic horror/psychological thriller because this is one of the genres I like to read. I wrote the first draft outlining events and then adapted Vogel's plan to suit my needs. That is the beauty of having the plan to follow. Far from creating a batch of identical stories, the plan is an existing plot structure that one can begin to subvert and experiment with.

I have enjoyed my three years writing at Edge Hill enormously. The workload has been demanding and every piece of work a roller coaster of emotions, but the satisfaction gained in having produced stories that have brought lots of people pleasure, has far outweighed any negative aspects. I have sought readers for the first time in my life, and discovered the importance of peer appraisals, which allow the writer to view their work through the eyes of others. Being too close to the work can render one unable to see continuity errors and the like, as what is in the head, does not always reach the paper. This in turn allows for more thorough drafting when one does not have the luxury of placing the manuscript in a drawer for two months.

And the future? I will always write. I do not feel as though I have a choice in that, but now I feel I will write with a view to submission, with a view to creating pieces of writing for other people to read and hopefully enjoy. As Obstfeld says in *Fiction First Aid*, 'Writers are neurotics; we write despite ourselves.'[3] I write despite the internal censor who says everything is rubbish. I write despite the fact sometimes I really do not want to be a writer. At least now, after these last three years I can write a lot better than I used to. I want to experiment with genre more, with postmodernism and science-fiction, with humour and the gothic. I hope to one day discover my 'writer's voice'. Until then I shall no doubt continue to be a jack of all trades, flitting from genre to genre, mastering none. If, however, all goes to plan, I shall be back for more as soon as I can find the time to start the Writing MA.[4]

Bibliography

W. Benjamin (2001) *One Way Street*: 'Caution: Steps' quoted in M. Cohen (ed.) *The Penguin Dictionary of Epigrams* (Harmondsworth: Penguin). This is a book of epigrams. What can I say? I am addicted to them.

J. Bell and P. Magrs (2001) *The Creative Writing Course Book* (London: Macmillan – now Palgrave Macmillan).
'How To Write...' books have certainly improved over the years and this collection of essays and advice is a jewel. It contains an essay by James Friel, one of our visiting writers, on drafting, which is very useful stuff. If you only have one book, I recommend this one

J. B. Kachuba (2001) *How To Write Funny* (London: Writer's Digest Books). This is the book I shall be using in the future when I try to write funny. A wonderful collection of different authors all lending useful, not to mention humorous, advice.

O. Kenyon (1989) *Women Writers Talk* (Oxford: Lennard Publishing). Not a 'how to' book but a 'how they do it' book. It is good to know how other writers work and this gives plenty of insights into how others work, showing that there are more ways than one to skin a literary cat.

S. King (2000) *On Writing* (London: Hodder & Stoughton). I like this book. I like the informal conversation tone and the fact that it contains a bit of everything...writer's craft, how King himself works, and a look at his own drafting technique with examples of his own work. The anecdotes are hilarious also, especially the one at the end where he describes being hit by a car driven by a character straight out of one of his own novels.

R. Obstfeld (2002) *Fiction First Aid* (Cincinnati: Writer's Digest Books). This is a very useful book for solving problems such as writer's block by addressing tired and predictable characters. My latest acquisition, I have yet to go through this book with a fine-tooth comb.

J. Saunders (1994) *How To Write Realistic Dialogue* (London: Allison & Busby).

Perhaps this book should be called 'How to write realistic dialogue for Mills and Boon and other Romances...' but even so, it does give valuable information as to layout of dialogue and how to use characters to tell the story.

Sol Stein (1999) *Practical Craft Techniques For Fiction and Non Fiction* (London: Souvenir Press).

This book is a real gem. It shows how you can take one sentence and rewrite it according to what it is you want to portray, or what mood you want to create. Seeing how one event, such as a man walking into a room, can be described in so many ways has been very useful to me in improving my own choice of words.

Magazines

Writer's News is a publication I have subscribed to for longer than I care to admit, especially as I have never submitted to it yet. It runs competitions and provides updates on the current market trends, bringing to light the fact that for many, writing is a business.

MsLexia is a little different. It prints far more readers' work than *Writer's News* does and has less of the marketplace. Written primarily for women, by women, the articles cover the practicalities of writing and rearing a family, and the politics of gender in the writing world. I hope to submit to this over the summer and see what happens.

Notes

1 Becoming a Writer

1 Stephen King (2000) *On Writing*. New English Library (London: Hodder and Stoughton).

3 Creativity

1 J. Rogers (1992) 'Teaching the Craft of Writing' in R. Miles and M. Monteith (eds), *Teaching Creative Writing*. (Buckingham: Open University Press), p. 108.
2 George Orwell (1946) 'Politics and the English Language' *Collected Essays, Vol. 1V: In Front of Your Nose 1945–1950*. (London: Secker and Warburg), pp. 127–40, p. 138.
3 Susan Greenfield (2000) *Brain Story* (London: BBC Worldwide), p. 161.
4 Ibid., p. 182.
5 Betty Edwards (1993) *Drawing on the Right Side of the Brain* (London: HarperCollins), p. xi.
6 Dorothea Brande (1934) *Becoming A Writer* (New York: Harcourt, Brace), pp. 72–3.
7 Guy Claxton (1997) *Hare Brain, Tortoise Mind* (London: Fourth Estate), p. 93.
8 Ibid., p. 14.
9 See David Galin's theories of creativity cited in *Drawing on the Right Side of the Brain* as well as Guy Claxton's model in *Hare Brain, Tortoise Mind*.

4 The Necessity of Mess

1 Robert Graves (2003) *The Collected Poems* (London: Penguin).

6 Dreams and Visions

1 Dorothea Brande (1934) *Becoming a Writer* (New York: Harcourt, Brace & Company).
2 Maura Dooley (ed.) (2000) *How Novelists Work* (London: Seren), p. 38.
3 Stephen King (2000) *On Writing* (London: Hodder and Stoughton), p. 139.
4 Brande, *Becoming a Writer*, pp. 72–3.
5 Steven Soderbergh, *Solaris* (2003) Twentieth Century Fox.

6   Larry and Andy Wachowski, *The Matrix* (1999) Warner Brothers.
7   Sigmund Freud, trans. Helen M. Downey (1993) *Delusion and Dream in Wilhelm Jensen's Gradiva* (Los Angeles: Sun and Moon Classics).

7   Journals and Notebooks

1   In Julia Bell and Paul Magrs (eds) (2001) *The Creative Writing Coursebook* (London: Macmillan – now Palgrave Macmillan), pp. 11–12.
2   Hallie Burnett and Whit Burnett (1975), *Fiction Writer's Handbook* (New York: Harper Perennial), p. 86.
3   Janet Burroway (1992) *Writing Fiction: A Guide To Narrative Craft* (New York: HarperCollins), p. 4.
4   Virginia Woolf (1953) *A Writer's Diary* (New York: Harcourt, Brace), quoted in Joyce Carol Oates (ed.) (1998) *Telling Stories: An Anthology for Writers* (New York: W.W Norton), p. 253.
5   Quoted in Mark Robert Waldman (ed.) (2001) *The Spirit of Writing: Classic and Contemporary Essays Celebrating the Writing Life* (New York: Jeremy P. Tarcher/Putnam), p. 28.
6   http://books.guardian.co.uk/review/story/0,12084,890545,00.html
7   Tristine Rainer (1986) *The New Diary: How to Use a Journal for Self Guidance and Expanded Creativity* (London: Angus and Robertson).
8   Jennifer Moon (1999) *Learning Journals* (London: Kogan Page), pp. 121–2.
9   Dorothea Brande (1934) *Becoming A Writer* (New York: Harcourt, Brace), pp. 72–3.
10   Bell and Magrs, *Creative Writing Coursebook*, p. 7.
11   Ibid., p. 13.
12   Jenny Newman, Edmund Cusick and Aileen La Tourette (eds) (2004) *The Writer's Workbook* (London: Arnold), p. 10.
13   Burnett, *Fiction Writer's Handbook*, p. 86.
14   Bell and Magrs, *Creative Writing Coursebook*, p. 10.

8   Reading as a Writer

1   J. Franzen (2000) *How to be Alone* (London: Fourth Estate).
2   T. Hughes (1972) *Selected Poems 1957–1967* (London: Faber).

9   Looking Your Words in the Face: Reflection

1   See also chapter 27, 'How Not Being Published Can Change Your Life'.
2   Will Blythe (ed.) (1998) *Why I Write: Thoughts on the Craft of Fiction* (London: Little, Brown), p. 33.

3   From Bonnie Lyons and Bill Oliver (eds) (1998) *Passion and Craft: Conversations With Notable Writers* (Urbana and Chicago: University of Illinois Press), p. 28.

10   Writing Together: Groups and Workshops

1   From J. Gardner (1999) *On Becoming a Novelist* (London: W.W. Norton), p. 77.
2   S. King (2000) *On Writing* (London: Hodder and Stoughton), p. 283. King took two university writing classes in his final year at the University of Maine, but he is sceptical about the value of his experience, believing that the classes appreciated and encouraged literary and whimsically emotional writing over his own embryo thrillers.
3   Although, of course, many libraries and bookshops create their very own apartheid systems by providing Crime/ Romance/ Sci-Fi sections. Interesting that they never offer sections called Clever Books. Except for *Classics* – Old Clever Books maybe.
4   D. Foster Wallace (1998) 'The Nature of the Fun', in W. Blyth (ed.), *Why I Write* (London: Little Brown).
5   D.M. Kaplan (1998) *Rewriting* (London: A & C Black).

11   Narrators: Whose Story Is It Anyway?

1   Quoted by Anne Lamott (1995) *Bird By Bird – Some Instructions on Writing and Life* (New York: Anchor Books), p. 49.
2   Shlomith Rimmon-Kenan (1989) *Narrative Fiction: Contemporary Poetics* (New York: Routledge), p. 95.
3   David Lodge (1990) *After Bakhtin: Essays on Fiction and Criticism* (London: Routledge), p. 47.
4   Sarah Waters (2002) *Fingersmith* (London: Virago), p. 7.
5   Jay McInerney (1985) *Bright Lights, Big City* (London: Jonathan Cape), p. 1.
6   Jeffrey Eugenides (1996) *The Virgin Suicides* (London: Bloomsbury), p. 8.
7   Oakley Hall (1985) *The Art and Craft of Novel Writing* (Cincinnati: Story Press), p. 28.
8   Orson Scott Card (1999) *Characters and Viewpoint* (London: Robinson Publishing), p. 163.
9   Collected in R.P. Blackmuir (1934) *The Art of The Novel* (New York: Charles Scribner's Sons), p. 320.
10   Card, *Characters and Viewpoint*, p. 107.
11   J.D. Salinger (1951) *The Catcher In the Rye* (London: Hamish Hamilton), p. 5.
12   Ibid., p. 31.

12 Your Travelling Companions: Characters

1 'The Art of Fiction', collected in Morris Shapira (ed.) (1963) *Henry James: Selected Literary Criticism* (Harmondsworth: Penguin), p. 131.
2 René Wellek and Austin Warren (1966) *Theory of Literature* (London: Jonathan Cape), p. 33.
3 Will Ferguson (2001) *Happiness* (Edinburgh: Canongate Books), p. 41.
4 Maggie O'Farrell (2002) *My Lover's Lover* (London: Review), p. 3.
5 Ibid., p. 9.
6 Jane Rogers, in Moira Monteith and Robert Miles (eds) (1992) *Teaching Creative Writing* (London: Open University Press), p. 114.
7 Michael Frayn (2002) *Spies* (London: Faber and Faber), p. 12.
8 Robert Scholes and Robert Kellog (1966) *The Nature of Narrative* (Oxford: Oxford University Press), p. 161.
9 David Lodge (1989) *Nice Work* (Harmondsworth: Penguin), pp. 148–9.
10 David Park (2002) *The Big Snow* (London: Bloomsbury), p. 151.
11 Ibid., p. 202.
12 Rob Watson (1999) *Extracts from a Work in Progress: Writing Life.* www.nawe.co.uk/forum.html

13 Setting

1 Graham Swift (1999) *Waterland* (London: Picador). Gerald Durrell (1969) *My Family and Other Animals* (Harmondsworth: Penguin).
2 Alan Paton (1983) *Cry, The Beloved Country* (Harmondsworth: Penguin), p. 7.
3 E. Annie Proulx (1994) *The Shipping News* (London: Fourth Estate), p. 24.
4 Ibid., p. 52.
5 William Gibson (1999) *Neuromancer* (New York: Vintage).
6 Anne Michaels (1997) *Fugitive Pieces* (London: Bloomsbury), p. 253.
7 Larry W. Phillips (ed.) *Ernest Hemingway on Writing* (New York: Touchstone: Simon and Schuster).
8 Umberto Eco (1994) *Six Walks in the Fictional Woods* (Cambridge, MA: Harvard University Press), p. 59.
9 Mickey Pearlman and Katherine Ushe Henderson (1990) *A Voice of One's Own: Conversations with America's Writing Women* (Boston: Houghlin Mifflin).
10 Jane Campion (1993) *The Piano* (New York: Miramax Books).
11 Ibid., p. 38.
12 James Frazer (1993) *The Golden Bough: A Study in Magic and Religion* (Wordsworth Reference S.) (London: Wordsworth Editions).
13 Phillips (ed.), *Ernest Hemingway on Writing*, p. 36

14 White Space: Page Design

1 Mike Sharples (1999) *How We Write* (London: Routledge), p. 139.
2 Ibid., p. 140.
3 John Haffenden (ed.) (1985) 'Fay Weldon', in *Novelists in Interview* (London: Methuen). pp. 305–20.
4 William Golding (1964) *The Spire* (London: Faber and Faber), p. 54.
5 Melissa Bank (2000) *The Girls' Guide to Hunting and Fishing* (Harmondsworth: Penguin Books), p. 57.

Style: Plain and Simple

1 Robert Clark (2001) *The English Style Book* (Norwich: University of East Anglia).
2 Anton Chekhov letter to Maxim Gorky, 3 September 1899, from *Anton Chekhov on Writing*, Nebraska Centre for Writers, http://mockingbird. creighton.edu/NCW/chekwrit.htm accessed 4 May 2004.

15 Your Vehicle: Plot

1 Anne Lamott (1995) *Bird By Bird – Some Instructions on Writing and Life* (New York: Anchor Books), p. 55.
2 Robert McKee (2003) *Story: Substance, Structure, Style, and the Principles of Screenwriting* (London: HarperCollins), p. 181.
3 Russell Hoban (1993) 'Telling Stories' in Duncan Minshull (ed.) *Telling Stories Vol. 2* (London: Coronet), p. 195.
4 Richard Ford (1990) *Wildlife* (London: Flamingo), p. 7.
5 In Ansen Dibell (1988) *Plot* (London: Robinson Publishing), p. 21.
6 Patricia Highsmith (1993) 'Thickening My Plots' in Clare Boylan (ed.), *The Agony and the Ego: The Art and Strategy of Fiction Writing Explored* (Harmondsworth: Penguin Books), p. 155.
7 Based on Michael Baldwin (1986) *The Way To Write Short Stories* (London: Elm Tree Books), pp. 3–4.
8 James N. Frey (1988) *How to Write a Damn Good Novel* (London: Macmillan), pp. 40–2.
9 Ibid., p. 34.
10 See also chapter 18, 'It's Showtime: Immediacy'.
11 David Lodge (1993) *The Art of Fiction* (Harmondsworth: Penguin), p. 10.
12 *In medias res* is Latin for in the middle of things. In other words, your story should start with the blue touch-paper burning – not with the trip down to the shops to buy fireworks.

13 You may have seen Robert McKee's legendary (or notorious) Ten Commandments for writers satirised in Charles Kaufman's script for the Spike Jonze film *Adaptation*. There the character Charlie Kaufman, the highbrow screenwriter, disdains his lowbrow twin Donald's devotion to McKee's screenwriting workshops. Charlie suggests that McKee disciples are like cult members.

Scaffolding

1 Christopher Nolan (2000) *Memento*. Twentieth Century Fox. Richard Kelly (2001) *Donnie Darko*. Metrodome. Tom Tykwer (1999) *Run Lola Run*. Columbia Tristar.
2 Kurt Vonnegut (2003) *Slaughterhouse 5* (London: Vintage) Martin Amis (2003) *Time's Arrow* (London: Vintage).

16 Scriptwriting for Nervous Beginners

1 James Schamus (1997) *The Ice Storm* (New York: Newmarket Press), p. xi.

17 Dialogue in Prose Fiction

1 Graham Swift (1996) *Last Orders* (London: Picador).

18 It's Showtime: Immediacy

1 Lubbock's *The Craft Of Fiction*, cited in Oakley Hall (1989) *The Art and Craft of Novel Writing* (Cincinnati: Story Press), p. 2.
2 Wayne C. Booth (1987) *The Rhetoric of Fiction* (Harmondsworth: Penguin), p. 21.
3 Monica Wood (1995) *Description* (Cincinnati: Writer's Digest Books), p. 55.
4 Kurt Vonnegut (2003) *Slaughterhouse 5* (London: Vintage), p. 1.
5 Anne Tyler (1992) *Dinner at the Homesick Restaurant* (London: Vintage), p. 57.
6 Renni Browne and Dave King (1991) *Self-Editing for Fiction Writers: Show and Tell* (New York: HarperCollins), p. 3.
7 Browne and King also suggest a way to avoid one kind of telling. They say that as editors they are prone to writing 'R.U.E.' in the margin of a manuscript: resist the urge to explain, ibid., pp. 48–50.
8 J.D. Salinger (1951) *The Catcher in the Rye* (London: Hamish Hamilton), p. 5.

19   Cut it Out, Put it In: Revision

1 Quoted in George Plimpton (ed.) (1992) *The Writer's Chapbook* (Harmondsworth: Penguin Books), p. 128.
2 Ibid., p. 128.
3 Bernard Malamud in Plimpton, *The Writers' Chapbook*, p. 133.
4 No reference for this, although one probably exists somewhere. I heard Frank Conroy use the 'Things You Make Them Carry' anecdote when I visited one of his classes at the Iowa Writer's Workshop in September 2001.
5 Jane Smiley (1999) 'What Stories Teach Their Writers: The Purpose and Practice of Revision' in Julie Checkoway (ed.) *Creating Fiction: Instruction and Insights from Teachers of the Associated Writing Programs* (Cincinnati: Story Press), p. 249.
6 Janet Burroway (1992) *Writing Fiction: A Guide to Narrative Craft* (New York: HarperCollins), p. 335.
7 From Kay Dick (ed.) (1972) *Writers At Work: Interviews from Paris Review* (Harmondsworth: Penguin Books), pp. 175–96.
8 Thomas McCormack (1988) *The Fiction Editor, the Novel, and the Novelist* (New York: St. Martin's Press), pp. 16–17.
9 Ibid., p.17.
10 Ibid.
11 Smiley, 'What Stories Teach', p. 251.

20   Poetry for People Who Don't Like Poetry

1 From Tony Harrison's poem *Them and [uz]*, in *Tony Harrison: Selected Poems* 2nd edn (Harmondsworth: Penguin Books, 1987).
2 The Beatles (1962) 'Love Me Do' (London: EMI).
3 Bob Dylan (1963) 'A Hard Rain's Gonna Fall'. From The Freewheeling Bob Dylan (Sony).
4 One of these terms means repeating consonants and the other means repeating vowels. I suggest that you look them up.
5 Sylvia Plath (1992) *Collected Poems* (New York: Harper).

21   Words and Images

1 Charlotte Brontë (2003) *Jane Eyre* (Harmondsworth: Penguin Books).
2 Thomas Hardy (1994) *The Complete Poems of Thomas Hardy* (London: Wordsworth Editions).
3 Catherine Phillips (ed.) (2002) *Gerard Manley Hopkins: The Major Works* (Oxford: Oxford University Press).

4 Tom Phillips (1998) *A Humument. A Treated Victorian Novel* (London: Thames and Hudson).
5 www.tomphillips.co.uk
6 Stanley Chapman (trans.), in Alastair Brotchie and Harry Matthews (eds) (1998) *Oulipo Compendium* (London: Atlas Press).
7 www.nottingham.ac.uk/critical theory/queneau

22 Trying Something Else: Poetry Writing

1 Basho (1985) *On Love and Barley: Haiku of Basho*, trans. Lucien Stryk (Harmondsworth: Penguin), p. 14.
2 Ibid., p. 14.
3 Ibid.
4 E. Pound, 'Imagisme', in P. Jones (1972) *Imagist Poetry* (Harmondsworth: Penguin), p. 129.
5 Ibid., p. 130.
6 Ibid.
7 Ibid., p. 129.
8 Ibid.
9 B. Bunting, *Cut Out Every Word You Dare*, fact sheet from the Basil Bunting Centre, University of Durham, p. 4.
10 Pound, 'Imagisme', p. 131.
11 W.C. Williams (1976) *Selected Poems* (Harmondsworth: Penguin), p. 133.
12 Pound's poem may be found in Peter Jones (1972) *Imagist Poetry* (Harmondsworth: Penguin), p. 95.
13 Pound, 'Imagisme', p. 129.
14 Ibid., p. 131.
15 G.O. Hartman (1980) *Free Verse: An Essay on Prosody* (Princeton, NJ: Princeton University Press), pp. 24–5.
16 'Imagisme', p. 133.
17 Ibid.
18 Bunting, *Cut Out Every Word You Dare*, p. 4.
19 Pound, 'Imagisme', p. 133.
20 Ibid.
21 W.C. Williams (1954) 'Author's Introduction to *The Wedge*', in *Selected Essays of William Carlos Williams* (New York: Random House), p. 256.
22 Derek Attridge, quoted in M. Perloff (1998) *Poetry On and Off the Page* (Evanston, IL: Northwestern University Press), p. 143.
23 G. Agamben (1995) *The Idea of Prose* (Albany, NY: SUNY Press), p. 40.
24 S. Burt (2002) 'Chicory and Daisies', *London Review of Books*, 7 March.
25 Bunting, *Cut Out Every Word You Dare*, p. 4.
26 Ibid.

23   Writing Play: On and Off the Page

1   Jeff Noon (2001) 'Why Can't Writers Have More Fun?', *Guardian*, 10 January. Also see Noon's whole Writer's Manifesto at: http://www.noonworld.co.uk/pages/manifesto.html
2   Jim Kalb's Palindrome Connection at http://www.palindromes.org/
3   Ibid. Thompson's review of the 2003 International Exhibition of Graphic and Comic Literature, at the London Institute of Contemporary Arts, directs you to some of these texts and useful websites.
4   Miyazaki Hiyao (1996) *Nausicaa* (London: Viz Communications) Nausicaa Fan Website: http://www.nausicaa.net/
5   Magan Sapnar and Ingrid Ankerson at www.Poemsthatgo.com
6   Vikram Seth (1986) *The Golden Gate: A Novel in Verse* (New York: Random House).

24   The Polyphonic Spree: Other Narrative Strategies

1   Wayne C. Booth (1961) *The Rhetoric of Fiction* (Chicago and London: University of Chicago Press), p. 191.
2   Peter Barry (1995) *Beginning Theory, An Introduction to Literary and Cultural Theory* (Manchester: Manchester University Press), p. 84.
3   Laurence Block (1970) 'Transitions and Breathing Space', in Frank A. Dickson and Sandra Smythe (eds) *The Writer's Digest Handbook of Short Story Writing* (Cincinnati: Writer's Digest Books), p. 214.
4   This analysis of traditional masculine plotting can be found in any number of texts which examine the writer's craft, most notably in Ansen Dibell's *Plot*, Janet Burroway's *Writing Fiction* and James N. Frey's *How to Write a Damn Good Novel*.
5   Ronald B. Tobias (1995) *20 Master Plots (And How to Build Them)* (London: Piatkus), pp. 160–7.
6   Judith Fetterley (1985) *Provisions* (Bloomington: Indiana University Press), pp. 14–15, cited in Elaine Showalter (1991) *Sister's Choice: Tradition and Change in American Women's Writing* (London: Clarenden Press), p. 153.
7   Ibid.
8   Ibid.
9   Ibid., pp. 158–9.
10 Kate Chopin (1983) 'Elizabeth Stock's One Story' in *The Awakening and Selected Stories* (London and New York: Penguin), p. 274.

25   Narrative Design: Pattern, Plant and Pay-Off

1   Quoted in Ann Charters (1995) *The Story and its Writer* (Bedford Books of St. Martin's Press, 1995), p. 1380.
2   Annie Dillard (2001) 'Ruining the Page' in Mark Robert Waldman (ed.), *The Spirit of Writing: Classic and Contemporary Essays Celebrating the Writing Life* (New York: Jeremy P. Tarcher/Putnam), pp. 17–18.
3   Mike Sharples (1999) *How We Write* (London: Routledge) pp. 71–3.
4   Rob Watson *Extracts from a Work in Progress: Writing Life* (www.nawe.co.uk/forum.html), accessed 28 April 2003.
5   Lucy Ellmann (1988) *Sweet Desserts* (London: Virago), p. 117.
6   Rose Tremain (1998) *The Way I Found Her* (London: Vintage), p. 7.
7   Ibid., p. 41.
8   Ibid., pp. 258–9.

26   Getting Published

1   *The Writers' and Artists' Yearbook 2004*, ed. Barry Turner (London: A & C Black). *The Writers' Handbook 2004* (London: Palgrave Macmillan).

27   Writing as Self-Invention

1   Alice Sebold (2003) *Lucky* and *The Lovely Bones* (London: Picador).
2   Maura Dooley (1999) *How Novelists Work* (Bridgend: Seren Books).

A Writer's Bookshelf

1   The mother of all books for writers? It doesn't set out to teach you much about craft, but it does teach you almost everything you need to know about understanding your writer's gifts. It has been in print most of the time from the 1930s onwards. In the UK this 1996 edition was the most recent, but is now out of print. Dorothea's day will come again (and again) but meantime, hunt this essential text down at e-bay or click on *New & Used* at Amazon.
2   Another job for e-bay or Amazon.
3   Around 1500 pages of short stories from across time and space, with wonderful essays about each other's craft by many masters and mistresses of the form.
4   For many, this and Volume 1 are all you need to know about poetry. Volume 2 is chosen because of its more recent focus.
5   63 pages long and more than any of you really need to know. (And don't make the mistake of thinking it's too basic for you. It ain't.)
6   Read it online at: http://www.bartleby.com/141/

Appendix

1 Creative Writing students at Edge Hill currently engage in two kinds of reflective writing. The first, a Self-Assessment / Annotated Bibliography, complements every piece of creative work, and reflects solely on that piece. The second, entitled a Reflection, focuses on at least one module, or one year of the programme – or it may, as Lisa's does, consider the whole three years.

2 Stephen King (2000) *On Writing* (London: Hodder & Stoughton), p. 114.

3 Raymond Obstfeld (2002) *Fiction First Aid* (Ohio:Writer's Digest Books), p. 24.

4 In October 2003, Lisa joined the most recent cohort of Edge Hill's MA in Writing Studies.

Index

Index of *Try This* – Writing Exercises